Students, Computers and Learning

MAKING THE CONNECTION

OECD
BETTER POLICIES FOR BETTER LIVES

Please cite this publication as:
OECD (2015), *Students, Computers and Learning: Making the Connection*, PISA, OECD Publishing.
http://dx.doi.org/10.1787/9789264239555-en

ISBN 978-92-64-23954-8 (print)
ISBN 978-92-64-23955-5 (PDF)

Photo credits:
© Flying Colours Ltd/Getty Images
© Jacobs Stock Photography/Kzenon
© khoa vu/Flickr/Getty Images
© Mel Curtis/Corbis
© Shutterstock/Kzenon
© Simon Jarratt/Corbis

Corrigenda to OECD publications may be found on line at: *www.oecd.org/publishing/corrigenda*.

Foreword

Information and communication technology (ICT) has revolutionised virtually every aspect of our life and work. Students unable to navigate through a complex digital landscape will no longer be able to participate fully in the economic, social and cultural life around them. Those responsible for educating today's "connected" learners are confronted with challenging issues, from information overload to plagiarism, from protecting children from online risks such as fraud, violations of privacy or online bullying to setting an adequate and appropriate media diet. We expect schools to educate our children to become critical consumers of Internet services and electronic media, helping them to make informed choices and avoid harmful behaviours. And we expect schools to raise awareness about the risks that children face on line and how to avoid them.

This report provides a first-of-its-kind internationally comparative analysis of the digital skills that students have acquired, and of the learning environments designed to develop these skills. This analysis shows that the reality in our schools lags considerably behind the promise of technology. In 2012, 96% of 15-year-old students in OECD countries reported that they have a computer at home, but only 72% reported that they use a desktop, laptop or tablet computer at school, and in some countries fewer than one in two students reported doing so. And even where computers are used in the classroom, their impact on student performance is mixed at best. Students who use computers moderately at school tend to have somewhat better learning outcomes than students who use computers rarely. But students who use computers very frequently at school do a lot worse in most learning outcomes, even after accounting for social background and student demographics.

The results also show no appreciable improvements in student achievement in reading, mathematics or science in the countries that had invested heavily in ICT for education. And perhaps the most disappointing finding of the report is that technology is of little help in bridging the skills divide between advantaged and disadvantaged students. Put simply, ensuring that every child attains a baseline level of proficiency in reading and mathematics seems to do more to create equal opportunities in a digital world than can be achieved by expanding or subsidising access to high-tech devices and services. Last but not least, most parents and teachers will not be surprised by the finding that students who spend more than six hours on line per weekday outside of school are particularly at risk of reporting that they feel lonely at school, and that they arrived late for school or skipped days of school in the two weeks prior to the PISA test.

One interpretation of all this is that building deep, conceptual understanding and higher-order thinking requires intensive teacher-student interactions, and technology sometimes distracts from this valuable human engagement. Another interpretation is that we have not yet become good enough at the kind of pedagogies that make the most of technology; that adding 21st-century technologies to 20th-century teaching practices will just dilute the effectiveness of teaching.

If students use smartphones to copy and paste prefabricated answers to questions, it is unlikely to help them to become smarter. If we want students to become smarter than a smartphone, we need to think harder about the pedagogies we are using to teach them. Technology can amplify great teaching but great technology cannot replace poor teaching.

The report leaves many questions unanswered. The impact of technology on education delivery remains sub-optimal, because we may overestimate the digital skills of both teachers and students, because of naïve policy design and implementation strategies, because of a poor understanding of pedagogy, or because of the generally poor quality of educational software and courseware. In fact, how many children would choose to play a computer game of the same quality as the software that finds its way into many classrooms around the world? Results suggest that the connections among students, computers and learning are neither simple nor hard-wired; and the real contributions ICT can make to teaching and learning have yet to be fully realised and exploited.

Still, the findings must not lead to despair. We need to get this right in order to provide educators with learning environments that support 21st-century pedagogies and provide children with the 21st-century skills they need to succeed in tomorrow's world. Technology is the only way to dramatically expand access to knowledge. Why should students be limited to a textbook that was printed two years ago, and maybe designed ten years ago, when they could have access to the world's best and most up-to-date textbook? Equally important, technology allows teachers and students to access specialised materials well beyond textbooks, in multiple formats, with little time and space constraints. Technology provides great platforms for collaboration in knowledge creation where teachers can share and enrich teaching materials. Perhaps most importantly, technology can support new pedagogies that focus on learners as active participants with tools for inquiry-based pedagogies and collaborative workspaces. For example, technology can enhance experiential learning, foster project-based and inquiry-based pedagogies, facilitate hands-on activities and cooperative learning, deliver formative real-time assessment and support learning and teaching communities, with new tools such as remote and virtual labs, highly interactive non-linear courseware based on state-of-the-art instructional design, sophisticated software for experimentation and simulation, social media and serious games.

To deliver on the promises technology holds, countries will need a convincing strategy to build teachers' capacity. And policy-makers need to become better at building support for this agenda. Given the uncertainties that accompany all change, educators will always opt to maintain the status quo. If we want to mobilise support for more technology-rich schools, we need to become better at communicating the need and building support for change. We need to invest in capacity development and change-management skills, develop sound evidence and feed this evidence back to institutions, and back all that up with sustainable financing. Last but not least, it is vital that teachers become active agents for change, not just in implementing technological innovations, but in designing them too.

Andreas Schleicher
Director
Directorate for Education and Skills

Acknowledgements

This report is the product of a collaboration among the countries participating in PISA and the OECD Secretariat. The report was prepared by Francesco Avvisati, with contributions from Judit Pál, and edited by Marilyn Achiron. Andreas Schleicher, Yuri Belfali, Francesca Borgonovi, Jenny Bradshaw, Tracey Burns, Alfonso Echazarra, Stuart Elliott, Carlos González-Sancho, Tue Halgreen, Miyako Ikeda, Noémie Le Donné, Mario Piacentini, Daniel Salinas, Shun Shirai and Pablo Zoido, from the OECD Secretariat, as well as Samuel Greiff, Johannes Naumann, Dara Ramalingam and Jean-François Rouet, provided valuable feedback at various stages of the report. Célia Braga-Schich, Claire Chetcuti, Vanessa Denis, Juliet Evans, Lorena Ortega Ferrand and Giannina Rech provided statistical, editorial and administrative support. The development of the report was steered by the PISA Governing Board, which is chaired by Lorna Bertrand (United Kingdom).

Table of Contents

BOX

FIGURES

Executive Summary

In 2012, 96% of 15-year-old students in OECD countries reported that they have a computer at home, but only 72% reported that they use a desktop, laptop or tablet computer at school. Only 42% of students in Korea and 38% of students in Shanghai-China reported that they use computers at school – and Korea and Shanghai-China were among the top performers in the digital reading and computer-based mathematics tests in the OECD Programme for International Student Assessment (PISA) in 2012. By contrast, in countries where it is more common for students to use the Internet at school for schoolwork, students' performance in reading declined between 2000 and 2012, on average.

These findings, based on an analysis of PISA data, tell us that, despite the pervasiveness of information and communication technologies (ICT) in our daily lives, these technologies have not yet been as widely adopted in formal education. But where they *are* used in the classroom, their impact on student performance is mixed, at best. In fact, PISA results show no appreciable improvements in student achievement in reading, mathematics or science in the countries that had invested heavily in ICT for education.

As these results show, the connections among students, computers and learning are neither simple nor hard-wired; and the real contributions ICT can make to teaching and learning have yet to be fully realised and exploited. But as long as computers and the Internet continue to have a central role in our personal and professional lives, students who have not acquired basic skills in reading, writing and navigating through a digital landscape will find themselves unable to participate fully in the economic, social and cultural life around them. Amidst the decidedly mixed messages that are drawn from the PISA data, a few critical observations emerge.

The foundation skills required in a digital environment can and should be taught.

Reading on line requires the same skills as reading a printed page – with the important addition of being able to navigate through and among pages/screens of text, and filtering the relevant and trustworthy sources from among a large amount of information. Korea and Singapore, the two highest-performing countries in digital reading, and among those countries whose students are the most proficient in navigating through the web, have excellent broadband infrastructure,

and their 15-year-old students use computers with ease in their daily lives. Yet students in these countries are not more exposed to the Internet at school than are students in other OECD countries. This suggests that many of the evaluation and task-management skills that are essential for online navigation may also be taught and learned with conventional, analogue pedagogies and tools.

Improve equity in education first.

In most countries, differences in computer access between advantaged and disadvantaged students shrank between 2009 and 2012; in no country did the gap widen. But results from the PISA computer-based tests show that once the so-called "first digital divide" (access to computers) is bridged, the remaining difference, between socio-economic groups, in the ability to use ICT tools for learning is largely, if not entirely, explained by the difference observed in more traditional academic abilities. So to reduce inequalities in the ability to benefit from digital tools, countries need to improve equity in education first. Ensuring that every child attains a baseline level of proficiency in reading and mathematics will do more to create equal opportunities in a digital world than can be achieved by expanding or subsidising access to high-tech devices and services.

Teachers, parents and students should be alerted to the possible harmful aspects of Internet use.

Those in charge of educating today's "connected" learners are confronted with a number of new (or newly relevant) issues, from information overload to plagiarism, from protecting children from online risks (fraud, violations of privacy, online bullying) to setting an adequate and appropriate media diet. In addition, many parents and teachers will not be surprised by the PISA finding that students who spend more than six hours on line per weekday outside of school are particularly at risk of reporting that they feel lonely at school, and that they arrived late for school or skipped days of school in the two weeks prior to the PISA test.

Schools can educate students to become critical consumers of Internet services and electronic media, helping them to make informed choices and avoid harmful behaviours. They can also raise awareness in families about the risks that children face on line and how to avoid them. Parents can help children to balance the use of ICT for entertainment and leisure with time for other recreational activities that do not involve screens, such as sports and, equally important, sleep.

To improve the effectiveness of investments in technology, learn from experience.

PISA data show that, in countries where mathematics lessons focus on formulating, and solving, real-world problems – whether in engineering, biology, finance or any problem that arises in everyday life and work – students reported that their teachers use computers to a greater extent in instruction. And among all teachers, those who are more inclined and better prepared for student-oriented teaching practices, such as group work, individualised learning, and project work, are more likely to use digital resources, according to students.

But while PISA results suggest that limited use of computers at school may be better than not using computers at all, using them more intensively than the current OECD average tends to be associated with significantly poorer student performance. ICT is linked to better student performance only in certain contexts, such as when computer software and Internet connections help to increase study time and practice.

One interpretation of these findings is that it takes educators time and effort to learn how to use technology in education while staying firmly focused on student learning. Meanwhile, online tools can help teachers and school leaders exchange ideas and inspire each other, transforming what used to be an individual's problem into a collaborative process. In the end, technology can amplify great teaching, but great technology cannot replace poor teaching.

■ Table 0.1 [Part 1/2] ■
SNAPSHOT OF HOME ICT EQUIPMENT AND INTERNET USE

- (dark shading) Countries/economies where home ICT equipment/time spent using the Internet is **above** the OECD average
- (no shading) Countries/economies where home ICT equipment/time spent using the Internet is not statistically different from the OECD average
- (light shading) Countries/economies where home ICT equipment/time spent using the Internet is **below** the OECD average

	Home ICT equipment				Time spent using the Internet			
	Students with at least one computer at home		Students with three or more computers at home		Average daily time spent using the Internet (lower bound)			Students who reported using the Internet outside of school for more than 6 hours during a typical weekday
	2012	Change between 2009 and 2012	2012	Change between 2009 and 2012	Outside of school, on weekdays	Outside of school, on weekend days	At school, on weekdays	
	%	% dif.	%	% dif.	Minutes	Minutes	Minutes	%
OECD average	95.8	**2.0**	42.8	**12.1**	104	138	25	7.2
Denmark	99.9	**0.2**	84.7	**9.9**	136	177	46	9.4
Netherlands	99.8	0.0	69.0	**10.0**	115	152	26	9.9
Finland	99.8	**0.3**	56.1	**17.2**	99	130	18	4.1
Slovenia	99.7	**0.5**	43.4	**15.9**	108	138	28	8.4
Sweden	99.6	**0.5**	74.8	**18.1**	144	176	39	13.2
Liechtenstein	99.6	-0.1	62.0	**20.7**	95	132	18	4.9
Hong Kong-China	99.6	**0.5**	31.8	**12.1**	111	164	11	7.0
Austria	99.5	**0.7**	45.3	**12.0**	96	119	29	6.6
Switzerland	99.5	**0.5**	58.9	**15.6**	88	121	16	4.6
Germany	99.4	**0.5**	54.0	**10.2**	114	144	14	8.6
Macao-China	99.4	**0.4**	25.4	**13.7**	112	178	14	7.0
Iceland	99.3	-0.2	70.7	**10.7**	124	160	20	7.7
Norway	99.1	-0.3	83.9	**12.1**	136	170	24	9.3
Luxembourg	99.1	0.2	56.6	**11.3**	m	m	m	m
Australia	99.0	0.2	64.6	**18.7**	130	158	58	9.9
France	99.0	**2.2**	45.0	**17.4**	m	m	m	m
Canada	98.9	0.3	53.0	**15.5**	m	m	m	m
Belgium	98.9	**0.5**	55.0	**14.7**	94	142	22	5.5
United Kingdom	98.8	-0.2	50.9	**10.2**	m	m	m	m
Italy	98.7	**2.0**	27.7	**12.7**	93	97	19	5.7
Ireland	98.7	**1.6**	36.0	**15.2**	74	100	16	3.4
Korea	98.6	-0.3	10.1	**3.4**	41	94	9	0.6
Estonia	98.5	**0.9**	37.3	**15.3**	138	170	23	9.0
Czech Republic	98.1	**1.0**	36.9	**17.0**	122	155	18	9.0
Spain	97.9	**6.7**	37.9	**17.1**	107	149	34	8.1
Chinese Taipei	97.7	**1.3**	30.0	**10.3**	74	153	23	5.8
United Arab Emirates	97.7	**14.3**	54.1	**16.4**	m	m	m	m
Poland	97.7	**3.1**	22.9	**12.2**	117	157	13	7.5
Croatia	97.5	**1.9**	16.2	**5.9**	103	143	23	7.4
Portugal	97.1	**-0.9**	36.6	**5.2**	99	149	24	6.1
Singapore	96.9	-0.1	47.9	**12.0**	102	152	20	7.6
New Zealand	96.8	0.5	41.6	**12.7**	98	125	25	6.2
Lithuania	96.6	**2.9**	16.3	**9.8**	m	m	m	m
Israel	96.5	**1.7**	44.6	**20.0**	106	133	25	8.9
Qatar	96.3	**-0.9**	59.7	**6.2**	m	m	m	m
Hungary	96.2	**2.3**	24.2	**8.7**	112	156	30	8.0
Serbia	95.7	**6.2**	10.7	**6.4**	110	136	20	9.9
Greece	94.6	**4.7**	18.4	**8.5**	108	139	42	9.4

Note: Countries/economies in which differences between 2009 and 2012 are statistically significant are marked in bold.
Countries and economies are ranked in descending order of the percentage of students with at least one computer at home in 2012.
Source: OECD, PISA 2012 Database, Tables 1.1 and 1.5a, b and c.
StatLink http://dx.doi.org/10.1787/888933253435

■ Table 0.1 [Part 2/2] ■
SNAPSHOT OF HOME ICT EQUIPMENT AND INTERNET USE

Countries/economies where home ICT equipment/time spent using the Internet is **above** the OECD average
Countries/economies where home ICT equipment/time spent using the Internet is not statistically different from the OECD average
Countries/economies where home ICT equipment/time spent using the Internet is **below** the OECD average

	Home ICT equipment				Time spent using the Internet			
	Students with at least one computer at home		Students with three or more computers at home		Average daily time spent using the Internet (lower bound)			Students who reported using the Internet outside of school for more than 6 hours during a typical weekday
	2012	Change between 2009 and 2012	2012	Change between 2009 and 2012	Outside of school, on weekdays	Outside of school, on weekend days	At school, on weekdays	
	%	% dif.	%	% dif.	Minutes	Minutes	Minutes	%
OECD average	95.8	**2.0**	42.8	**12.1**	104	138	25	7.2
United States	94.5	1.1	37.6	**7.2**	m	m	m	m
Latvia	94.5	**3.5**	19.9	**11.1**	117	147	17	7.6
Slovak Republic	94.4	**4.1**	26.4	**15.7**	116	152	32	8.1
Bulgaria	93.5	**6.3**	17.0	**10.0**	m	m	m	m
Montenegro	93.3	**8.0**	10.1	**5.8**	m	m	m	m
Russian Federation	92.8	**13.0**	10.5	**7.7**	130	161	34	13.7
Japan	92.4	**3.7**	17.1	**2.9**	70	111	13	4.5
Shanghai-China	91.9	**10.2**	17.6	**10.5**	39	106	10	2.2
Uruguay	89.6	**12.3**	20.4	**12.6**	118	144	30	11.0
Chile	88.3	**12.2**	20.9	**12.0**	106	148	30	9.3
Romania	87.1	**2.7**	8.7	**4.7**	m	m	m	m
Jordan	86.5	**11.9**	13.0	**7.2**	69	110	23	6.4
Argentina	83.3	**16.4**	18.7	**11.9**	m	m	m	m
Costa Rica	75.0	**11.3**	13.2	**5.7**	91	113	29	6.6
Malaysia	74.0	**10.6**	13.9	**4.9**	m	m	m	m
Brazil	73.5	**20.2**	9.4	**6.2**	m	m	m	m
Turkey	70.7	**9.4**	4.1	**2.4**	52	78	15	2.5
Kazakhstan	68.1	**14.8**	2.4	**1.6**	m	m	m	m
Thailand	65.6	**10.1**	6.1	**1.7**	m	m	m	m
Albania	65.4	**16.2**	3.5	**1.6**	m	m	m	m
Colombia	62.9	**15.2**	5.2	**2.9**	m	m	m	m
Tunisia	59.6	**14.3**	5.2	**3.4**	m	m	m	m
Mexico	58.5	**8.9**	9.1	**4.3**	80	91	26	5.3
Peru	52.8	**14.6**	6.2	**2.5**	m	m	m	m
Viet Nam	38.9	m	2.0	m	m	m	m	m
Indonesia	25.8	4.7	1.9	1.1	m	m	m	m

Note: Countries/economies in which differences between 2009 and 2012 are statistically significant are marked in bold.
Countries and economies are ranked in descending order of the percentage of students with at least one computer at home in 2012.
Source: OECD, PISA 2012 Database, Tables 1.1 and 1.5a, b and c.
StatLink http://dx.doi.org/10.1787/888933253435

■ Table 0.2 [Part 1/2] ■
SNAPSHOT OF ICT EQUIPMENT AND USE AT SCHOOL

- (dark shading) Countries/economies where the number of students per school computer is **below** the OECD average/ICT use is **above** the OECD average
- (no shading) Countries/economies where the number of students per school computer/ICT use is not statistically different from the OECD average
- (light shading) Countries/economies where the number of students per school computer is **above** the OECD average/ICT use is **below** the OECD average

	Number of students per school computer	ICT use at and for school						
		Students using computers at school		Students browsing the Internet for schoolwork at least once a week				Students who reported the use of computers in mathematics lessons during the month prior to the PISA test
				At school		Outside of school		
	2012	2012	Change between 2009 and 2012	2012	Change between 2009 and 2012	2012	Change between 2009 and 2012	2012
	Mean	%	% dif.	%	% dif.	%	% dif.	%
OECD average	4.7	72.0	**1.3**	41.9	**3.4**	54.9	**9.5**	31.6
Australia	0.9	93.7	**2.1**	80.8	**15.8**	75.6	**7.8**	40.0
New Zealand	1.2	86.4	**3.0**	59.3	**9.1**	66.1	**14.5**	28.6
Macao-China	1.3	87.6	**7.5**	26.7	1.5	44.2	**12.9**	34.0
United Kingdom	1.4	m	m	m	m	m	m	m
Czech Republic	1.6	83.2	**4.1**	47.6	**9.8**	61.6	**15.8**	25.6
Norway	1.7	91.9	-1.1	69.0	-0.2	68.8	**5.4**	73.1
United States	1.8	m	m	m	m	m	m	m
Lithuania	1.9	m	m	m	m	m	m	m
Slovak Republic	2.0	80.2	0.9	43.1	0.0	50.3	**11.1**	33.3
Singapore	2.0	69.9	**7.2**	30.4	**4.5**	56.0	**12.8**	34.4
Liechtenstein	2.1	91.8	0.9	41.3	**-14.5**	43.9	**10.1**	37.9
Estonia	2.1	61.0	**5.2**	28.9	**7.3**	64.0	**13.7**	39.2
Hong Kong-China	2.2	83.8	1.1	22.7	**-5.5**	50.3	**6.2**	16.8
Spain	2.2	73.2	**7.7**	51.1	**8.5**	61.9	**13.7**	29.4
Luxembourg	2.2	m	m	m	m	m	m	m
Hungary	2.2	74.7	**5.3**	35.7	**-4.7**	52.7	2.4	25.9
Latvia	2.2	52.4	**5.1**	23.1	**5.9**	54.4	**13.6**	30.8
Denmark	2.4	86.7	**-6.3**	80.8	**6.6**	74.3	**13.2**	58.3
Kazakhstan	2.5	m	m	m	m	m	m	m
Ireland	2.6	63.5	0.6	32.4	**6.4**	45.4	**16.7**	17.6
Bulgaria	2.6	m	m	m	m	m	m	m
Netherlands	2.6	94.0	**-2.6**	67.5	0.2	65.8	**12.7**	20.2
Switzerland	2.7	78.3	2.6	32.5	**-2.9**	46.0	**8.6**	29.6
Belgium	2.8	65.3	**2.5**	29.4	**12.6**	57.1	**14.0**	25.6
Canada	2.8	m	m	m	m	m	m	m
France	2.9	m	m	m	m	m	m	m
Shanghai-China	2.9	38.3	m	9.7	m	38.5	m	8.6
Austria	2.9	81.4	-2.7	48.0	2.8	53.0	**10.5**	38.3
Russian Federation	3.0	80.2	**7.9**	20.3	**3.5**	62.9	**29.4**	52.6
Thailand	3.1	m	m	m	m	m	m	m
Finland	3.1	89.0	1.6	34.9	**4.2**	28.3	**10.5**	19.1
Slovenia	3.3	57.2	-1.0	41.6	**7.3**	58.8	**14.6**	29.6
Japan	3.6	59.2	0.0	11.3	-1.6	16.5	**7.7**	23.8
Colombia	3.7	m	m	m	m	m	m	m
Sweden	3.7	87.0	-2.1	66.6	**6.3**	58.5	**11.2**	20.0
Portugal	3.7	69.0	**13.8**	38.1	-2.2	67.4	**6.9**	28.8
Poland	4.0	60.3	-0.3	30.3	**3.6**	66.4	**10.0**	23.3
Iceland	4.1	81.9	**2.4**	28.9	**-9.0**	35.8	**4.5**	33.5

Note: Countries/economies in which differences between 2009 and 2012 are statistically significant are marked in bold.
Countries and economies are ranked in ascending order of the number of students per school computer in 2012.
Source: OECD, PISA 2012 Database, Tables 2.1, 2.3, 2.5, 2.7 and 2.11.
StatLink http://dx.doi.org/10.1787/888933253441

■ Table 0.2 [Part 2/2] ■

SNAPSHOT OF ICT EQUIPMENT AND USE AT SCHOOL

Countries/economies where the number of students per school computer is **below** the OECD average/ICT use is **above** the OECD average
Countries/economies where the number of students per school computer/ICT use is not statistically different from the OECD average
Countries/economies where the number of students per school computer is **above** the OECD average/ICT use is **below** the OECD average

	Number of students per school computer	ICT use at and for school						
		Students using computers at school		Students browsing the Internet for schoolwork at least once a week				Students who reported the use of computers in mathematics lessons during the month prior to the PISA test
				At school		Outside of school		
	2012	2012	Change between 2009 and 2012	2012	Change between 2009 and 2012	2012	Change between 2009 and 2012	2012
	Mean	%	% dif.	%	% dif.	%	% dif.	%
OECD average	4.7	72.0	**1.3**	41.9	**3.4**	54.9	**9.5**	31.6
Italy	4.1	66.8	**3.0**	28.8	1.3	49.1	**3.6**	40.4
Qatar	4.2	m	m	m	m	m	m	m
United Arab Emirates	4.2	m	m	m	m	m	m	m
Germany	4.2	68.7	**4.1**	28.9	2.3	51.3	**11.5**	26.9
Romania	4.6	m	m	m	m	m	m	m
Israel	4.7	55.2	4.0	30.6	**3.3**	49.0	**6.4**	30.7
Chile	4.7	61.7	**4.9**	44.5	0.3	64.7	**17.7**	28.3
Jordan	5.0	79.7	**5.7**	32.6	2.0	42.7	**14.7**	69.6
Croatia	5.0	78.3	**10.3**	31.4	**3.4**	59.2	**18.9**	23.7
Korea	5.3	41.9	**-20.9**	11.0	**-2.6**	31.3	**-10.6**	9.8
Chinese Taipei	5.8	78.8	m	28.6	m	25.9	m	9.3
Montenegro	7.7	m	m	m	m	m	m	m
Peru	7.9	m	m	m	m	m	m	m
Greece	8.2	65.9	**8.0**	44.9	**9.7**	54.4	**13.7**	33.3
Viet Nam	8.6	m	m	m	m	m	m	m
Uruguay	8.7	49.9	2.2	40.0	**11.2**	73.2	**19.6**	39.4
Serbia	8.8	82.0	**10.7**	24.9	**7.0**	48.7	**21.3**	33.4
Albania	8.9	m	m	m	m	m	m	m
Argentina	14.1	m	m	m	m	m	m	m
Mexico	15.5	60.6	m	39.5	m	67.0	m	41.4
Indonesia	16.4	m	m	m	m	m	m	m
Malaysia	16.7	m	m	m	m	m	m	m
Costa Rica	17.7	57.4	m	38.3	m	64.8	m	25.6
Brazil	22.1	m	m	m	m	m	m	m
Turkey	44.9	48.7	-2.1	28.0	0.0	50.2	-1.9	41.7
Tunisia	53.1	m	m	m	m	m	m	m

Note: Countries/economies in which differences between 2009 and 2012 are statistically significant are marked in bold.
Countries and economies are ranked in ascending order of the number of students per school computer in 2012.
Source: OECD, PISA 2012 Database, Tables 2.1, 2.3, 2.5, 2.7 and 2.11.
StatLink http://dx.doi.org/10.1787/888933253441

▪ Table 0.3 ▪
SNAPSHOT OF PERFORMANCE IN COMPUTER-BASED ASSESSMENTS

Countries/economies with performance **above** the OECD average
Countries/economies with performance not statistically different from the OECD average
Countries/economies with performance **below** the OECD average

	Performance in digital reading			**Performance in computer-based mathematics**		
	Mean score in PISA 2012	Change between 2009 and 2012	Relative performance in digital reading, compared with students around the world with similar performance in print reading	Mean score in PISA 2012	Solution rate on tasks that do not require the use of computers to solve problems	Solution rate on tasks that require the use of computers to solve problems
	Mean score	Score dif.	Score dif.	Mean score	% correct	% correct
OECD average	497	1	-5	497	38.1	26.6
Singapore	567	m	32	566	55.2	41.8
Korea	555	**-12**	24	553	50.2	37.8
Hong Kong-China	550	**35**	12	550	49.7	36.6
Japan	545	**26**	13	539	47.8	36.5
Canada	532	m	11	523	42.4	32.4
Shanghai-China	531	m	-26	562	52.5	39.6
Estonia	523	m	7	516	42.2	29.0
Australia	521	**-16**	9	508	41.0	29.8
Ireland	520	**11**	-1	493	37.9	24.6
Chinese Taipei	519	m	-2	537	46.8	35.2
Macao-China	515	**23**	5	543	45.9	34.7
United States	511	m	10	498	36.9	27.2
France	511	**17**	4	508	42.3	26.9
Italy	504	m	11	499	38.0	25.2
Belgium	502	-5	-7	512	41.9	28.6
Norway	500	0	-6	498	38.6	27.0
Sweden	498	**-12**	9	490	36.8	24.7
Denmark	495	6	-5	496	38.6	26.0
Portugal	486	m	-7	489	35.5	25.2
Austria	480	m	-15	507	38.5	27.9
Poland	477	**13**	-40	489	37.3	24.2
Slovak Republic	474	m	1	497	36.0	25.8
Slovenia	471	m	-17	487	34.0	24.3
Spain	466	-9	-25	475	33.3	21.5
Russian Federation	466	m	-17	489	34.8	24.9
Israel	461	m	-31	447	29.5	20.2
Chile	452	**18**	-4	432	26.0	15.5
Hungary	450	**-18**	-43	470	31.3	21.1
Brazil	436	m	3	421	23.6	16.2
United Arab Emirates	407	m	-50	434	25.2	18.1
Colombia	396	**27**	-30	397	19.1	11.5

Note: Countries/economies in which differences between 2009 and 2012 are statistically significant are marked in bold.
Countries and economies are ranked in descending order of mean performance in digital reading in 2012.
Source: OECD, PISA 2012 Database, Tables 3.2, 3.6, 3.8 and 3.11.
StatLink http://dx.doi.org/10.1787/888933253454

■ Table 0.4 ■
SNAPSHOT OF STUDENT NAVIGATION IN DIGITAL READING

- Countries/economies with performance/navigation **above** the OECD average
- Countries/economies with performance/navigation not statistically different from the OECD average
- Countries/economies with performance/navigation **below** the OECD average

	Performance in digital reading	Navigation in digital reading[1]	
		Overall browsing activity	Task-oriented browsing
	Mean score	Mean percentile rank	Mean percentile rank
OECD average	497	48	50
Singapore	567	68	64
Korea	555	77	58
Hong Kong-China	550	72	55
Japan	545	65	53
Canada	532	51	57
Shanghai-China	531	76	49
Estonia	523	54	49
Australia	521	48	58
Ireland	520	50	56
Chinese Taipei	519	76	48
Macao-China	515	76	49
United States	511	51	57
France	511	51	54
Italy	504	56	49
Belgium	502	46	50
Norway	500	43	49
Sweden	498	43	50
Denmark	495	47	50
Portugal	486	45	50
Austria	480	46	48
Poland	477	41	47
Slovak Republic	474	44	41
Slovenia	471	39	46
Spain	466	42	43
Russian Federation	466	44	40
Israel	461	39	46
Chile	452	40	42
Hungary	450	35	41
Brazil	436	28	37
United Arab Emirates	407	32	37
Colombia	396	29	33

1. To describe the navigation behaviour of students in the digital reading test, students' complete browsing sequences were divided into elementary sequences ("steps"), with an origin and a destination page. Two indices were derived from step counts.

A first index measures the quantity of navigation steps. To make this comparable across students who took different test forms, the *index of overall browsing activity* is computed as a percentile rank on the distribution of all students who were administered the same questions. A student with a value of, say, 73 on this index can be said to have browsed more pages than 73% of the students who took his or her same test form.

A second index relates to the quality of navigation steps. Not all pages available for browsing in the digital reading tests led students to information that was helpful or necessary for the specific task given to them. The *index of task-oriented browsing* measures how well students' navigation sequences conform to expectations, given the demands of the task. High values on this index correspond to long navigation sequences that contain a high number of task-relevant steps (steps from a relevant page to another relevant page) and few or no missteps or task-irrelevant steps (steps leading to non-relevant pages).

Countries and economies are ranked in descending order of mean performance in digital reading.

Source: OECD, PISA 2012 Database, Tables 3.2 and 4.1.

StatLink http://dx.doi.org/10.1787/888933253464

■ Table 0.5 [Part 1/2] ■

SNAPSHOT OF SOCIO-ECONOMIC DIFFERENCES IN ICT ACCESS AND USE

- (dark shading) Countries/economies where Internet access/time spent using the Internet/use of computers is **above** the OECD average among disadvantaged students
- (no shading) Countries/economies where Internet access/time spent using the Internet/use of computers is not statistically different from the OECD average among disadvantaged students
- (light shading) Countries/economies where Internet access/time spent using the Internet/use of computers is **below** the OECD average among disadvantaged students

	Internet access		Time spent using the Internet		Use of computers			
					Students using computers outside of school at least once a week to...			
	Students with a link to the Internet at home		Average daily time spent using the Internet, outside of school, during weekend days (lower bound)		...obtain practical information from the Internet		... play one-player games	
	Disadvantaged students	Difference between advantaged and disadvantaged students	Disadvantaged students	Difference between advantaged and disadvantaged students	Disadvantaged students	Difference between advantaged and disadvantaged students	Disadvantaged students	Difference between advantaged and disadvantaged students
	%	% dif.	Minutes	Minutes	%	% dif.	%	% dif.
OECD average	85.2	**13.4**	124	**7**	55.6	**18.6**	39.4	0.5
Denmark	99.3	**0.7**	154	0	67.3	**19.1**	36.0	-1.6
Iceland	99.1	**0.9**	160	**-18**	70.8	**11.1**	39.1	-3.1
Finland	98.8	**1.1**	109	-6	65.2	**9.1**	49.5	-3.8
Hong Kong-China	98.7	**0.9**	171	**-34**	53.5	**21.1**	36.1	2.1
Netherlands	98.6	**1.3**	148	-3	49.0	**18.4**	41.3	3.3
Norway	98.6	**1.3**	169	**-14**	71.3	**11.5**	44.0	-0.5
Switzerland	98.1	**1.5**	128	**-18**	61.3	**15.0**	27.9	-2.2
Sweden	98.1	**1.9**	170	-10	63.0	**12.6**	37.5	0.4
Slovenia	97.6	**2.1**	136	-7	61.0	**16.5**	50.8	**-8.8**
Estonia	97.4	**2.4**	167	-1	73.6	**12.3**	40.2	-0.5
Austria	97.1	**2.6**	120	-8	56.3	**18.0**	33.7	-1.6
United Kingdom	96.7	**3.2**	m	m	m	m	m	m
Germany	96.7	**3.2**	143	**-17**	57.6	**14.6**	33.4	-3.1
Macao-China	96.6	**2.5**	175	-5	54.0	**16.9**	40.2	2.2
Liechtenstein	95.8	4.2	132	-13	59.1	**26.4**	37.6	-2.2
France	95.6	**4.1**	m	m	m	m	m	m
Luxembourg	95.4	**4.2**	m	m	m	m	m	m
Belgium	95.3	**4.6**	130	**-11**	53.9	**14.9**	40.1	**-4.2**
Ireland	94.8	**4.6**	100	-5	41.9	**18.5**	37.3	**-5.3**
Canada	94.8	**5.0**	m	m	m	m	m	m
Korea	94.0	**5.7**	101	**-18**	43.1	**11.9**	30.9	-2.0
Australia	93.1	**6.6**	152	1	54.0	**22.2**	46.0	**-5.3**
Italy	92.9	**6.3**	94	**-7**	66.2	**13.1**	42.0	-2.1
Czech Republic	92.7	**7.0**	143	6	70.3	**16.4**	46.0	2.0
Singapore	91.8	**7.9**	150	0	56.7	**21.3**	35.7	0.3
Chinese Taipei	90.6	**8.6**	168	**-42**	49.0	**14.1**	40.4	-3.0
Croatia	89.2	**9.8**	135	4	57.9	**17.4**	45.7	3.8
Portugal	87.9	**11.5**	127	**16**	53.2	**23.8**	52.0	-4.2
Spain	85.7	**13.8**	140	3	51.6	**16.2**	29.6	-2.8
Poland	85.6	**14.0**	134	**25**	67.2	**19.0**	46.1	0.3
United Arab Emirates	84.0	**15.7**	m	m	m	m	m	m
Qatar	83.2	**15.6**	m	m	m	m	m	m

Notes: Countries/economies in which differences between advantaged and disadvantaged students are statistically significant are marked in bold. Advantaged students refers to students in the top quarter of the *PISA index of economic, social and cultural status;* disadvantaged students refers to students in the bottom quarter of that index.

Countries and economies are ranked in descending order of the percentage of disadvantaged students with a link to the Internet at home.

Source: OECD, PISA 2012 Database, Tables 5.1a, 5.11 and 5.12.

StatLink http://dx.doi.org/10.1787/888933253475

■ Table 0.5 [Part 2/2] ■
SNAPSHOT OF SOCIO-ECONOMIC DIFFERENCES IN ICT ACCESS AND USE

- Countries/economies where Internet access/time spent using the Internet/use of computers is **above** the OECD average among disadvantaged students
- Countries/economies where Internet access/time spent using the Internet/use of computers is not statistically different from the OECD average among disadvantaged students
- Countries/economies where Internet access/time spent using the Internet/use of computers is **below** the OECD average among disadvantaged students

	Internet access		Time spent using the Internet		Use of computers			
	Students with a link to the Internet at home		Average daily time spent using the Internet, outside of school, during weekend days (lower bound)		Students using computers outside of school at least once a week to…			
					…obtain practical information from the Internet		… play one-player games	
	Disadvantaged students	Difference between advantaged and disadvantaged students	Disadvantaged students	Difference between advantaged and disadvantaged students	Disadvantaged students	Difference between advantaged and disadvantaged students	Disadvantaged students	Difference between advantaged and disadvantaged students
	%	% dif.	Minutes	Minutes	%	% dif.	%	% dif.
OECD average	85.2	**13.4**	124	**7**	55.6	**18.6**	39.4	0.5
Lithuania	82.5	**16.7**	m	m	m	m	m	m
Israel	80.9	**18.3**	95	**29**	64.4	**13.7**	35.8	**5.2**
Hungary	80.8	**18.5**	137	7	58.6	**19.5**	52.5	-4.4
New Zealand	80.0	**19.6**	114	7	47.6	**26.4**	40.2	-0.4
United States	79.8	**19.9**	m	m	m	m	m	m
Russian Federation	79.5	**19.4**	144	**20**	50.9	**27.3**	42.5	-0.9
Bulgaria	79.0	**20.5**	m	m	m	m	m	m
Latvia	78.4	**20.9**	129	13	61.8	**19.7**	37.5	-0.5
Slovak Republic	76.9	**22.4**	125	**26**	53.6	**24.0**	40.0	3.2
Japan	75.3	**21.9**	109	-8	41.0	**15.9**	48.6	-1.5
Serbia	73.5	**25.5**	116	**23**	45.1	**23.5**	57.1	1.5
Greece	69.2	**28.8**	124	7	53.3	**15.9**	53.5	2.6
Montenegro	68.2	**31.2**	m	m	m	m	m	m
Shanghai-China	62.8	**34.7**	107	**-17**	37.9	**25.9**	29.1	2.2
Uruguay	57.7	**40.8**	85	**69**	45.7	**32.5**	33.5	**12.9**
Romania	52.1	**45.4**	m	m	m	m	m	m
Brazil	44.7	**51.1**	m	m	m	m	m	m
Argentina	44.4	**51.1**	m	m	m	m	m	m
Chile	44.0	**52.2**	95	**77**	35.8	**39.3**	27.0	**14.4**
Costa Rica	30.2	**66.6**	52	**97**	26.6	**40.3**	19.3	**27.6**
Jordan	29.8	**62.2**	54	**84**	34.9	**27.6**	31.4	**16.6**
Malaysia	27.6	**66.5**	m	m	m	m	m	m
Turkey	21.5	**64.2**	43	**58**	33.1	**26.5**	29.2	**18.4**
Kazakhstan	19.4	**65.4**	m	m	m	m	m	m
Colombia	17.4	**68.4**	m	m	m	m	m	m
Tunisia	15.8	**71.2**	m	m	m	m	m	m
Thailand	13.2	**71.4**	m	m	m	m	m	m
Peru	7.4	**71.0**	m	m	m	m	m	m
Mexico	6.0	**80.2**	35	**103**	28.0	**42.7**	11.0	**21.3**
Indonesia	6.0	**50.2**	m	m	m	m	m	m
Viet Nam	2.9	**70.4**	m	m	m	m	m	m

Notes: Countries/economies in which differences between advantaged and disadvantaged students are statistically significant are marked in bold. Advantaged students refers to students in the top quarter of the *PISA index of economic, social and cultural status;* disadvantaged students refers to students in the bottom quarter of that index.
Countries and economies are ranked in descending order of the percentage of disadvantaged students with a link to the Internet at home.
Source: OECD, PISA 2012 Database, Tables 5.1a, 5.11 and 5.12.
StatLink http://dx.doi.org/10.1787/888933253475

■ Table 0.6 ■

SNAPSHOT OF THE RELATION BETWEEN COMPUTER USE AT SCHOOL AND PERFORMANCE IN COMPUTER-BASED ASSESSMENTS

- Countries/economies with performance **above** the OECD average
- Countries/economies with performance not statistically different from the OECD average
- Countries/economies with performance **below** the OECD average

	Digital reading			Computer-based mathematics		
		Difference in performance, by frequency of browsing the Internet for schoolwork at school, after accounting for the socio-economic status of students and schools			Difference in performance, by use of computers in mathematics lessons, after accounting for the socio-economic status of students and schools	
	Mean score in PISA 2012	"Once or twice a month" minus "never or hardly ever"	"Once a week or more" minus "once or twice a month"	Mean score in PISA 2012	"Students did at least one task" minus "computers were not used"	"Only the teacher demonstrated the use of computers" minus "computers were not used"
	Mean score	Score dif.	Score dif.	Mean score	Score dif.	Score dif.
OECD average	497	**13**	**-8**	497	**-12**	**-6**
Singapore	567	**-6**	**-29**	566	**-27**	**10**
Korea	555	-4	-6	553	-11	-11
Hong Kong-China	550	**8**	**-21**	550	**-31**	-1
Japan	545	**10**	-2	539	**-12**	**-22**
Canada	532	m	m	523	m	m
Shanghai-China	531	**9**	**-19**	562	**-22**	-3
Estonia	523	3	**-23**	516	**-23**	-6
Australia	521	**30**	**11**	508	2	0
Ireland	520	**11**	3	493	**-16**	**10**
Chinese Taipei	519	**13**	-5	537	**-13**	**-15**
Macao-China	515	**6**	4	543	**-20**	4
United States	511	m	m	498	m	m
France	511	m	m	508	m	m
Italy	504	-2	**-13**	499	**-9**	-3
Belgium	502	**15**	**-11**	512	4	**7**
Norway	500	**49**	-2	498	**19**	-3
Sweden	498	**48**	**-13**	490	**-34**	**-18**
Denmark	495	**36**	-3	496	**15**	**-12**
Portugal	486	**-11**	**-15**	489	**-19**	2
Austria	480	**14**	-4	507	-5	**-13**
Poland	477	2	**-23**	489	**-27**	**-19**
Slovak Republic	474	**18**	2	497	**-32**	-9
Slovenia	471	3	**-8**	487	**-13**	**-10**
Spain	466	**12**	8	475	-1	10
Russian Federation	466	**-12**	**-19**	489	**-19**	**-9**
Israel	461	8	**-28**	447	**-37**	-12
Chile	452	4	**-8**	432	**-27**	-5
Hungary	450	3	**-21**	470	**-21**	-7
Brazil	436	m	m	421	m	m
United Arab Emirates	407	m	m	434	m	m
Colombia	396	m	m	397	m	m

Note: Countries/economies in which score differences are statistically significant are marked in bold.
Countries and economies are ranked in descending order of mean performance in digital reading in 2012.
Source: OECD, PISA 2012 Database, Tables 3.1, 3.8, 6.3c and 6.5h.
StatLink http://dx.doi.org/10.1787/888933253481

Reader's Guide

Data underlying the figures

The data tables are listed in Annex B and available on line at http://dx.doi.org/10.1787/edu-data-en.

Four symbols are used to denote missing data:

a The category does not apply in the country concerned. Data are therefore missing.

c There are too few observations or no observation to provide reliable estimates (i.e. there are fewer than 30 students or less than five schools with valid data).

m Data are not available. These data were not submitted by the country or were collected but subsequently removed from the publication for technical reasons.

w Data have been withdrawn or have not been collected at the request of the country concerned.

Country coverage

This publication features data on 64 countries and economies: 34 OECD countries (indicated in black in the figures) and 30 partner countries and economies (indicated in blue in the figures).

Calculating international averages

An OECD average was calculated for most indicators presented in this report. The OECD average corresponds to the arithmetic mean of the respective country estimates. Readers should, therefore, keep in mind that the term "OECD average" refers to the OECD countries included in the respective comparisons.

Rounding figures

Because of rounding, some figures in tables may not exactly add up to the totals. Totals, differences and averages are always calculated on the basis of exact numbers and are rounded only after calculation. All standard errors in this publication have been rounded to one or two decimal places. Where the value 0.00 is shown, this does not imply that the standard error is zero, but that it is smaller than 0.005.

Bolding of estimates

This report discusses only statistically significant differences or changes (statistical significance at the 5% level). These are denoted in darker colours in figures and in bold in tables.

Reporting student data

The report uses "15-year-olds" as shorthand for the PISA target population. PISA covers students who are aged between 15 years 3 months and 16 years 2 months at the time of assessment and who have completed at least 6 years of formal schooling, regardless of the type of institution in which they are enrolled and of whether they are in full-time or part-time education, of whether they attend academic or vocational programmes, and of whether they attend public or private schools or foreign schools within the country.

Reporting school data

The principals of the schools in which students were assessed provided information on their schools' characteristics by completing a school questionnaire. Where responses from school principals are presented in this publication, they are weighted so that they are proportionate to the number of 15-year-olds enrolled in the school.

Indices used in this report

Some analyses in this report are based on synthetic indices. Student questionnaire indices summarise information from several related questionnaire responses into a single global measure. The construction of the following indices is detailed in the *PISA 2012 Technical Report* (OECD, 2014):

- *Index of ICT use at school*
- *Index of ICT use outside of school for leisure*
- *Index of ICT use outside of school for schoolwork*
- *Index of computer use in mathematics lessons*
- *Four indices of mathematics teachers' behaviour (student orientation, formative assessment, structuring practices, cognitive activation strategies)*
- *Index of disciplinary climate in mathematics lessons*
- *PISA index of economic, social and cultural status*

In addition, two indices used in Chapter 4 of this report were derived to describe students' interactions with digital reading tasks in the computer-based assessment of digital reading:

- *Index of overall browsing activity*
- *Index of task-oriented browsing*

Abbreviations used in this report

% dif.	Percentage-point difference	ICT	Information and communication technology
Dif.	Difference	PPP	Purchasing power parity
ESCS	PISA index of economic, social and cultural status	S.E.	Standard error
GDP	Gross domestic product		

Further documentation

For further information on the PISA assessment instruments and the methods used in PISA, see the *PISA 2012 Technical Report* (OECD, 2014).

StatLinks

This report uses the OECD StatLinks service. Below each table and chart is a url leading to a corresponding Excel™ workbook containing the underlying data. These urls are stable and will remain unchanged over time. In addition, readers of the e-books will be able to click directly on these links and the workbook will open in a separate window, if their Internet browser is open and running.

Note regarding Israel

The statistical data for Israel are supplied by and under the responsibility of the relevant Israeli authorities. The use of such data by the OECD is without prejudice to the status of the Golan Heights, East Jerusalem and Israeli settlements in the West Bank under the terms of international law.

Reference

OECD (2014), *PISA 2012 Technical Report*, PISA, OECD, Paris, www.oecd.org/pisa/pisaproducts/pisa2012technicalreport.htm.

1

How Students' Use of Computers has Evolved in Recent Years

Children access and use information and communication technology (ICT) earlier than ever before. This chapter uses data from PISA 2012 to examine how students' access to ICT devices, and their experience in using these technologies, evolved in recent years. It explores the frequency and variety of uses of ICT at home, and the differences in students' use of computers between countries. The chapter also discusses how students' use of computers and the Internet at home is changing the way they engage with learning and school.

In recent years, information and communication technology (ICT) has modified the world in which students grow and learn. More and more families own an increasing number of computers, most of which are now connected to the Internet. New devices, such as tablet computers and smartphones, offer the possibility of accessing the Internet (almost) anytime, anywhere. This, in turn, means that children access and use ICT earlier than ever before – and increasingly by themselves, without adult supervision.

The rapid development of ICT has driven much of this change. In just three years, between 2008 and 2011, the volume of Internet traffic, measured in bytes, increased more than three-fold. The rolling out of broadband infrastructures has meant an expansion in the bandwidth available for all types of services whose primary activity is the transfer of information. Greater availability of bandwidth, in turn, has driven many services to online platforms that can increasingly be accessed with mobile devices. These services, including not only traditional telecommunication, such as telephony, but also broadcast TV and radio, video and book publishing, as well as banking and money transfer services, can now be – and increasingly are – consumed "on the go" (OECD, 2013a). To access this wealth of services, households have invested in upgrading their ICT equipment.

As a result, new technologies have transformed not only our professional lives, but our private lives too – the way we read, socialise and play. Young generations are at the forefront of this transformation. For them, ICT devices and the Internet are usually first experienced as a platform for communicating, playing games and sharing hobbies, through participation in social networks, e-mail or chat. Only later, and to a lesser extent, do they engage in formal learning activities on computers.

What the data tell us

- In 49 out of 63 countries and economies, the number of computer-equipped households among the PISA student population increased between 2009 and 2012. In all but one of the remaining 14 countries and economies, the number of home computers to which students had access increased.
- On average across OECD countries, students spend over 2 hours on line each day. The most common online activity is browsing the Internet for fun, with 88% of students doing this at least once a week – 6% more than in 2009, on average.
- Students who spend more than 6 hours on line per weekday, outside of school, are particularly at risk of reporting that they feel lonely at school, and that they arrived late for school or skipped days of school.

This chapter uses PISA 2012 data to investigate how students' access to ICT devices and experience in using these technologies evolved in recent years. It also explores the frequency and variety of uses of ICT at home, and differences between countries in how students use information and communication technology. Finally, it shows that these changes are not without consequences on the way students engage with learning and school.

Box 1.1. **How information on students' familiarity with ICT was collected**

PISA collects internationally comparable information on students' access to and use of computers and their attitudes towards the use of computers for learning. In PISA 2012, 29 OECD countries and 13 partner countries and economies chose to distribute the optional ICT familiarity component of the student questionnaire. In 2012, this component contained 12 questions, some of which were retained from the previous PISA survey (2009) to allow for comparisons across time. New questions focus on the age at first use of computers and the Internet; the amount of time spent on the Internet; and, since mathematics was the major domain assessed in PISA 2012, on the use of computers during mathematics lessons.

The OECD countries that participated were Australia, Austria, Belgium, Chile, the Czech Republic, Denmark, Estonia, Finland, Germany, Greece, Hungary, Iceland, Ireland, Israel, Italy, Japan, Korea, Mexico, the Netherlands, New Zealand, Norway, Poland, Portugal, the Slovak Republic, Slovenia, Spain, Sweden, Switzerland and Turkey.

The partner countries and economies that participated were Costa Rica, Croatia, Hong Kong-China, Jordan, Latvia, Liechtenstein, Macao-China, the Russian Federation, Serbia, Shanghai-China, Singapore, Chinese Taipei and Uruguay.

With the exception of Costa Rica, Mexico, Shanghai-China and Chinese Taipei, all other countries and economies had also distributed the ICT familiarity module as part of the student questionnaire in 2009. Trends based on this module are therefore available for 28 OECD countries and 10 partner countries and economies.

Additional information on the availability and use of ICT at home and at school, as well as on school policies on using ICT, was collected through the main student and school questionnaires, and is available for all participants in PISA 2012. In the student questionnaire, students answered questions on whether or not they have a home computer to use for schoolwork, educational software, and a link to the Internet; how many computers they have at home; whether they program computers; and how many hours, on average, they spend repeating and training content from school lessons by working on a computer (e.g. learning vocabulary with training software). As part of the school questionnaire, principals provided information on the availability of computers at their schools and on whether they feel that a lack of computers hindered instruction in their school. A new question in PISA 2012 also asked school principals to report on the extent to which students are expected to access the Internet to perform school-related work.

STUDENTS' ACCESS TO ICT AT HOME

Earlier publications on ICT have often emphasised the "digital divide" that separates those who live in a digital and connected world from those who are left behind on the analogue side of the divide. Students' use of ICT is conditional upon the accessibility of devices and the availability of a connection to the Internet. PISA data show that in a majority of participating countries, access to computers had, by 2012, become nearly universal. However, important between-country differences exist in the quantity and quality of devices accessible, and in the experience acquired in using them. This chapter focuses on these differences in computer access and use.

■ Figure 1.1 ■

Change between 2009 and 2012 in access to computers at home

Percentage of students who reported having at least one computer or three or more computers at home

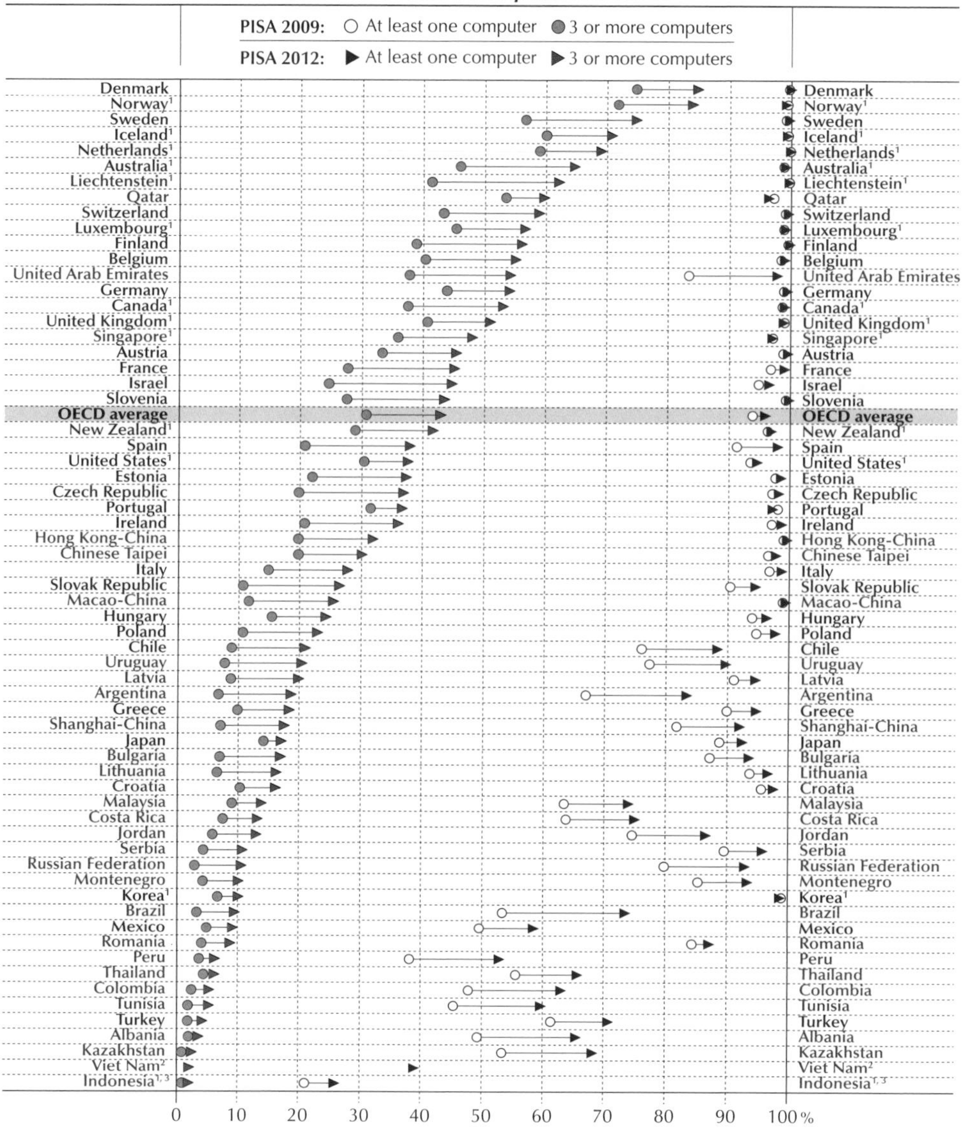
PISA 2009: At least one computer 3 or more computers
PISA 2012: At least one computer 3 or more computers
Denmark
Norway[1]
Sweden
Iceland[1]
Netherlands[1]
Australia[1]
Liechtenstein[1]
Qatar
Switzerland
Luxembourg[1]
Finland
Belgium
United Arab Emirates
Germany
Canada[1]
United Kingdom[1]
Singapore[1]
Austria
France
Israel
Slovenia
OECD average
New Zealand[1]
Spain
United States[1]
Estonia
Czech Republic
Portugal
Ireland
Hong Kong-China
Chinese Taipei
Italy
Slovak Republic
Macao-China
Hungary
Poland
Chile
Uruguay
Latvia
Argentina
Greece
Shanghai-China
Japan
Bulgaria
Lithuania
Croatia
Malaysia
Costa Rica
Jordan
Serbia
Russian Federation
Montenegro
Korea[1]
Brazil
Mexico
Romania
Peru
Thailand
Colombia
Tunisia
Turkey
Albania
Kazakhstan
Viet Nam[2]
Indonesia[1, 3]
0
10
20
30
40
50
60
70
80
90
100 %

1. The share of students with at least one computer at home is not significantly different in 2009 and 2012.
2. PISA 2009 data are missing for Viet Nam.
3. The share of students with three or more computers at home is not significantly different in 2009 and 2012.

Countries and economies are ranked in descending order of the percentage of students who reported having three or more computers at home in 2012.

Source: OECD, PISA 2012 Database, Table 1.1.

StatLink http://dx.doi.org/10.1787/888933252593

Access to a home computer

Data collected from students participating in the PISA assessment show that by 2012, computers were present in almost every household across most OECD countries, and often in large numbers. On average across OECD countries, only 4% of 15-year-old students lived in homes where no computer was present, and 43% of them lived in homes with three or more computers. However, this country average masks large disparities. For instance, among OECD countries, 42% of students in Mexico and 29% of students in Turkey did not have a computer in their homes (and these shares exclude 15-year-olds who are not in school).[1] Meanwhile, more than half of students in the partner countries Indonesia (74%) and Viet Nam (61%) did not have a computer at home. In these countries, the so-called "first digital divide", between "have" and "have nots", has not yet been closed (Table 1.1).

Between 2009 and 2012, more students gained access to computers, and the share of students with no computer at home declined. In 49 out of the 63 countries and economies with comparable data for 2009 and 2012, the number of computer-equipped households increased, and where it did not – sometimes because almost all students already had computers at home by 2009 – the number of home computers to which students had access increased. For instance, in Albania, Argentina, Brazil and Colombia, the share of students with a computer at home increased by 15 percentage points or more. In Denmark, Iceland, the Netherlands, Norway and Sweden, where fewer than 1% of 15-year-old students had no computer at home in 2009, the share of students who reported having more than three home computers increased by around 10 percentage points or more over the three-year period. By 2012, more than two out of three students in these countries had three computers or more at home (Figure 1.1 and Table 1.1).

Home Internet access

Home ICT devices today are mostly used to access services offered on the Internet, such as computer-mediated communication (Internet telephony, e-mail, instant messaging, chat, etc.), web-based services (social network and online community services, news websites, e-commerce, online banking, etc.) and cloud computing services based on data transfer systems (software-as-a-service, file storage, video streaming, etc.). Many of these services can support formal and informal learning. As a result, home computers or mobile devices connected to the Internet also offer users a host of educational resources, both in terms of content and applications, and often for free. Without a connection to the Internet, students have only limited, if any, ICT tools that support collaboration; and they do not have access to online encyclopaedias or other multimedia content in native and foreign languages. An Internet connection at home thus represents a substantial difference in the educational resources available to students.

Figure 1.2 shows the percentage of students in each country who reported having access to the Internet at home. On average across OECD countries, 93% of students reported that they had a link to the Internet at home. In Denmark, Finland, Hong Kong-China, Iceland, the Netherlands, Norway, Slovenia, Sweden and Switzerland, at least 99% of students' homes had Internet access. Only in five countries that participated in the PISA 2012 survey – Indonesia, Mexico, Peru, Thailand and Viet Nam – did fewer than one in two homes have Internet access.

■ Figure 1.2 ■

Change between 2009 and 2012 in Internet access at home

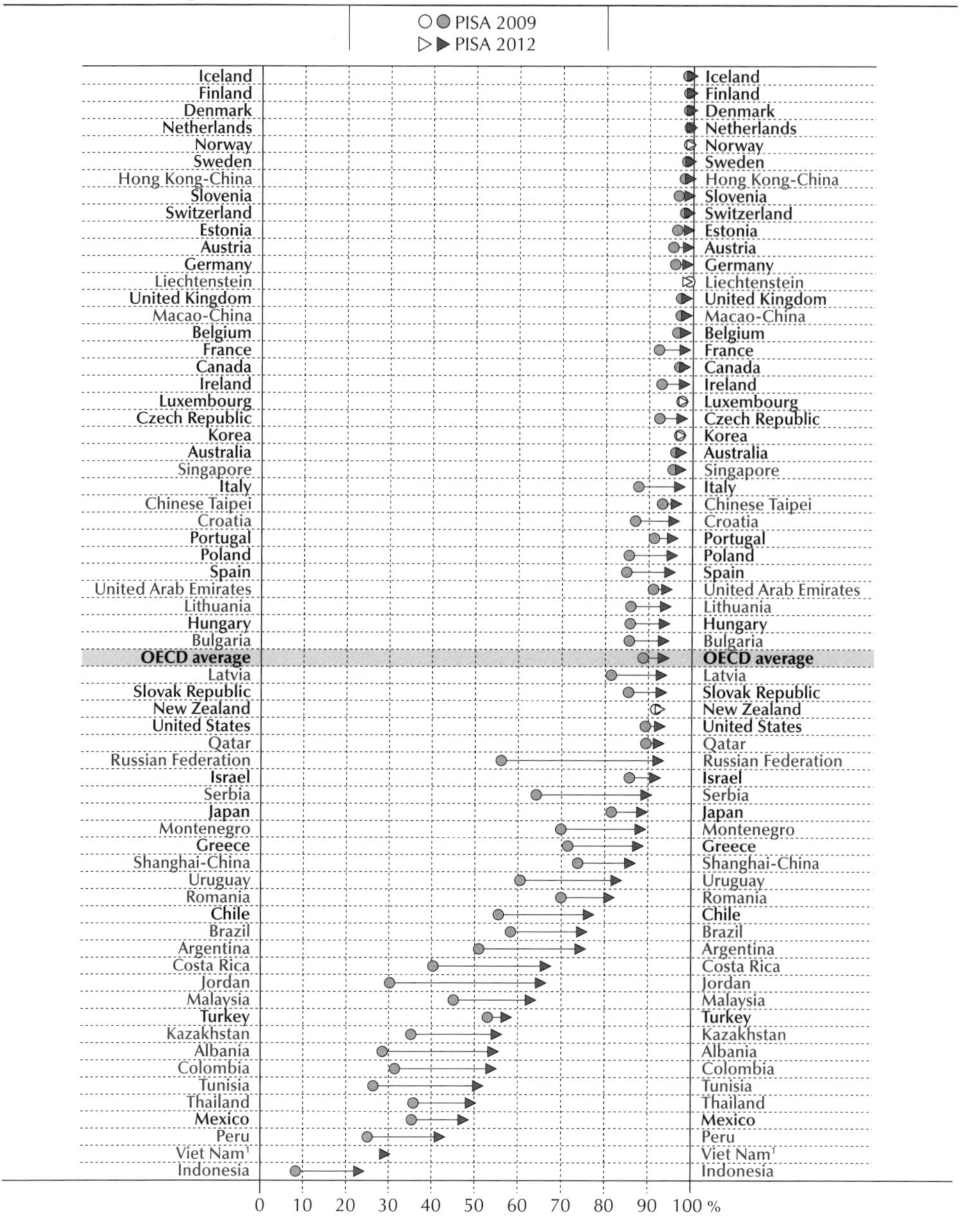
PISA 2009
PISA 2012
Iceland
Finland
Denmark
Netherlands
Norway
Sweden
Hong Kong-China
Slovenia
Switzerland
Estonia
Austria
Germany
Liechtenstein
United Kingdom
Macao-China
Belgium
France
Canada
Ireland
Luxembourg
Czech Republic
Korea
Australia
Singapore
Italy
Chinese Taipei
Croatia
Portugal
Poland
Spain
United Arab Emirates
Lithuania
Hungary
Bulgaria
OECD average
Latvia
Slovak Republic
New Zealand
United States
Qatar
Russian Federation
Israel
Serbia
Japan
Montenegro
Greece
Shanghai-China
Uruguay
Romania
Chile
Brazil
Argentina
Costa Rica
Jordan
Malaysia
Turkey
Kazakhstan
Albania
Colombia
Tunisia
Thailand
Mexico
Peru
Viet Nam1
Indonesia
0
10
20
30
40
50
60
70
80
90
100 %

1. PISA 2009 data are missing for Viet Nam.

Note: White symbols indicate differences between PISA 2009 and PISA 2012 that are not statistically significant.

Countries and economies are ranked in descending order of the percentage of students accessing the Internet at home in 2012.

Source: OECD, PISA 2012 Database, Table 1.2.

StatLink http://dx.doi.org/10.1787/888933252605

In almost all countries, Internet access increased between 2009 and 2012. The OECD average increase was 5 percentage points. The expansion in Internet access was largest in Albania, Costa Rica, Jordan, the Russian Federation and Serbia, with increases of more than 25 percentage points (Figure 1.2 and Table 1.2).

Students' experience using computers

At what age did students begin using computers? When did they first access the Internet? How many of them have never used a computer or accessed the Internet? Because the narrowing of the "first digital divide" is a recent trend, large gaps across and within countries emerge when examining the age at which students who were 15 in 2012 had started using computers (Figures 1.3 and 1.4).

■ Figure 1.3 ■

Age at first use of computers

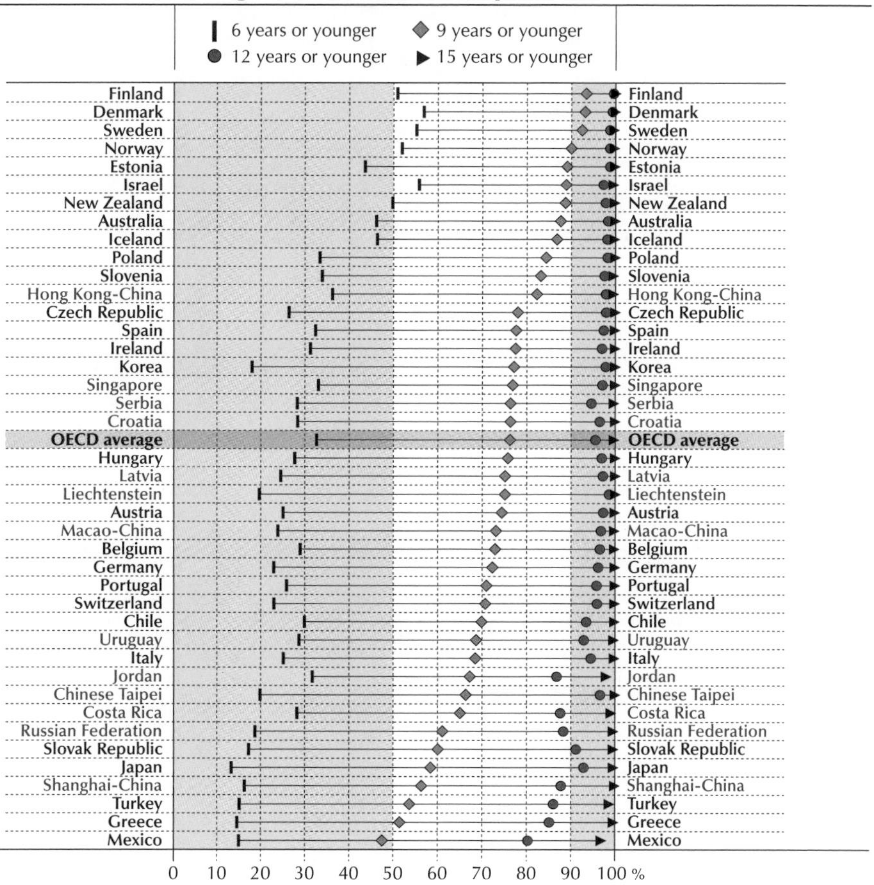
6 years or younger
9 years or younger
12 years or younger
15 years or younger
Finland
Denmark
Sweden
Norway
Estonia
Israel
New Zealand
Australia
Iceland
Poland
Slovenia
Hong Kong-China
Czech Republic
Spain
Ireland
Korea
Singapore
Serbia
Croatia
OECD average
Hungary
Latvia
Liechtenstein
Austria
Macao-China
Belgium
Germany
Portugal
Switzerland
Chile
Uruguay
Italy
Jordan
Chinese Taipei
Costa Rica
Russian Federation
Slovak Republic
Japan
Shanghai-China
Turkey
Greece
Mexico
0
10
20
30
40
50
60
70
80
90
100 %

Countries and economies are ranked in descending order of the percentage of students who started using computers at age 9 or younger.

Source: OECD, PISA 2012 Database, Table 1.3.

StatLink http://dx.doi.org/10.1787/888933252619

Age at first use of computers

The typical 15-year-old student in 2012 had at least five years of experience using computers. Across all countries and economies analysed, except Mexico, more than one in two students reported that they were 9 years old or younger when they used a computer for the first time. In five countries – Denmark, Finland, Israel, Norway and Sweden – a majority of 15-year-olds reported having first used computers at age 6 or younger, and therefore had started using computers in the early 2000s. These early users had already gained some familiarity with ICT tools when they were taught to read and write. More than nine out of ten students in Denmark, Finland and Sweden had started using computers by the time they turned 10 (Figure 1.3).

■ Figure 1.4 ■

Age at first use of the Internet

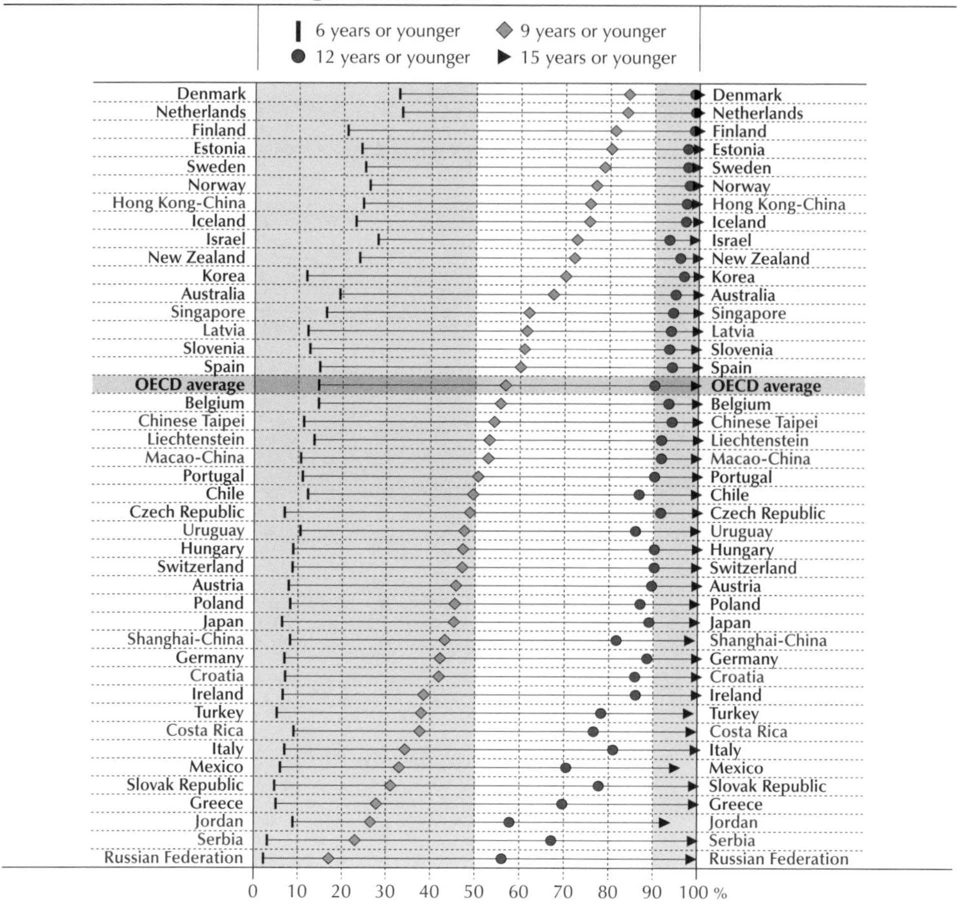
6 years or younger
9 years or younger
12 years or younger
15 years or younger
Denmark
Netherlands
Finland
Estonia
Sweden
Norway
Hong Kong-China
Iceland
Israel
New Zealand
Korea
Australia
Singapore
Latvia
Slovenia
Spain
OECD average
Belgium
Chinese Taipei
Liechtenstein
Macao-China
Portugal
Chile
Czech Republic
Uruguay
Hungary
Switzerland
Austria
Poland
Japan
Shanghai-China
Germany
Croatia
Ireland
Turkey
Costa Rica
Italy
Mexico
Slovak Republic
Greece
Jordan
Serbia
Russian Federation
0
10
20
30
40
50
60
70
80
90
100 %

Countries and economies are ranked in descending order of the percentage of students who started using the Internet at age 9 or younger.

Source: OECD, PISA 2012 Database, Table 1.4.

StatLink http://dx.doi.org/10.1787/888933252625

By contrast, more than one in ten students in Costa Rica, Greece, Jordan, Mexico, the Russian Federation, Shanghai-China and Turkey had no or only limited experience in using computers in 2012 when they were 15. These students first used a computer at age 13 or older – or, more rarely, they had never used one. Some 3% of students in Mexico, 2% in Jordan, and 1% of students in Costa Rica and Turkey had never used a computer; these students were overwhelmingly from the bottom quarter of disadvantaged students. In all other countries and economies, well under 1% of students had never used a computer (Table 1.3).

Age at first use of the Internet

At 15, students have typically had at least five years of experience with the Internet, although for many students, the first computer they used did not have Internet access. A comparison of students' answers about computer use, in general, and Internet use, in particular, implies that students typically accessed the Internet for the first time one-and-a-half years after they started using computers.[2] On average across OECD countries, 57% of students had accessed the Internet for the first time when they were younger than 10 (at that age, 76% of students were already using computers). In Denmark and the Netherlands, more than 30% of students had accessed the Internet for the first time before they turned 7 (Figure 1.4).

In some countries, large shares of students who had participated in PISA 2012 had accessed the Internet only recently, if at all. In Jordan, the Russian Federation and Serbia, more than 30% of students accessed the Internet for the first time after they turned 13 – i.e. after 2009. This is consistent with the observation that, in these countries, home Internet access expanded rapidly between the PISA 2009 and PISA 2012 surveys (see Figure 1.2). In Jordan and Mexico, a significant number of students (more than 5%) reported in 2012 that they had had no experience in accessing the Internet (Table 1.4).

STUDENTS' USE OF COMPUTERS AND THE INTERNET OUTSIDE OF SCHOOL

PISA data show that students spend far more time on line outside of school than while at school. Many of the students who were 15 years old in 2012 had started using computers before they even went to school. This section explores how students use ICT devices outside of school.

How much time students spend on line

For the first time, PISA 2012 measured how much time, within a typical school week, students spend using the Internet at school and at home, both during school days and during weekends. Because the answers were given on a categorical scale, it is not possible to compute exactly the average time students spend on line. However, it is possible to establish with confidence a lower bound for the number of minutes students spend on online activities, whereby the answer "between one and two hours", for instance, is converted into "61 minutes at least". Self-reports show that, on average across OECD countries, students typically spend over two hours on line each day on school days as well as during weekends (Figure 1.5).

During weekdays, in Australia, Denmark, Estonia, Norway, the Russian Federation and Sweden, more than one in four students (25%) spend over four hours per day on line outside of school. On average, students in these countries, as well as in the Czech Republic and Iceland, spend at least two hours (120 minutes) on line outside of school, during weekdays (Table 1.5a).

■ Figure 1.5 ■

Time spent on line in school and outside of school

Minutes per day spent using the Internet (lower bound on the average)

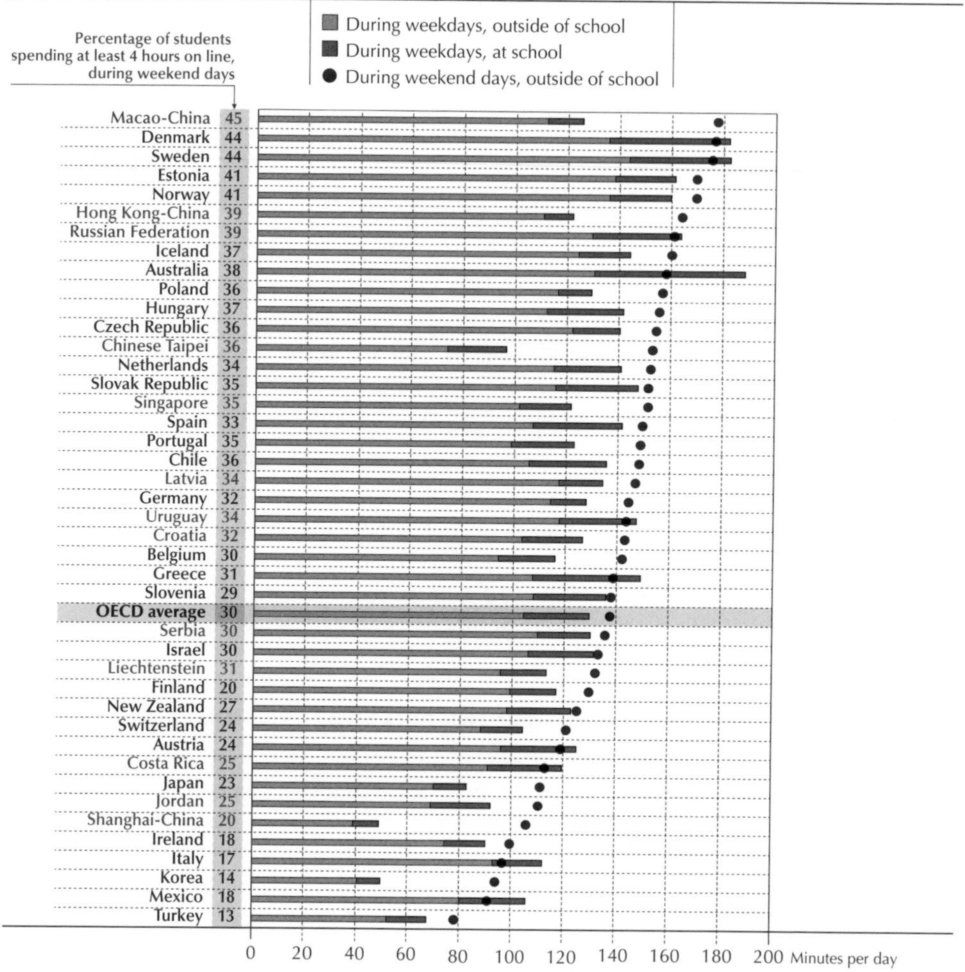
During weekdays, outside of school
During weekdays, at school
During weekend days, outside of school
Percentage of students spending at least 4 hours on line, during weekend days
Macao-China 45
Denmark 44
Sweden 44
Estonia 41
Norway 41
Hong Kong-China 39
Russian Federation 39
Iceland 37
Australia 38
Poland 36
Hungary 37
Czech Republic 36
Chinese Taipei 36
Netherlands 34
Slovak Republic 35
Singapore 35
Spain 33
Portugal 35
Chile 36
Latvia 34
Germany 32
Uruguay 34
Croatia 32
Belgium 30
Greece 31
Slovenia 29
OECD average 30
Serbia 30
Israel 30
Liechtenstein 31
Finland 20
New Zealand 27
Switzerland 24
Austria 24
Costa Rica 25
Japan 23
Jordan 25
Shanghai-China 20
Ireland 18
Italy 17
Korea 14
Mexico 18
Turkey 13
0 20 40 60 80 100 120 140 160 180 200 Minutes per day

Countries and economies are ranked in descending order of the average time students spend using the Internet during weekend days, outside of school.

Source: OECD, PISA 2012 Database, Tables 1.5a, b and c.

StatLink http://dx.doi.org/10.1787/888933252638

During weekends, the share of students who spend more than four hours per day on line exceeds 40% in Denmark, Estonia, Macao-China, Norway and Sweden. At the opposite extreme are Ireland, Italy, Korea, Mexico and Turkey, where this share is below 20%, and about 60% or more students spend less than two hours on line during a typical weekend day (Figure 1.5 and Table 1.5b). While in Mexico and Turkey the lack of Internet access at home may represent the main constraint (see Figure 1.2 above), in Ireland, Italy and Korea, very few students have no

Internet access at home, and most students use the Internet at least to some extent – but rarely for more than two hours per day. Assuming that weekends are mostly devoted to social activities, these do not (yet) take place on line in the latter group of countries.

In most countries, boys spend more time on line than girls during weekends. In Denmark, Germany, Korea, Liechtenstein, Portugal, Sweden and Chinese Taipei, the estimated difference in favour of boys is at least 40 minutes per day (the average difference in favour of boys is at least 18 minutes across OECD countries). But there are exceptions: in Chile, Japan, Mexico and Spain, girls spend more time on line during weekends than boys (Table 1.5b).

Students' ICT-related activities outside of school

In PISA 2012, students were asked how often they use a computer outside of school for ten different leisure tasks (six of which were included in the PISA 2009 questionnaire). In the following section, students who reported that they engage in any activity at least once a week are considered frequent users of computers for that task.

■ Figure 1.6 ■

Use of ICT for leisure

Percentage of students who reported engaging in each activity at least once a week

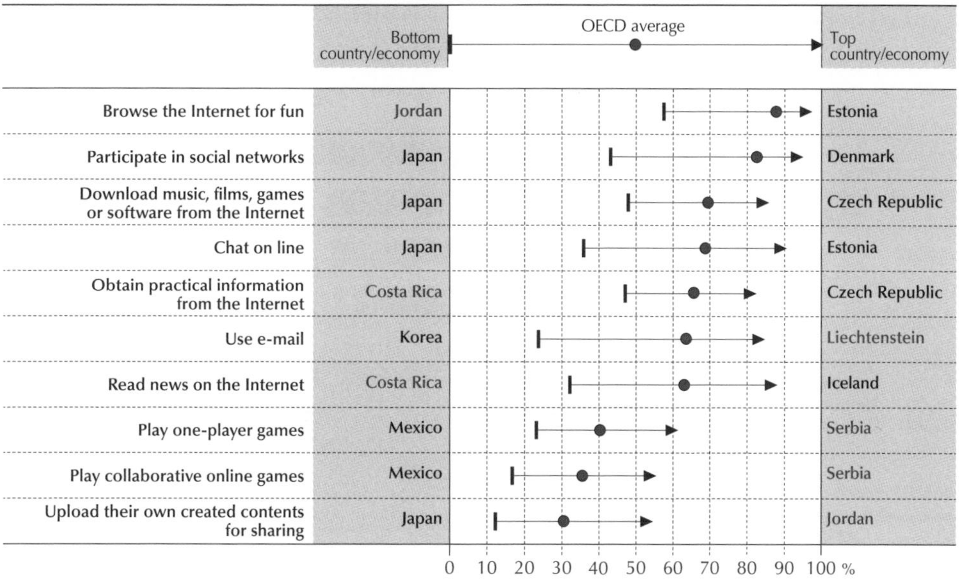
Bottom country/economy
OECD average
Top country/economy
Browse the Internet for fun
Jordan
Estonia
Participate in social networks
Japan
Denmark
Download music, films, games or software from the Internet
Japan
Czech Republic
Chat on line
Japan
Estonia
Obtain practical information from the Internet
Costa Rica
Czech Republic
Use e-mail
Korea
Liechtenstein
Read news on the Internet
Costa Rica
Iceland
Play one-player games
Mexico
Serbia
Play collaborative online games
Mexico
Serbia
Upload their own created contents for sharing
Japan
Jordan
0 10 20 30 40 50 60 70 80 90 100 %

Source: OECD, PISA 2012 Database, Table 1.6.
StatLink http://dx.doi.org/10.1787/888933252645

Computer use for leisure

Across OECD countries, the most common leisure activity using computers is browsing the Internet for fun. Some 88% of students do this at least once a week. This is followed by participating in social networks (83% of students), downloading music, films, games or software from the

Internet (70%) and chatting online (69%). More than one in two students also use the Internet at least weekly to obtain practical information (66%), read or send e-mails (64%), or read news on the Internet (63%). Two in five students (40%) also play one-player games on computers, while 36% play online collaborative games. Only 31% of students use computers at least once a week to upload their own content, such as music, poetry, videos or computer programs (Figure 1.6).

Among the activities listed in both the 2009 and 2012 questionnaires, e-mail and chat use are on the decline, probably replaced by the use of social networking services and other web-based messaging tools. Participation in social networks was more popular than sending e-mail or using chat in 2012, but was not among the activities listed in the 2009 PISA questionnaire. Thus this trend does not reflect a decline in the use of ICT for communication and sharing interests, but rather a convergence of different forms of communication on new integrated platforms that require greater bandwidths. A second trend shows a decline in one-player games, which is partly offset by the emergence of online collaborative games. By contrast, the share of students who frequently browse the Internet for fun or download music, films, games or software from the Internet has increased significantly (Figure 1.7).

■ Figure 1.7 ■

Change between 2009 and 2012 in ICT use for entertainment

Percentage of students who reported engaging in each activity at least once a week (OECD average)

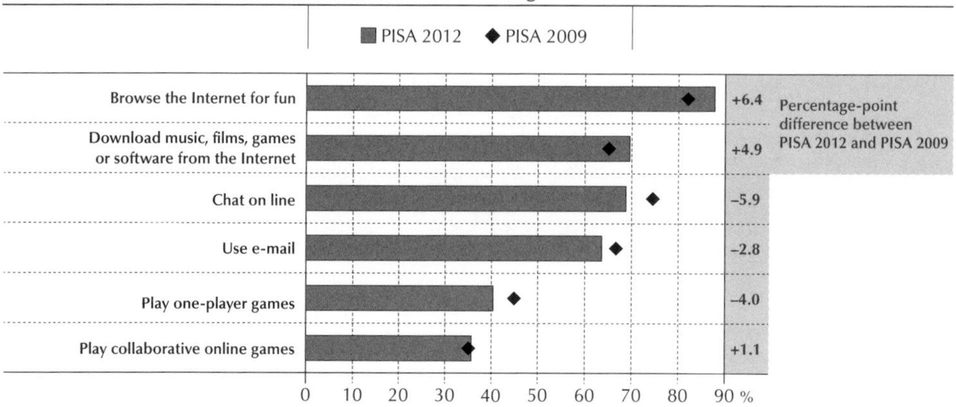
PISA 2012
PISA 2009
Browse the Internet for fun
Download music, films, games or software from the Internet
Chat on line
Use e-mail
Play one-player games
Play collaborative online games
+6.4
+4.9
-5.9
-2.8
-4.0
+1.1
Percentage-point difference between PISA 2012 and PISA 2009
0
10
20
30
40
50
60
70
80
90 %

Notes: The difference between 2012 and 2009 is based on OECD countries with data in both PISA cycles. In contrast, the OECD average values for 2009 and 2012 are based on all countries with available data.
All reported differences between 2012 and 2009 are statistically significant.
Source: OECD, PISA 2012 Database, Table 1.6.
StatLink http://dx.doi.org/10.1787/888933252655

Within countries and economies, however, uses and trends can differ markedly from the OECD average. In Japan, for instance, the use of e-mail (79% of students) is more widespread among 15-year-olds than participation in social networks (43% of students), and has increased quickly. Computer games – both one-player games and online collaborative games – are more popular in Serbia than in any other PISA-participating country/economy: in Serbia, more students play

games using computers than use e-mail. More than 80% of students in the Czech Republic, Hungary, Latvia and the Russian Federation use computers to download music, films, games or software from the Internet. In Hong Kong-China, Korea, Macao-China and Singapore, the share of students who regularly use computers for gaming (one-player or collaborative games) or communication (chat, e-mail) has shrunk faster than in other countries/economies (Table 1.6).

When students' use of computers for leisure is summarised in the *index of ICT use outside of school for leisure*, clear and large differences between and within countries emerge. According to this composite index, computer use for entertainment is greatest (as measured by the frequency and variety of entertainment activities in which students engage) in the Czech Republic and Estonia. In these countries, for instance, more than 75% of students chat on line, more than 80% of students read news on the Internet, more than 75% of students use e-mail, and more than 40% of students play collaborative online games at least once or twice a week. The least use of computers for entertainment is found in Japan, Korea and Mexico.[3] The difference between the country that uses computers the most for entertainment and the country that uses them the least for entertainment is over one standard deviation (Table 1.7).

In all countries surveyed, boys make significantly more use of computers for entertainment activities than girls. The largest differences are found in Liechtenstein, Portugal, Sweden and Turkey (Table 1.7).

HOW STUDENTS' USE OF THE INTERNET OUTSIDE OF SCHOOL IS RELATED TO THEIR SOCIAL WELL-BEING AND ENGAGEMENT WITH SCHOOL

While children gain access to a host of educational resources and engaging experiences through ICT devices and the Internet, they also need to be protected from the potential negative consequences of using ICT. Risks include exposure to harmful content or contacts (including cyberbullying; see Box 1.2), consumer-related risks, such as online fraud or abusive marketing practices, and privacy-related risks, such as identity theft (OECD, 2012 and 2011). Many of these risks existed well before the Internet, but measures to protect children from the corresponding offline threats (such as physical barriers, age-related norms that prevent access to certain spaces, and adult supervision) are difficult to migrate and enforce in a virtual space that is inherently open. Education can thus empower children and parents to evaluate and minimise the risks.

Excessive use of the Internet has also been found to be related to various problems among adolescents, including poor academic performance, family and interpersonal problems, and even physical weakness (Park, Kang and Kim, 2014). While the causal direction is not always established, excessive use of the Internet for leisure can harm academic achievement and health, as it reduces the time available for sleep, study or physical activity. Conversely, students who feel excluded from school-based socialisation may retreat to online activities. In these cases, excessive use of the Internet is more a symptom than a cause of their problems. Acknowledging emerging concerns over adolescents' use of the Internet for online gaming, the fifth edition of the Diagnostic and Statistical Manual for Mental Disorders (DSM-5) identifies Internet Gaming Disorder as a condition warranting more clinical research (American Psychiatric Association, 2013).

Box 1.2. **Cyberbullying**

Cyberbullying, which occurs when a young person is repeatedly threatened, harassed, or embarrassed by another person using the Internet, has emerged as a public health problem and a threat to young people's social and emotional development (David-Ferdon and Feldman Hertz, 2007; Raskauskas and Stoltz, 2007; OECD, 2013b; OECD, 2014a). According to a survey carried out in 2010 in European countries, 6% of children aged 9-16 had been victims of cyberbullying in the preceding year (Livingstone et al., 2011). When the survey was repeated four years later, in 2014, the proportion had risen significantly (to 12%) for the seven countries involved (Mascheroni and Ólafsson, 2014).

Cyberbullying is often a continuation and extension of offline bullying behaviours, with the same children involved as bullies, victims and bystanders (Raskauskas and Stoltz, 2007; Katzer, Fetchenhauer and Belschak, 2009; Tokunaga, 2010; Salmivalli and Pöyhönen, 2012). In such cases, school-based programmes that are effective in reducing bullying (Ttofi and Farrington, 2011) may help to prevent cyberbullying as well. Other studies however document significant differences between (traditional) bullying and cyberbullying (Kubiszewski et al., 2015).

PISA data may be used to shed light on some of the associations between extreme use of the Internet (defined here as "using the Internet for more than six hours per day outside of school, during school days") and students' sense of belonging at school and engagement with learning.

Students' sense of belonging at school, which is related to their social well-being, is measured in PISA by asking students whether they agree with the following statements: I feel like an outsider at school; I make friends easily at school; I feel like I belong at school; I feel awkward and out of place at school; other students seem to like me; I feel lonely at school.

When the answers of students are related to the time they spend on line outside of school during weekdays, results clearly indicate lower levels of well-being among students who spend more than six hours per day on line. Extreme Internet users, who spend six or more hours per day on line during weekdays are twice as likely as moderate Internet users (those who spend between one and two hours per day on line) to report that they feel lonely at school (14% compared to 7%). Conversely, students who are well-integrated at school are less likely to spend more than six hours per day on line (Figure 1.8, Tables 1.8 and 1.9).

PISA data also show that extreme Internet users are particularly at risk of being less engaged with school. For instance, while 32% of students who spend less than one hour per day on line during weekdays arrived late for school in the two weeks prior to the PISA test, 45% of students who spend more than six hours per day on line arrived late. Lower levels of engagement with school may be related to less sense of belonging at school. It is also possible that truancy and arriving late for school are the consequence of lack of sleep among extreme Internet users (Figure 1.9 and Table 1.10).

■ Figure 1.8 ■

Students' sense of belonging at school, by amount of time spent on the Internet outside of school during weekdays

Percentage of students who agreed or strongly agreed with the statement "I feel lonely at school"

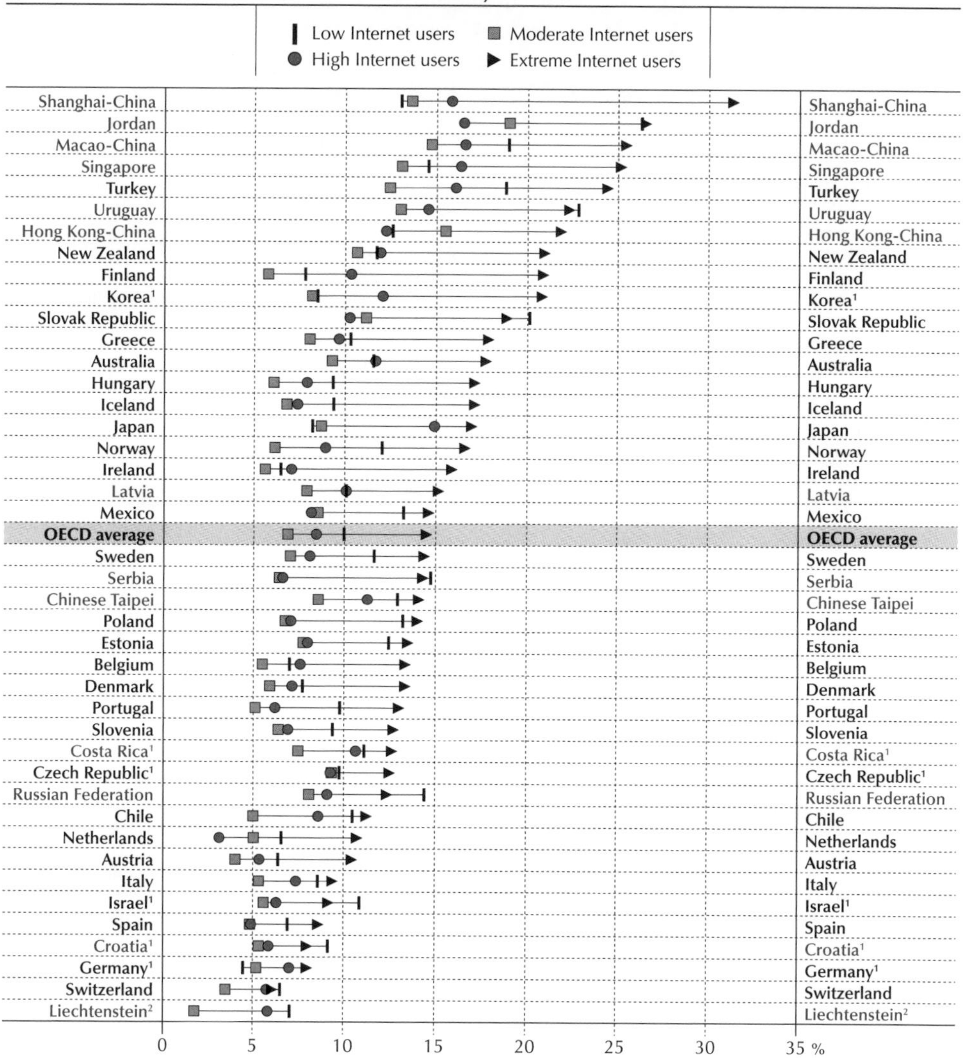
Low Internet users
Moderate Internet users
High Internet users
Extreme Internet users
Shanghai-China
Jordan
Macao-China
Singapore
Turkey
Uruguay
Hong Kong-China
New Zealand
Finland
Korea[1]
Slovak Republic
Greece
Australia
Hungary
Iceland
Japan
Norway
Ireland
Latvia
Mexico
OECD average
Sweden
Serbia
Chinese Taipei
Poland
Estonia
Belgium
Denmark
Portugal
Slovenia
Costa Rica[1]
Czech Republic[1]
Russian Federation
Chile
Netherlands
Austria
Italy
Israel[1]
Spain
Croatia[1]
Germany[1]
Switzerland
Liechtenstein[2]
0
5
10
15
20
25
30
35 %

1. The difference between moderate and extreme Internet users is not statistically significant.
2. In Liechtenstein, the sample size for extreme Internet users is too small to report.

Note: Categories of Internet users are based on students' responses about how much time they spend on line, outside of school, during a typical weekday. Low Internet users: one hour or less; moderate Internet users: 1 to 2 hours; high Internet users: 2 to 6 hours; extreme Internet users: more than 6 hours.

Countries and economies are ranked in descending order of the percentage of extreme Internet users expressing feelings of loneliness/not belonging at school.

Source: OECD, PISA 2012 Database, Table 1.8.

StatLink http://dx.doi.org/10.1787/888933252665

■ Figure 1.9 ■

Students arriving late for school, by amount of time spent on the Internet outside of school during weekdays

Percentage of students who reported arriving late at least once in the two weeks prior to PISA test

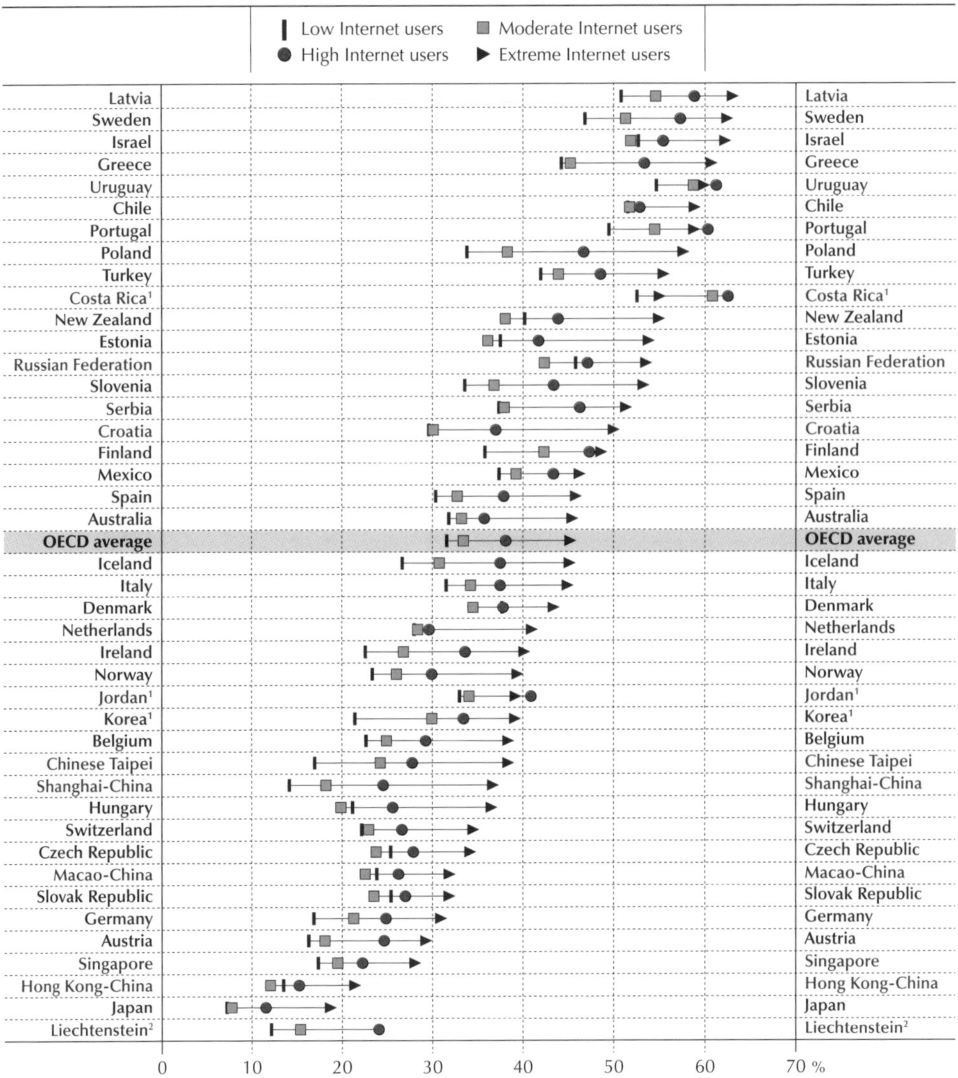
Low Internet users
Moderate Internet users
High Internet users
Extreme Internet users
Latvia
Sweden
Israel
Greece
Uruguay
Chile
Portugal
Poland
Turkey
Costa Rica1
New Zealand
Estonia
Russian Federation
Slovenia
Serbia
Croatia
Finland
Mexico
Spain
Australia
OECD average
Iceland
Italy
Denmark
Netherlands
Ireland
Norway
Jordan1
Korea1
Belgium
Chinese Taipei
Shanghai-China
Hungary
Switzerland
Czech Republic
Macao-China
Slovak Republic
Germany
Austria
Singapore
Hong Kong-China
Japan
Liechtenstein2
0
10
20
30
40
50
60
70 %

1. The difference between low and extreme Internet users is not statistically significant.
2. In Liechtenstein, the sample size for extreme Internet users is too small to report.

Note: Categories of Internet users are based on students' responses about how much time they spend on line, outside of school, during a typical weekday. Low Internet users: one hour or less; moderate Internet users: 1 to 2 hours; high Internet users: 2 to 6 hours; extreme Internet users: more than 6 hours.

Countries and economies are ranked in descending order of the percentage of extreme Internet users arriving late for school.

Source: OECD, PISA 2012 Database, Table 1.10.

StatLink http://dx.doi.org/10.1787/888933252670

Notes

1. In 2012, 24% of 15-year-olds in Turkey, and 30% of 15-year-olds in Mexico, were not enrolled in school or had not completed six years of formal education (OECD, 2014b).

2. Assuming that the age when students started using computers follows a normal distribution, the best fit to the frequencies reported in Tables 1.3 and 1.4 for the OECD average implies a mean age of 8.2 years for the age of first use of computers, and 9.6 years for the age of first access to the Internet (standard deviations are 2.7 and 2.5, respectively).

3. Infrequent use of computers for entertainment in Japan and Korea may have different explanations. While students also consistently report spending less time on the Internet than on average across OECD countries (Figure 1.5), Japan and Korea have excellent broadband infrastructure, and are leaders in the use of handheld devices for accessing Internet services (OECD, 2014c, pp. 28 and 43). In 2013, Korea had the highest average broadband speed (22 Mbit/s); in 2012, 87.3% of households had access to the Internet, and 99.7% of them through a smartphone. Japan and Korea, together with Australia, Denmark, Finland, Sweden and the United States, are among the seven countries in which in June 2014 there were more mobile broadband subscriptions than inhabitants (OECD, 2014d). Korea and Japan also have excellent fixed broadband infrastructure, with more than 20 subscriptions to fibre connection providers per 100 inhabitants (OECD, 2014d). It may therefore be that some of the typical online and offline entertainment activities are done with smartphones, rather than with computers (questionnaires did not define the term "computer").

Chapter 1 tables are available on line at http://dx.doi.org/10.1787/edu-data-en.

Note regarding Israel

The statistical data for Israel are supplied by and under the responsibility of the relevant Israeli authorities. The use of such data by the OECD is without prejudice to the status of the Golan Heights, East Jerusalem and Israeli settlements in the West Bank under the terms of international law.

References

American Psychiatric Association (2013), "Internet Gaming Disorder", in *Diagnostic and Statistical Manual of Mental Disorders* (5th ed.), American Psychiatric Publishing, Arlington, VA,. pp. 797-798.

David-Ferdon, C. and **M. Feldman Hertz** (2007), "Electronic Media, violence, and adolescents: an emerging public health problem", *Journal of Adolescent Health,* Vol. 41/6, S. 1-5.

Katzer, C., D. Fetchenhauer and **F. Belschak** (2009), "Cyberbullying: Who are the victims? A comparison of victimization in internet chatrooms and victimization in school", *Journal of Media Psychology,* Vol. 21/1, pp. 25-36.

Kubiszewski, V., R. Fontaine, C. Potard and **L. Auzoult** (2015), "Does cyberbullying overlap with school bullying when taking modality of involvement into account?", *Computers in Human Behavior*, 43, pp. 49-57.

Livingstone, S., L. Haddon, A. Görzig and **K. Ólafsson** (2011), *Risks and Safety on the Internet: the Perspective of European Children: Full Findings*, EU Kids Online, LSE, London.

Mascheroni, G. and **K. Ólafsson** (2014), *Net Children Go Mobile: Risks and Opportunities (Second edition)*, Educatt, Milan, Italy.

OECD (2014a), *Trends Shaping Education 2014 Spotlight 5: Infinite Connections*, OECD, Paris, www.oecd.org/edu/ceri/Spotlight%205-%20Infinite%20Connections.pdf.

OECD (2014b), *PISA 2012 Technical Report*, PISA, OECD, Paris, www.oecd.org/pisa/pisaproducts/pisa2012technicalreport.htm.

OECD (2014c), *Measuring the Digital Economy: A New Perspective*, OECD Publishing, Paris, http://dx.doi.org/10.1787/9789264221796-en.

OECD (2014d), *Fixed and Wireless Broadband Subscriptions per 100 Inhabitants* (indicator 1.2), OECD Publishing, Paris, www.oecd.org/sti/broadband/oecdbroadbandportal.htm (accessed 3 June 2015).

OECD (2013a), "Main trends in the communications industry", in *OECD Communications Outlook 2013*, OECD Publishing, Paris, http://dx.doi.org/10.1787/comms_outlook-2013-en.

OECD (2013b), *Trends Shaping Education 2013*, OECD Publishing, Paris, http://dx.doi.org/10.1787/trends_edu-2013-en.

OECD (2012), *The Protection of Children Online: Recommendation of the OECD Council: Report on Risks Faced by Children Online and Policies to Protect Them*, OECD Publishing, Paris, www.oecd.org/sti/ieconomy/childrenonline_with_cover.pdf.

OECD (2011), *The Protection of Children Online: Risks Faced by Children Online and Policies to Protect Them*, OECD Digital Economy Papers, No. 179, OECD Publishing, Paris, http://dx.doi.org/10.1787/5kgcjf71pl28-en.

Park, S., M. Kang and **E. Kim** (2014), "Social relationship on problematic Internet use (PIU) among adolescents in South Korea: A moderated mediation model of self-esteem and self-control", *Computers in Human Behavior,* Vol. 38, pp. 349-57.

Raskauskas, J. and **A.D. Stoltz** (2007), "Involvement in traditional and electronic bullying among adolescents", *Developmental Psychology*, Vol. 43/3, pp. 564-75.

Salmivalli, C. and **V. Pöyhönen** (2012), "Cyberbullying in Finland", in Qing, L, D. Cross and P.K. Smith (eds.), *Cyberbullying in the Global Playground*, Wiley-Blackwell, pp. 57-72.

Tokunaga, R.S. (2010), "Following you home from school: A critical review and synthesis of research on cyberbullying victimization", *Computers in Human Behavior,* Vol. 26/3, pp. 277-87.

Ttofi, Maria M. and **D.P. Farrington** (2011), "Effectiveness of school-based programs to reduce bullying: A systematic and meta-analytic review", *Journal of Experimental Criminology,* Vol. 7/1, pp. 27-56.

2

Integrating Information and Communication Technology in Teaching and Learning

This chapter discusses how education systems and schools are integrating information and communication technology (ICT) into students' learning experiences, and examines trends since 2009. It provides an overview of country differences in schools' ICT resources and how these are related to computer use; and it shows how the use of ICT in school not only depends on its availability, but on policies related to teachers and curricula.

With computers and the Internet increasingly part of the environment in which young adults grow and learn, schools and education systems are urged to reap the educational benefits of information and communication technology (ICT). Co-ordinated ICT policies often exist at the school, district or national level. They help schools and teachers to keep abreast of the constant flow of technological novelty, and to manage the change and disruption that some new tools may introduce.

Education policies that aim to embed ICT more deeply into schools and teachers' practices are often justified on one of several grounds. First, as a tool, ICT devices and the Internet hold the promise of enhancing the (traditional) learning experiences of children and adolescents, and perhaps of acting as a catalyst for wider change where such change is desired. Second, the widespread presence of ICT in society, used for everyday work and leisure activities, and the increasing number of goods and services whose production relies on ICT, create a demand for digital competencies, which are, arguably, best learned in context. Third, while learning with and about ICT may well take place outside of school, initial education can play a key role in ensuring that everyone can use these technologies and benefit from them, bridging the divide between rich and poor. Finally, school ICT policies may be based on the desire to reduce administrative and other costs. Where teacher shortages exist or can be expected, ICT policies may also complement other actions taken to attract and retain teachers in the profession.

What the data tell us

- On average, seven out of ten students use computers at school – a proportion unchanged since 2009. Among these students, the frequency of computer use increased in most countries during the period.
- The countries with the greatest integration of ICT in schools are Australia, Denmark, the Netherlands and Norway. Rapid increases in the share of students doing school work on computers can often be related to large-scale laptop-acquisition programmes, such as those observed in Australia, Chile, Greece, New Zealand, Sweden and Uruguay.
- The level of ICT use in mathematics lessons is related to both the content and the quality of instruction. Countries and economies where students are more exposed to real-world applications of mathematics tend to use computers more. There is also a specific association between mathematics teachers' use of student-oriented practices, such as individualised instruction, group work and project-based learning, and their willingness and ability to integrate ICT into mathematics lessons.

Information and communication technologies can support and enhance learning. With access to computers and the Internet, students can search for information and acquire new knowledge beyond what is available through teachers and textbooks. ICT also provide students with new ways to practice their skills – e.g. maintaining a personal webpage or online publication, programming computers, talking and listening to native speakers when learning a second language, and/or preparing a multimedia presentation, whether alone or as part of a remotely connected team. ICT devices bring together traditionally separated education media (books, writing, audio recordings, video recordings, databases, games, etc.), thus extending or integrating the range of time and places where learning can take place (Livingstone, 2011).

The widespread presence of ICT in everyday lives also creates a need for specific skills and literacies. At the very least, education can raise awareness in children and their families about the risks that they face online and how to avoid them (OECD, 2012). But as a dynamic and changing technology that requires its users to update their knowledge and skills frequently, ICT also invites education to rethink the content and methods of teaching and learning. Users of ICT – as we all are today – often must adjust to a new device or software or to new functions of their existing devices and applications. As a result, ICT users must learn, and unlearn, at a rapid pace. Only those who can direct this process of learning themselves, solving unfamiliar problems as they arise, fully reap the benefits of a technology-rich world.

More specifically, education may prepare young people for working in the sectors where new jobs are expected to be created in the coming years. Today, ICT is used across all sectors of the economy, and many of the sectors with high levels of ICT use, such as financial services and health, are also those that have increased their share of employment over the past several decades (OECD, 2013a). Other sectors of the economy that were shielded from international competition, such as retail trade or news dissemination, have been transformed by the rise of the corresponding online services. And whatever their desired jobs are, when today's students leave school or university, they will most likely search and apply for jobs on line. As a consequence, a high level of familiarity with ICT among the workforce can be a competitive advantage for countries in the new service economy.

This chapter investigates how education systems and schools are integrating ICT into students' learning experiences, and examines changes since 2009. It provides an overview of country differences in schools' ICT resources and how these are related to computer use. It shows that the use of ICT clearly depends on the availability of adequate infrastructure – equipping schools with more and better ICT resources – but is also related to the wider context shaped by teacher and curricular policies.

STUDENTS' USE OF COMPUTERS AT SCHOOL

A basic indicator of how integrated ICT devices are in teaching and learning is the share of students who use computers at school, particularly if this use is regular and occurs at least once a week.

In PISA 2012, as in PISA 2009, students reported whether they use computers at school, and how frequently they engaged in nine activities using computers at school: chat on line; use e-mail; browse the Internet for schoolwork; download, upload or browse material from the school's website; post work on the school's website; play simulations at school; practice and repeat lessons, such as for learning a foreign language or mathematics; do individual homework on a school computer; and use school computers for group work and to communicate with other students. On average across OECD countries, 72% of students reported using desktop, laptop or tablet computers at school (by comparison, 93% of students reported that they use computers at home). As in 2009, the task most frequently performed on school computers was browsing the Internet for schoolwork, with 42% of students, on average, doing so once a week or more often. The activity performed the least frequently was playing simulations at school (11% of students on average across OECD countries) (Figure 2.1 and Table 2.3).

■ Figure 2.1 ■

Use of ICT at school

Percentage of students who reported engaging in each activity at least once a week

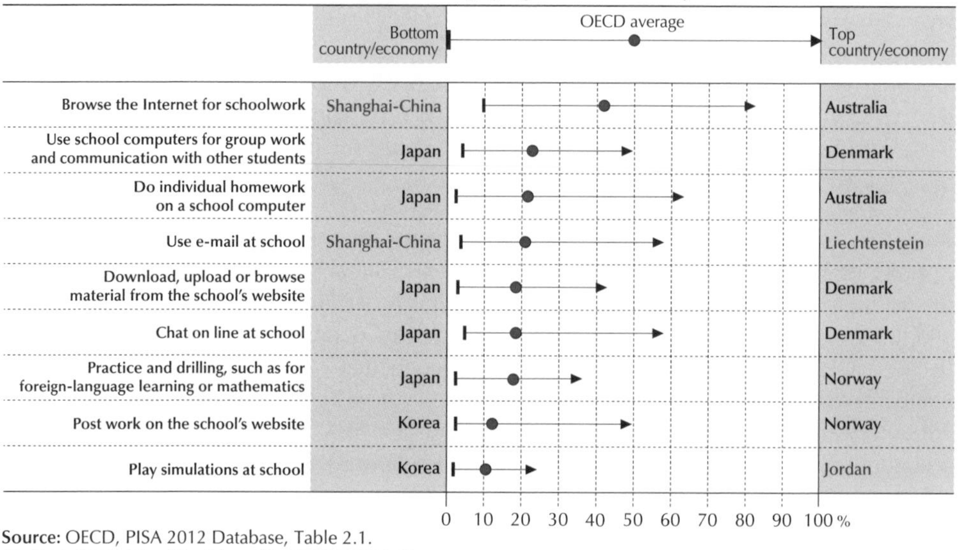
Bottom country/economy
OECD average
Top country/economy
Browse the Internet for schoolwork
Shanghai-China
Australia
Use school computers for group work and communication with other students
Japan
Denmark
Do individual homework on a school computer
Japan
Australia
Use e-mail at school
Shanghai-China
Liechtenstein
Download, upload or browse material from the school's website
Japan
Denmark
Chat on line at school
Japan
Denmark
Practice and drilling, such as for foreign-language learning or mathematics
Japan
Norway
Post work on the school's website
Korea
Norway
Play simulations at school
Korea
Jordan
0 10 20 30 40 50 60 70 80 90 100 %

Source: OECD, PISA 2012 Database, Table 2.1.
StatLink http://dx.doi.org/10.1787/888933252687

■ Figure 2.2 ■

Change between 2009 and 2012 in ICT use at school

Percentage of students who reported engaging in each activity at least once a week (OECD average)

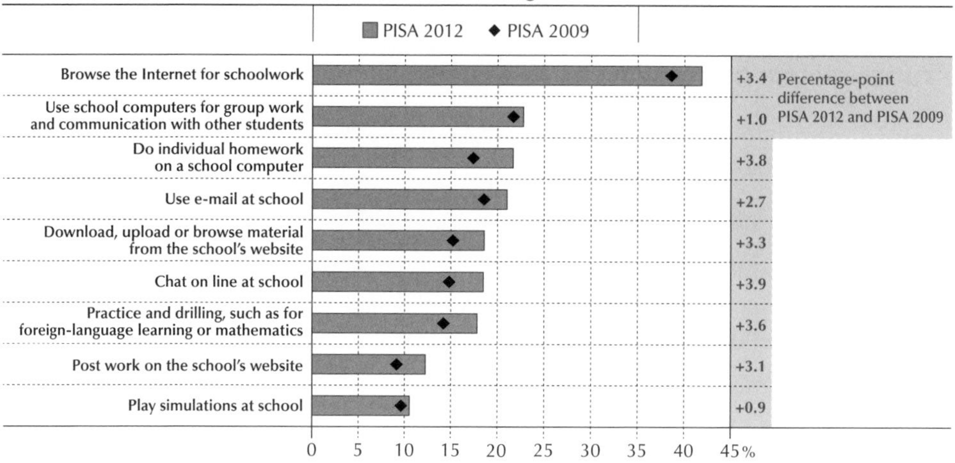
PISA 2012
PISA 2009
Browse the Internet for schoolwork
+3.4
Percentage-point difference between PISA 2012 and PISA 2009
Use school computers for group work and communication with other students
+1.0
Do individual homework on a school computer
+3.8
Use e-mail at school
+2.7
Download, upload or browse material from the school's website
+3.3
Chat on line at school
+3.9
Practice and drilling, such as for foreign-language learning or mathematics
+3.6
Post work on the school's website
+3.1
Play simulations at school
+0.9
0 5 10 15 20 25 30 35 40 45 %

Notes: PISA 2012 and PISA 2009 values are based on all OECD countries with available data. The difference between 2012 and 2009 is based on OECD countries with data in both waves.

All reported differences between PISA 2012 and PISA 2009 are statistically significant.

Source: OECD, PISA 2012 Database, Table 2.1.
StatLink http://dx.doi.org/10.1787/888933252698

While the average share of students who use computers at school did not increase much over the period (in 2009, 71% of students reported using computers at school, only 1 percentage point less than in 2012 – see Figure 2.4), the type and intensity of use did change over the period. Indeed, across all the school-related activities performed on computers listed in PISA 2009 and PISA 2012, the average share of students across OECD countries who frequently engage in these activities increased significantly over the three-year period (Figure 2.2).

Perhaps reflecting the increased availability of laptop and other mobile computers at school (see Table 2.9), the use of computers for activities in which students work individually (online chats, practice and drilling, and doing individual homework) increased the most among all the listed activities between 2009 and 2012. The share of students who engaged in each of these activities at least once a week grew by about 4 percentage points during the period (Figure 2.2).

■ Figure 2.3 ■

Index of ICT use at school

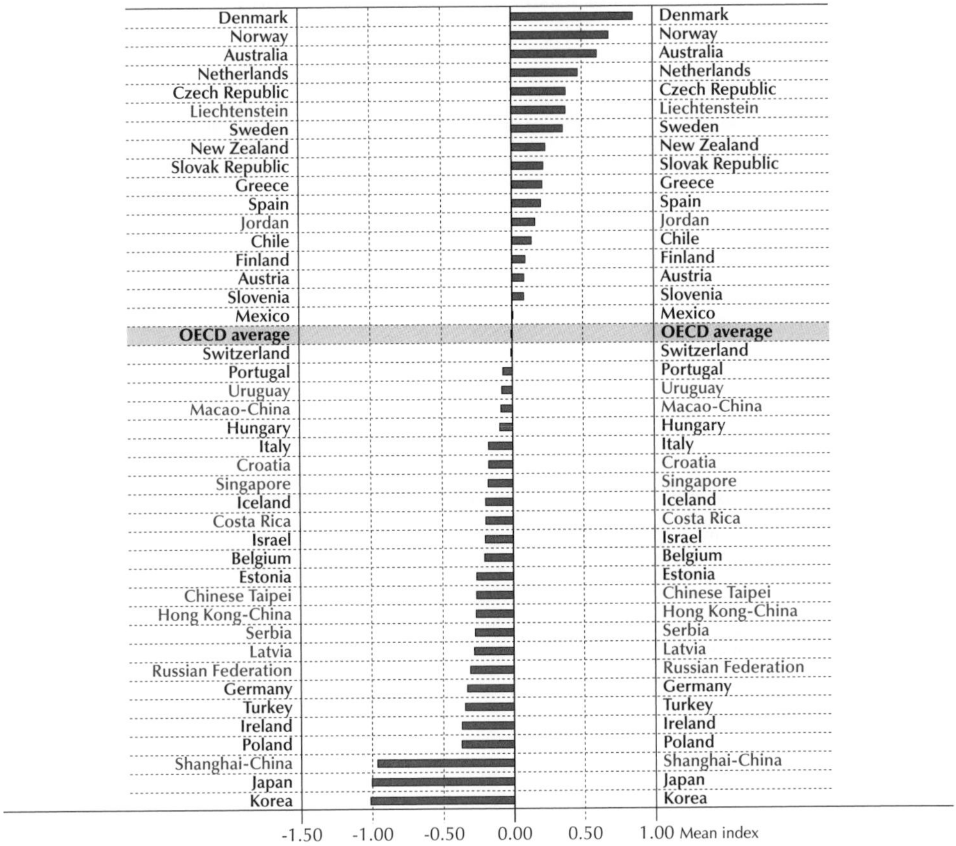
Denmark
Norway
Australia
Netherlands
Czech Republic
Liechtenstein
Sweden
New Zealand
Slovak Republic
Greece
Spain
Jordan
Chile
Finland
Austria
Slovenia
Mexico
OECD average
Switzerland
Portugal
Uruguay
Macao-China
Hungary
Italy
Croatia
Singapore
Iceland
Costa Rica
Israel
Belgium
Estonia
Chinese Taipei
Hong Kong-China
Serbia
Latvia
Russian Federation
Germany
Turkey
Ireland
Poland
Shanghai-China
Japan
Korea
-1.50
-1.00
-0.50
0.00
0.50
1.00
Mean index

Countries and economies are ranked in descending order of the mean index of ICT use at school.
Source: OECD, PISA 2012 Database, Table 2.2.
StatLink http://dx.doi.org/10.1787/888933252700

When all nine activities are summarised in the *index of ICT use at school*,[1] the countries with the highest mean values are Australia, Denmark, the Netherlands and Norway. In contrast, students in Japan, Korea and Shanghai-China make significantly less use of computers at school than students in any other country/economy, according to students' reports (Figure 2.3).[2]

When students report infrequent use of computers at school, it should not be assumed that ICT equipment is not used at all. Students in Shanghai-China, for instance, use computers during mathematics lessons the least (see Figure 2.7). However, they also report, more often than students in OECD countries do, that teachers use ICT equipment during lessons (perhaps projectors and smartboards). Such teacher-centred approaches to integrating ICT into education are only imperfectly covered by PISA measures. Similarly, the use of smartphones at school may not be captured by the questions referring to "computer" use.

■ Figure 2.4 ■

Change between 2009 and 2012 in the share of students using computers at school

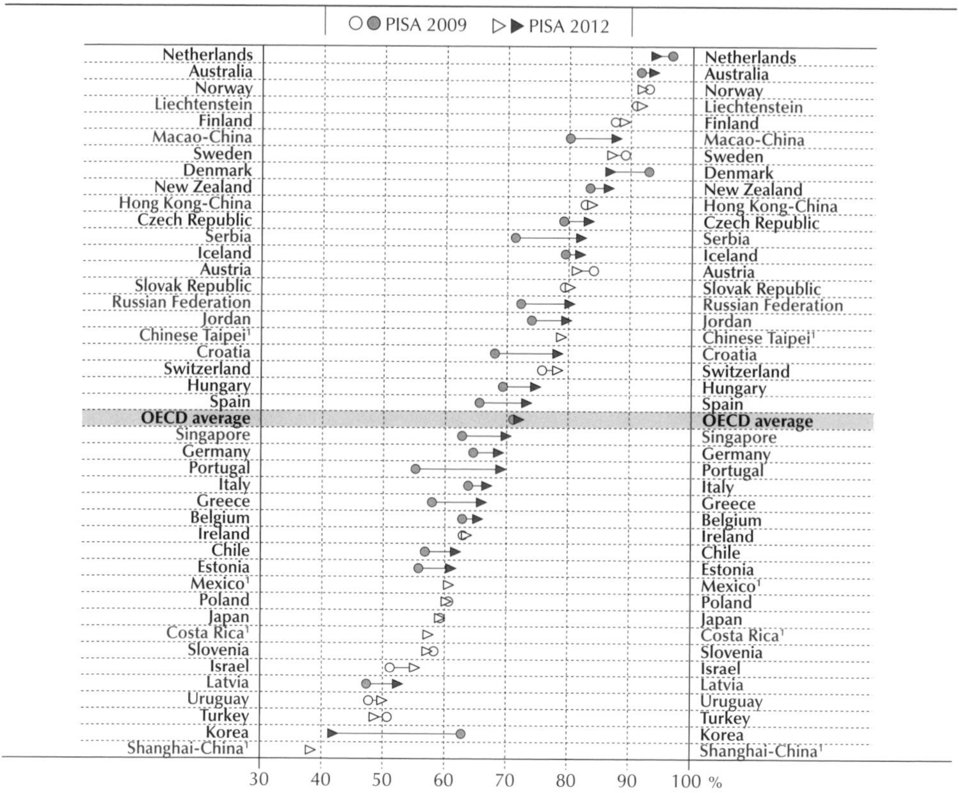
PISA 2009
PISA 2012
Netherlands
Australia
Norway
Liechtenstein
Finland
Macao-China
Sweden
Denmark
New Zealand
Hong Kong-China
Czech Republic
Serbia
Iceland
Austria
Slovak Republic
Russian Federation
Jordan
Chinese Taipei1
Croatia
Switzerland
Hungary
Spain
OECD average
Singapore
Germany
Portugal
Italy
Greece
Belgium
Ireland
Chile
Estonia
Mexico1
Poland
Japan
Costa Rica1
Slovenia
Israel
Latvia
Uruguay
Turkey
Korea
Shanghai-China1
30
40
50
60
70
80
90
100 %

1. PISA 2009 data are missing for Costa Rica, Mexico, Shanghai-China and Chinese Taipei.

Note: White symbols indicate differences between PISA 2009 and PISA 2012 that are not statistically significant.

Countries and economies are ranked in descending order of the percentage of students using computers at school in 2012.

Source: OECD, PISA 2012 Database, Table 2.3.

StatLink http://dx.doi.org/10.1787/888933252710

Still, not all trends point towards a greater use of computers at school.[3] When the shares of students using computers at school are compared across PISA cycles, a large decline (-21 percentage points) is observed in Korea between 2009 and 2012. In 2012, only 42% of students in Korea reported that they use computers at school – the second smallest proportion among the 42 countries/economies surveyed, after Shanghai-China (38%). In Denmark, where the share of students who use computers at school was second only to the Netherlands in 2009, this share shrank by 6 percentage points to below 90% in 2012 (Figure 2.4 and Table 2.3).

Internet use at school

Students' self-reports show that, on average across OECD countries, students typically spend at least 25 minutes on line each day at school. In Australia, the time spent on line at school is more than twice the average (58 minutes); in Denmark students spend an average of 46 minutes on line per day at school, in Greece they spend 42 minutes, and in Sweden 39 minutes (Figure 2.5).

■ Figure 2.5 ■

Time spent on line at school

Average time students spend using the Internet at school (lower bound)

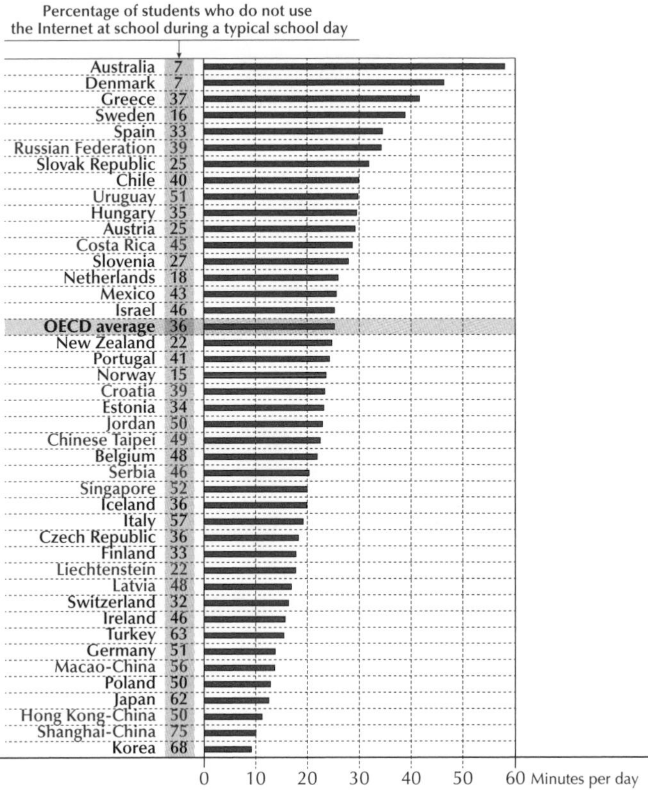
Percentage of students who do not use the Internet at school during a typical school day
Australia 7
Denmark 7
Greece 37
Sweden 16
Spain 33
Russian Federation 39
Slovak Republic 25
Chile 40
Uruguay 51
Hungary 35
Austria 25
Costa Rica 45
Slovenia 27
Netherlands 18
Mexico 43
Israel 46
OECD average 36
New Zealand 22
Portugal 41
Norway 15
Croatia 39
Estonia 34
Jordan 50
Chinese Taipei 49
Belgium 48
Serbia 46
Singapore 52
Iceland 36
Italy 57
Czech Republic 36
Finland 33
Liechtenstein 22
Latvia 48
Switzerland 32
Ireland 46
Turkey 63
Germany 51
Macao-China 56
Poland 50
Japan 62
Hong Kong-China 50
Shanghai-China 75
Korea 68
0
10
20
30
40
50
60 Minutes per day

Countries and economies are ranked in descending order of the average time students spend using the Internet at school.

Source: OECD, PISA 2012 Database, Table 1.5c.

StatLink http://dx.doi.org/10.1787/888933252720

In 11 countries and economies, namely Germany, Italy, Japan, Jordan, Korea, Macao-China, Poland, Shanghai-China, Singapore, Turkey and Uruguay, on a typical school day, a majority of students do not use the Internet at school (Figure 2.5).

Computer use during mathematics instruction

PISA 2009 showed that computers were used less frequently during classroom lessons in mathematics than in either language or science classes, with only about 15% of students using computers at least once a week in mathematics classes, on average across OECD countries (OECD, 2011, Figure VI.5.21).

PISA 2012 took a closer look at whether and how students use computers during mathematics lessons. Students were given a list of seven possible mathematics tasks on computers and were asked to report whether, during the month preceding the survey, they (or their classmates) had performed any of those tasks during mathematics lessons, whether teachers demonstrated the task, or whether they had not encountered the task at all. The tasks included: drawing the graph of a function; calculating with numbers; constructing geometric figures; entering data in a spreadsheet; rewriting algebraic expressions and solving equations; drawing histograms; and finding out how the graph of a function changes, depending on its parameters.

■ Figure 2.6 ■

Use of computers during mathematics lessons

Percentage of students who reported that a computer was used in mathematics lessons in the month prior to the PISA test, by task (OECD average)

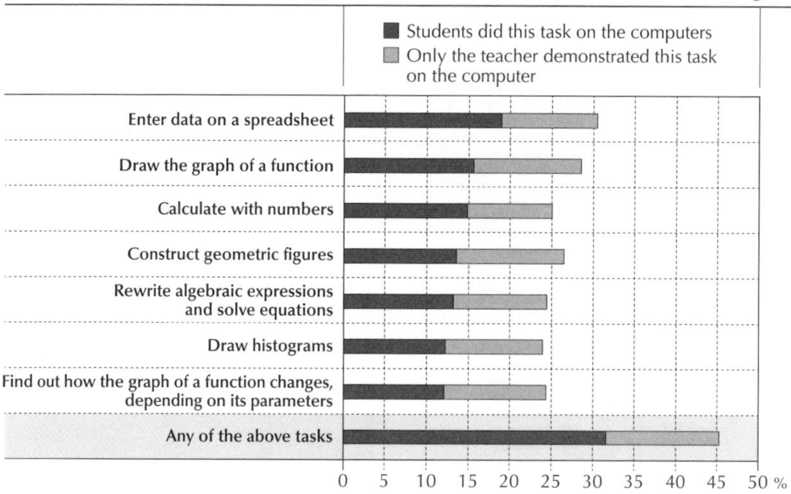
Students did this task on the computers
Only the teacher demonstrated this task on the computer
Enter data on a spreadsheet
Draw the graph of a function
Calculate with numbers
Construct geometric figures
Rewrite algebraic expressions and solve equations
Draw histograms
Find out how the graph of a function changes, depending on its parameters
Any of the above tasks
0
5
10
15
20
25
30
35
40
45
50 %

Source: OECD, PISA 2012 Database, Table 2.5.
StatLink http://dx.doi.org/10.1787/888933252733

On average across OECD countries, only a minority of students saw any of these tasks performed in their mathematics class during the month preceding the PISA test. This is consistent with the finding that computers are infrequently used during mathematics instruction. For 14% of students, on average, only teachers demonstrated the use of computers; 32% of students reported that they, or their classmates, did at least one of the tasks. However, in some countries, computer use during mathematics lessons was much more common. More than two out of three students in Norway (82% of students), Jordan (80%) and Denmark (71%) saw at least one of these tasks demonstrated by their teachers; often, the students themselves performed the task on computer (Figures 2.6 and 2.7).

■ Figure 2.7 ■

Students and teachers using computers during mathematics lessons

Percentage of students who reported that a computer was used in mathematics lessons in the month prior to the PISA test

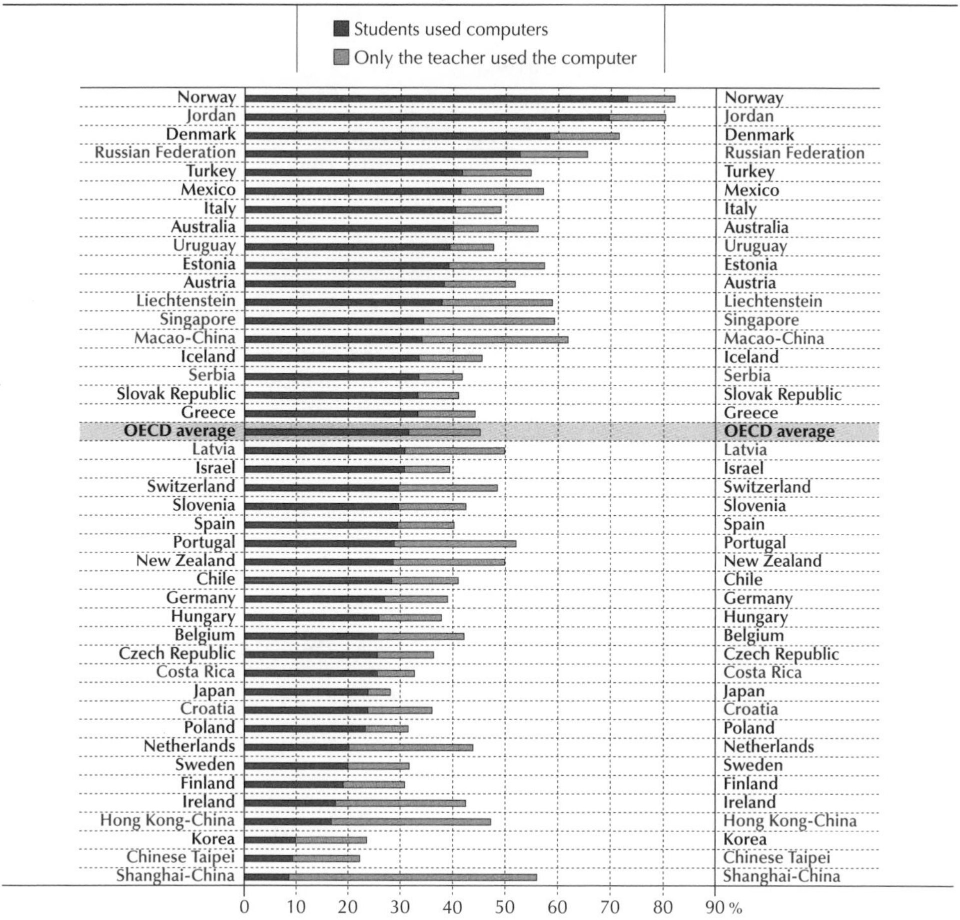
Students used computers
Only the teacher used the computer
Norway
Jordan
Denmark
Russian Federation
Turkey
Mexico
Italy
Australia
Uruguay
Estonia
Austria
Liechtenstein
Singapore
Macao-China
Iceland
Serbia
Slovak Republic
Greece
OECD average
Latvia
Israel
Switzerland
Slovenia
Spain
Portugal
New Zealand
Chile
Germany
Hungary
Belgium
Czech Republic
Costa Rica
Japan
Croatia
Poland
Netherlands
Sweden
Finland
Ireland
Hong Kong-China
Korea
Chinese Taipei
Shanghai-China
0
10
20
30
40
50
60
70
80
90 %

Note: This figure shows the percentage of students who reported that a computer was used in mathematics lessons during the month prior to the PISA test for at least one of seven mathematics tasks (see Figure 2.6 for the list of tasks).
Countries and economies are ranked in descending order of the percentage of students who used computers during mathematics lessons.
Source: OECD, PISA 2012 Database, Table 2.5.
StatLink http://dx.doi.org/10.1787/888933252749

Some 19% of students, on average across OECD countries, reported that they had entered data on a spreadsheet during mathematics lessons in the month prior to the PISA test; in Norway, over 67% of students so reported. The second most common activity, drawing the graph of a function, was performed by16% of students on average, and only 31% of Norwegian students (Figure 2.6 and Table 2.5).

Finland, Japan, Korea, Poland and Chinese Taipei, all high-performing countries/economies in PISA, show the least frequent use of computers in mathematics lessons; and in Shanghai-China, students reported that teachers demonstrate certain tasks on computers relatively frequently, but the share of students who perform any of the tasks themselves is the smallest among all countries and economies (Figure 2.7). The relationship between computer use and performance is further explored in Chapter 6.

Use of home computers for schoolwork

With ICT devices readily available at home and within the community, the school day can be expanded beyond the physical classroom. Learning activities can be offered on line and off line, on site (at school) and off site (outside of school). In PISA 2012, students were asked whether they use computers for seven school-related tasks (six of which were also included in the PISA 2009 questionnaire) outside of school. An index was generated to summarise schoolwork-related activities that take place outside of school.

■ Figure 2.8 ■

Use of ICT outside of school for schoolwork

Percentage of students who reported engaging in each activity at least once a week

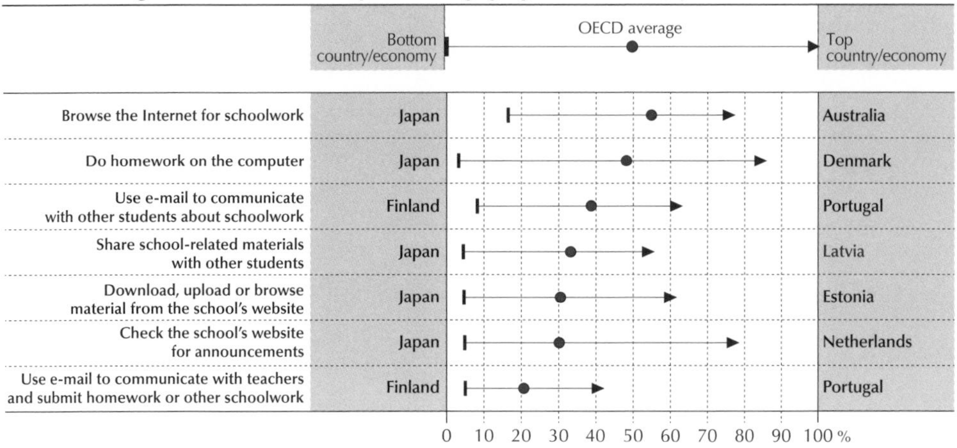
Bottom country/economy
OECD average
Top country/economy
Browse the Internet for schoolwork
Japan
Australia
Do homework on the computer
Japan
Denmark
Use e-mail to communicate with other students about schoolwork
Finland
Portugal
Share school-related materials with other students
Japan
Latvia
Download, upload or browse material from the school's website
Japan
Estonia
Check the school's website for announcements
Japan
Netherlands
Use e-mail to communicate with teachers and submit homework or other schoolwork
Finland
Portugal
0
10
20
30
40
50
60
70
80
90
100 %

Source: OECD, PISA 2012 Database, Table 2.7.
StatLink http://dx.doi.org/10.1787/888933252758

In general, students more frequently use their home computers (or other computers outside of school) for schoolwork than they use school computers. For instance, while 42% of students browse the Internet for schoolwork at least once a week at school, 55% of students do so outside of school, on average across OECD countries (Tables 2.1 and 2.7). Still, only a minority of students engages in school-related activities on computers at least once a week, except for browsing the Internet to help with schoolwork (55% of students). On average across OECD countries only 48% of students do homework on a computer, 38% use e-mail to communicate with other students about schoolwork, and 33% share school-related materials with other students via computer. The least common activities are those that require a corresponding online presence by the school or the teacher. For example, 30% of students check their school's website for announcements, 30% download, upload or browse material from the school's website, and only 21% use e-mail to communicate with teachers or submit schoolwork (Figure 2.8).

The share of students who regularly perform tasks that require an online presence of teachers and school leaders grew faster than the share of students who perform the remaining school-related activities. Three out of ten students in 2012 check the school website for announcements at least once a week – 10% more, on average, than in 2009 (Figure 2.9). Overall, however, these tasks are still relatively infrequent.

When all activities are combined to form an *index of ICT use outside of school for schoolwork*, the highest values on the index are observed in Denmark, Estonia, the Netherlands and Uruguay. More than 70% of students in Denmark and Uruguay browse the Internet for schoolwork and do homework on computers at least once a week. Meanwhile, a large majority of students in Estonia and the Netherlands regularly checks the school's website for announcements or uses a computer to download, upload or browse materials from the school's website (Figure 2.10 and Table 2.7).

■ Figure 2.9 ■

Change between 2009 and 2012 in ICT use outside of school for schoolwork

Percentage of students who reported engaging in each activity at least once a week (OECD average)

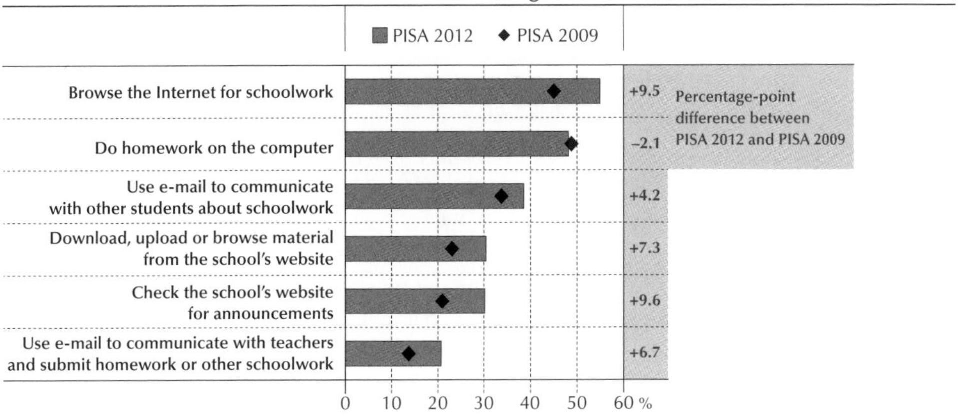
PISA 2012
PISA 2009
Browse the Internet for schoolwork
Do homework on the computer
Use e-mail to communicate with other students about schoolwork
Download, upload or browse material from the school's website
Check the school's website for announcements
Use e-mail to communicate with teachers and submit homework or other schoolwork
+9.5
–2.1
+4.2
+7.3
+9.6
+6.7
Percentage-point difference between PISA 2012 and PISA 2009
0
10
20
30
40
50
60 %

Notes: PISA 2012 and PISA 2009 values are based on all OECD countries with available data. The difference between 2012 and 2009 is based on OECD countries with data in both waves.
All reported differences between PISA 2012 and PISA 2009 are statistically significant.
Source: OECD, PISA 2012 Database, Table 2.7.
StatLink http://dx.doi.org/10.1787/888933252765

■ Figure 2.10 ■

Index of ICT use outside of school for schoolwork

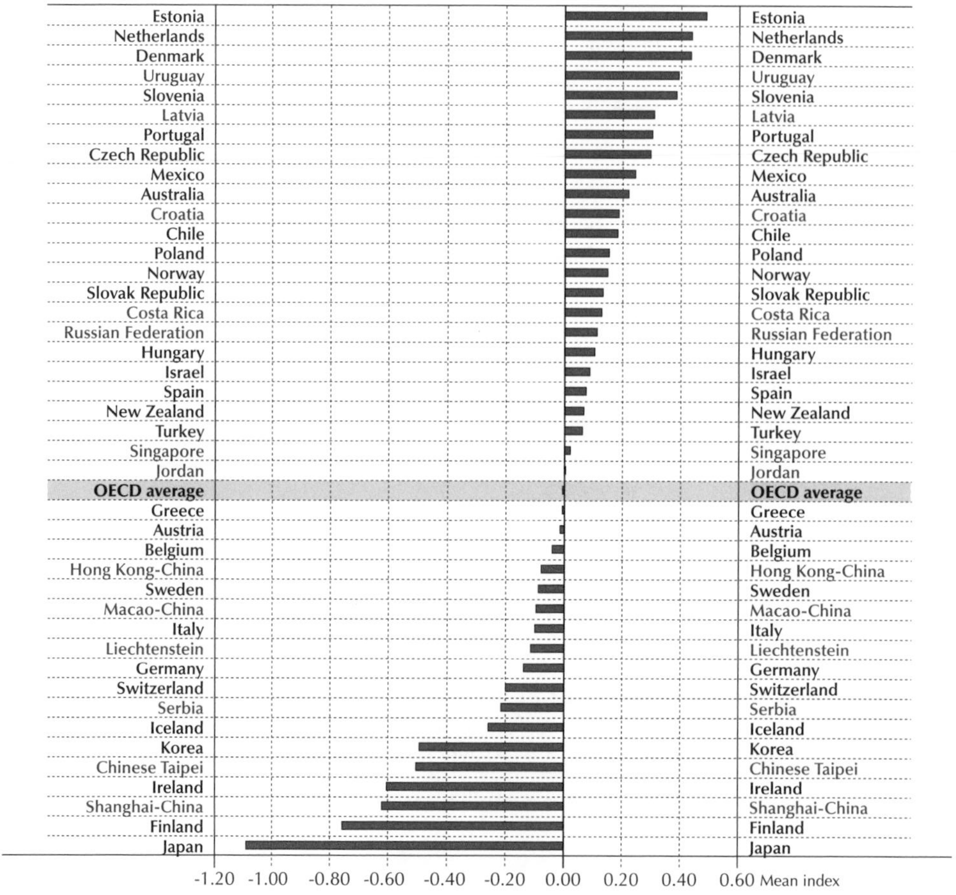
Estonia
Netherlands
Denmark
Uruguay
Slovenia
Latvia
Portugal
Czech Republic
Mexico
Australia
Croatia
Chile
Poland
Norway
Slovak Republic
Costa Rica
Russian Federation
Hungary
Israel
Spain
New Zealand
Turkey
Singapore
Jordan
OECD average
Greece
Austria
Belgium
Hong Kong-China
Sweden
Macao-China
Italy
Liechtenstein
Germany
Switzerland
Serbia
Iceland
Korea
Chinese Taipei
Ireland
Shanghai-China
Finland
Japan
-1.20
-1.00
-0.80
-0.60
-0.40
-0.20
0.00
0.20
0.40
0.60
Mean index

Countries and economies are ranked in descending order of the mean index of ICT use outside of school for schoolwork.
Source: OECD, PISA 2012 Database, Table 2.8.
StatLink http://dx.doi.org/10.1787/888933252770

Finland and Japan are the two countries where students make the least use of computers outside of school for schoolwork. Some of this may be related to homework policies: students in Finland and Japan are typically assigned little, if any, homework (OECD, 2013b, Figure IV.3.10).

As can be expected, there is a positive relationship between the extent to which students use ICT at school for schoolwork and the extent to which they use other ICT resources outside of school for schoolwork. However, in several countries where ICT use at school is below average, ICT use outside of school – for school-related reasons – is above average, most notably in Croatia, Estonia, Latvia, Portugal and Uruguay (Figure 2.11).

■ Figure 2.11 ■

Relationship between use of ICT outside of school for schoolwork and use of ICT at school

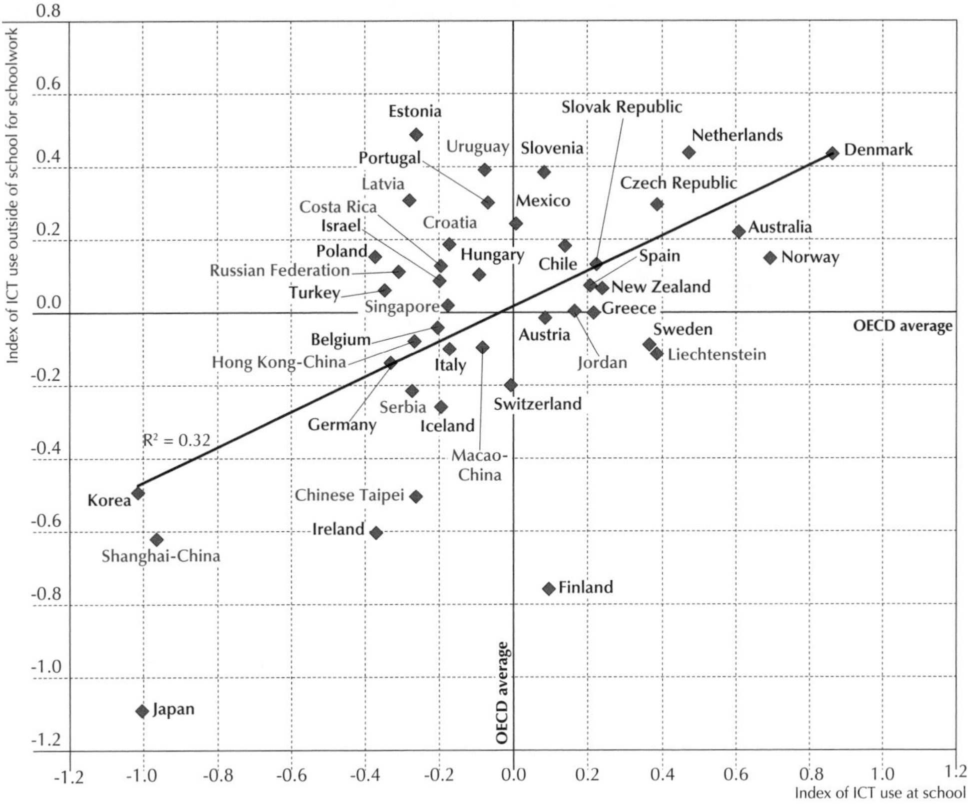
Index of ICT use outside of school for schoolwork
0.8
0.6
0.4
0.2
0.0
-0.2
-0.4
-0.6
-0.8
-1.0
-1.2
-1.2
-1.0
-0.8
-0.6
-0.4
-0.2
0.0
0.2
0.4
0.6
0.8
1.0
1.2
Index of ICT use at school
OECD average
OECD average
$R^2 = 0.32$
Estonia
Slovak Republic
Netherlands
Denmark
Uruguay
Slovenia
Portugal
Latvia
Czech Republic
Costa Rica
Mexico
Israel
Croatia
Australia
Poland
Hungary
Chile
Spain
Norway
Russian Federation
Turkey
New Zealand
Singapore
Greece
Sweden
Belgium
Austria
Liechtenstein
Hong Kong-China
Italy
Jordan
Serbia
Switzerland
Germany
Iceland
Macao-China
Korea
Chinese Taipei
Ireland
Shanghai-China
Finland
Japan

Source: OECD, PISA 2012 Database, Tables 2.2 and 2.8.
StatLink http://dx.doi.org/10.1787/888933252787

DRIVERS AND BARRIERS TO INTEGRATING ICT INTO TEACHING AND LEARNING

Previous sections described large differences between countries in the extent to which 15-year-olds use computers in schools. What drives these differences?

The absence or difficulty of accessing ICT devices and connecting them to the Internet is certainly a barrier to integrating ICT in teaching and learning. Differences in the devices available to schools indicate either a deliberate choice not to invest in the integration of ICT in teaching and learning, or a lack of sufficient resources to do so.

At the same time, not all between- and within-country differences in the use of ICT devices at school can be traced back to disparities in their availability. Other variables influence how willing and ready schools and teachers are to integrate new devices into their practices.

Indeed, to harness the potential of ICT, teachers and industry must create and develop new educational resources (software, textbooks, lesson plans, etc.). They may find encouragement and support to do so in changes in related education policies, including curricula, student- and teacher-assessment frameworks, initial teacher training (Tondeur et al., 2012) and professional development activities for teachers, as well as in school practices that support collaboration and encourage teachers to take risks and share lessons learned (Little, 1982; Frost and Durrant, 2003; Harris, 2005; Horn and Little, 2010; Resnick et al., 2010; Avvisati et al., 2013).

While PISA data cannot be used to characterise initial teacher training, professional development, and teachers' working conditions,[4] it can illustrate how ICT use at school is related to other drivers of/barriers to innovation, such as variations in infrastructure and curricula.

The school ICT infrastructure

As part of the ICT familiarity questionnaire, students were asked if there are computers available for them to use at school. On average across OECD countries, 92% of students reported that they have access to a computer (in 2012, computers include desktop, laptop and tablet computers). This proportion declined by 0.6 percentage points, on average across OECD countries with comparable data, between 2009 and 2012. The largest declines in access to computers at school were observed in Slovenia (by 8 percentage points), and in Belgium, Japan and Korea (by 5 percentage points). In contrast, in Greece, Jordan, Portugal, Serbia, Spain, Turkey and Uruguay, more students had access to computers in 2012 than in 2009. Among this group of countries, Portugal had the highest rate of access to school computers in 2012 (98%); only Australia, Denmark, Hong Kong-China, Liechtenstein, the Netherlands, New Zealand, Norway and Singapore had similar (or sometimes higher) rates in 2012 (Figure 2.12).

Similarly, in 2012, nine in ten students, on average, reported that they have an Internet connection available at school – a slightly smaller proportion than in 2009. Between 2009 and 2012, the proportion of students with access to the Internet at school declined by two percentage points, on average across OECD countries. Still, in all countries more than 70% of students reported that they have access to an Internet connection at school (Figure 2.13).

Some of the apparent declines in access may be due to changes in the reference frame of students. Given the rapid improvements in broadband infrastructure between 2009 and 2012 (see Chapter 1), it is possible that, when answering the question in 2012, some students may not have considered slow or difficult-to-access Internet connections in the same way as their peers did in 2009.

Indeed, principals' reports about their schools' ICT resources paint a somewhat different picture. The number of computers in schools did not change significantly across OECD countries, on average, but the share of school computers connected to the Internet increased between 2009 and 2012 (Figures 2.14 and 2.15)

In 2012 as in 2009 there were between four and five students to every school computer, on average across the OECD. The number of computers available to 15-year-old students increased in 17 countries/economies (as reflected in lower student/computer ratios), and decreased in six – most notably in Turkey. At the same time, the share of school computers that were not connected to the Internet decreased, from about 4% to less than 3%, on average.

■ Figure 2.12 ■

Change between 2009 and 2012 in the share of students with access to computers at school

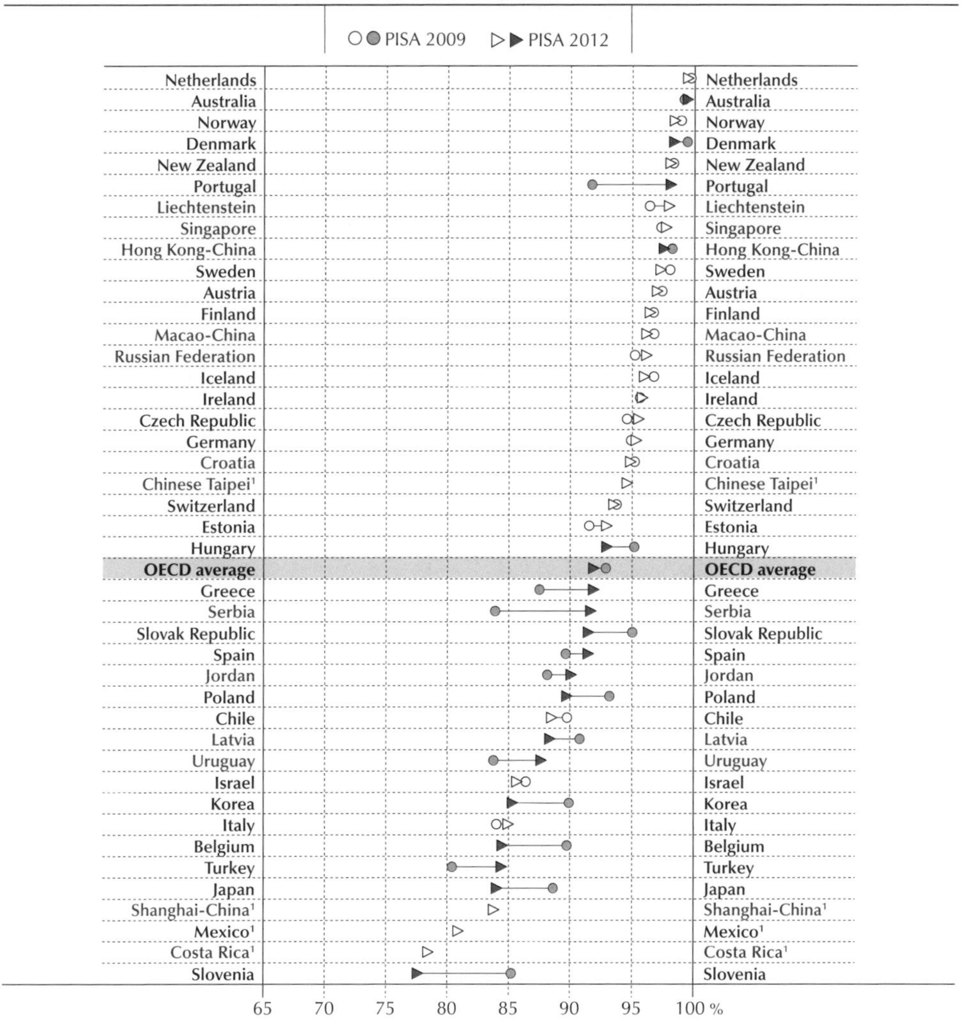
PISA 2009
PISA 2012
Netherlands
Australia
Norway
Denmark
New Zealand
Portugal
Liechtenstein
Singapore
Hong Kong-China
Sweden
Austria
Finland
Macao-China
Russian Federation
Iceland
Ireland
Czech Republic
Germany
Croatia
Chinese Taipei1
Switzerland
Estonia
Hungary
OECD average
Greece
Serbia
Slovak Republic
Spain
Jordan
Poland
Chile
Latvia
Uruguay
Israel
Korea
Italy
Belgium
Turkey
Japan
Shanghai-China1
Mexico1
Costa Rica1
Slovenia
65
70
75
80
85
90
95
100 %

1. PISA 2009 data are missing for Costa Rica, Mexico, Shanghai-China and Chinese Taipei.

Note: White symbols indicate differences between PISA 2009 and PISA 2012 that are not statistically significant.

Countries and economies are ranked in descending order of the percentage of students with access to a computer at school in 2012.

Source: OECD, PISA 2012 Database, Table 2.9.

StatLink http://dx.doi.org/10.1787/888933252791

■ Figure 2.13 ■

Change between 2009 and 2012 in the share of students with access to the Internet at school

PISA 2009
PISA 2012
Denmark
Australia
Hong Kong-China
Portugal
Netherlands
New Zealand
Sweden
Finland
Norway
Austria
Estonia
Latvia
Ireland
Chinese Taipei¹
Greece
Croatia
Czech Republic
Russian Federation
Liechtenstein
Spain
Korea
Singapore
Germany
Hungary
Switzerland
Iceland
OECD average
Slovak Republic
Uruguay
Poland
Macao-China
Chile
Slovenia
Belgium
Turkey
Israel
Jordan
Serbia
Italy
Japan
Mexico¹
Shanghai-China¹
Costa Rica¹
65
70
75
80
85
90
95
100 %

1. PISA 2009 data are missing for Costa Rica, Mexico, Shanghai-China and Chinese Taipei.
Note: White symbols indicate differences between PISA 2009 and PISA 2012 that are not statistically significant.
Countries and economies are ranked in descending order of the percentage of students using the Internet at school in 2012.
Source: OECD, PISA 2012 Database, Table 2.10.
StatLink http://dx.doi.org/10.1787/888933252808

Still, a stable, or even declining, share of students reporting access to computers and the Internet at school implies that any increase in the average extent to which students used computers in school between 2009 and 2012 (Figure 2.2) results from changes in the frequency and variety of uses rather than from changes in the share of students using computers at school.

■ Figure 2.14 ■

Change between 2009 and 2012 in the number of students per school computer

Mean student-computer ratio for 15-year-old students in the modal grade

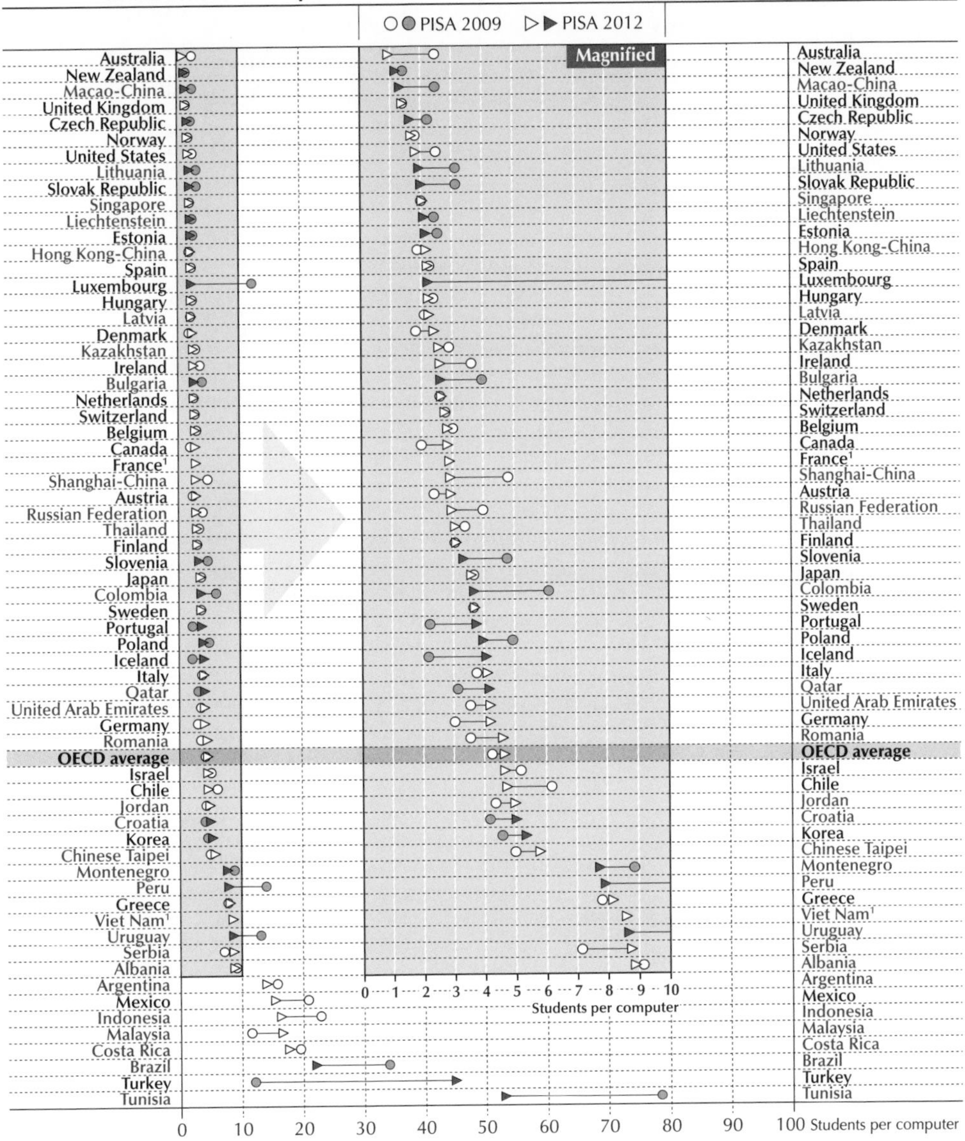
○● PISA 2009 ▷▶ PISA 2012
Magnified
Australia
New Zealand
Macao-China
United Kingdom
Czech Republic
Norway
United States
Lithuania
Slovak Republic
Singapore
Liechtenstein
Estonia
Hong Kong-China
Spain
Luxembourg
Hungary
Latvia
Denmark
Kazakhstan
Ireland
Bulgaria
Netherlands
Switzerland
Belgium
Canada
France¹
Shanghai-China
Austria
Russian Federation
Thailand
Finland
Slovenia
Japan
Colombia
Sweden
Portugal
Poland
Iceland
Italy
Qatar
United Arab Emirates
Germany
Romania
OECD average
Israel
Chile
Jordan
Croatia
Korea
Chinese Taipei
Montenegro
Peru
Greece
Viet Nam¹
Uruguay
Serbia
Albania
Argentina
Mexico
Indonesia
Malaysia
Costa Rica
Brazil
Turkey
Tunisia
0 1 2 3 4 5 6 7 8 9 10
Students per computer
0 10 20 30 40 50 60 70 80 90 100 Students per computer

1. PISA 2009 data are missing for France and Viet Nam.

Notes: White symbols indicate differences between PISA 2009 and PISA 2012 that are not statistically significant.

Only schools with at least 10 students in the national modal grade for 15-year-olds are included. The number of students per computer is based on principals' reports about the number of students in the national modal grade for 15-year-olds and on the number of computers available for these students. In schools where no computer is available, the number of students per computer is set at the number of students reported by the principal plus 1.

Countries and economies are ranked in ascending order of the student-computer ratio in 2012.

Source: OECD, PISA 2012 Database, Table 2.11.

StatLink http://dx.doi.org/10.1787/888933252810

■ Figure 2.15 ■

Change between 2009 and 2012 in the share of school computers that are connected to the Internet

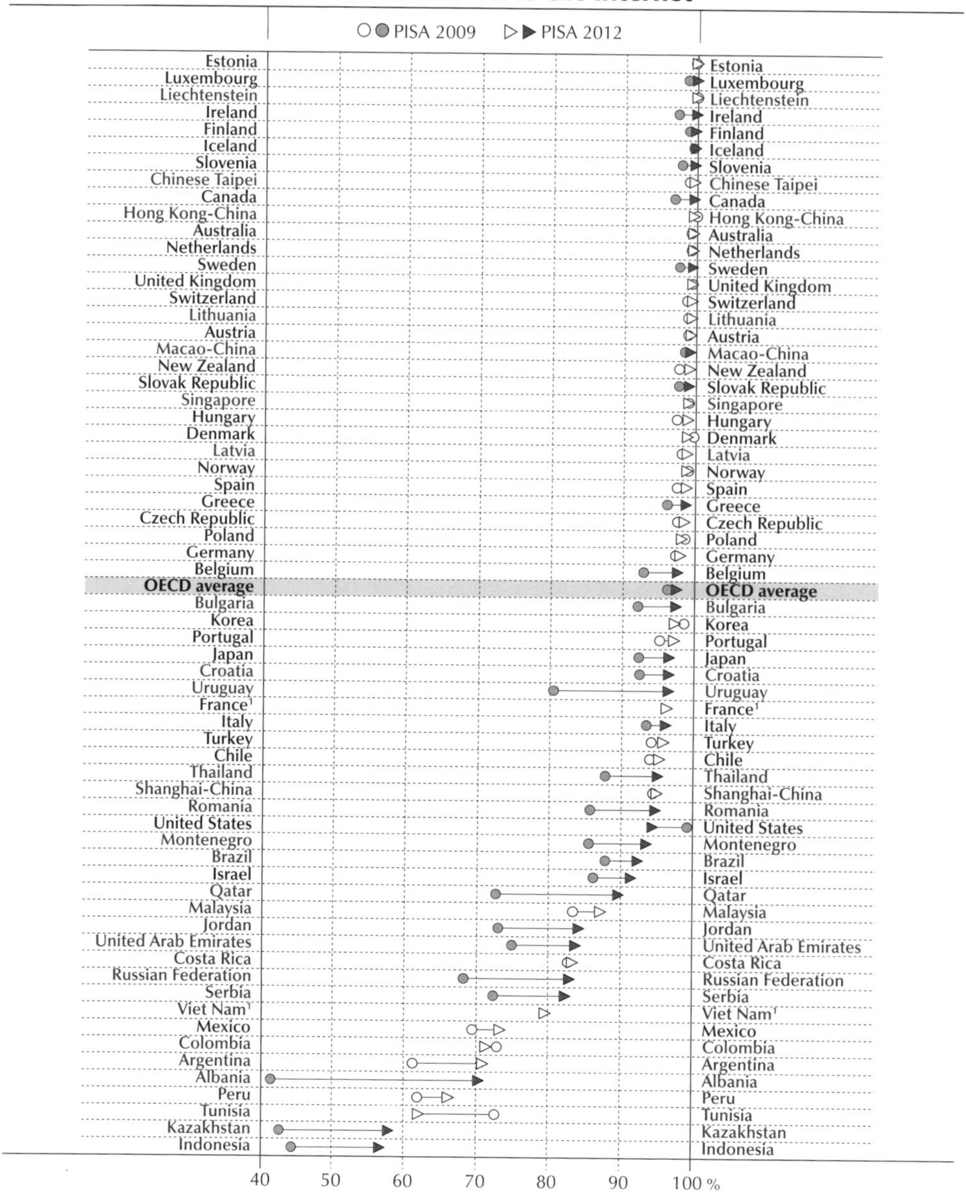
PISA 2009
PISA 2012
Estonia
Luxembourg
Liechtenstein
Ireland
Finland
Iceland
Slovenia
Chinese Taipei
Canada
Hong Kong-China
Australia
Netherlands
Sweden
United Kingdom
Switzerland
Lithuania
Austria
Macao-China
New Zealand
Slovak Republic
Singapore
Hungary
Denmark
Latvia
Norway
Spain
Greece
Czech Republic
Poland
Germany
Belgium
OECD average
Bulgaria
Korea
Portugal
Japan
Croatia
Uruguay
France[1]
Italy
Turkey
Chile
Thailand
Shanghai-China
Romania
United States
Montenegro
Brazil
Israel
Qatar
Malaysia
Jordan
United Arab Emirates
Costa Rica
Russian Federation
Serbia
Viet Nam[1]
Mexico
Colombia
Argentina
Albania
Peru
Tunisia
Kazakhstan
Indonesia
40
50
60
70
80
90
100 %

1. PISA 2009 data are missing for France and Viet Nam.

Note: White symbols indicate differences between PISA 2009 and PISA 2012 that are not statistically significant.

Countries and economies are ranked in descending order of the share of school computers that are connected to the Internet in 2012.

Source: OECD, PISA 2012 Database, Table 2.11.

StatLink http://dx.doi.org/10.1787/888933252826

The rise of mobile computers in schools

Even if the quantity of resources did not change, increases in the intensity of computer use may still be related to improvements in the quality of schools' ICT infrastructure. Whether students can access computers in their classrooms or only in separate computer labs or at the school library makes a big difference in teachers' willingness to use computers in their teaching. Laptop and tablet computers offer much greater flexibility than desktop computers, and PISA data show that more and more schools have opted for these mobile computing solutions (Table 2.9).[5]

In 2012, desktop computers remained the most common form of computers in schools in every country. But the share of students with access to laptop computers at school increased by 8 percentage points between 2009 and 2012, on average across OECD countries, while over the same period the share of students with access to desktop computers declined by 3 percentage points. By 2012, 43% of students, on average, had access to laptops at school, and 11% had access to tablets. In 2012, the highest rates of student access to school laptops were observed in Denmark (91%), Australia (89%), Norway (87%), Sweden (75%) and the Russian Federation (64%). Laptop-acquisition programmes have expanded access to laptops by over 20 percentage points in Australia, Chile, Sweden and Uruguay. School tablets, on the other hand, were available to more than one in five students in Denmark (35%), Jordan (29%), Singapore (23%) and Australia (21%) in 2012 (Table 2.9).

Only in a few cases have laptop- or tablet-acquisition programmes actually expanded access to computers in schools; in most cases, tablets or laptops seem to have entered those schools where desktop computers were already available, thus broadening the variety of ICT devices. The most notable exceptions are Australia, Spain and Uruguay, where the increased availability of computers at school is entirely attributable to laptop or tablet computers (Table 2.9).

Although not considered computers, other ICT devices also entered schools between 2009 and 2012. Among these, e-book readers were available at school for more than one in five students in Jordan (39%), Greece (37%), Serbia (23%), Mexico (22%), Chile and Hungary (20%) (Table 2.9).

How school infrastructure trends are related to the use of ICT

PISA data on the types of devices available to students at school indirectly confirm that school ICT-acquisition programmes between 2009 and 2012 increasingly favoured mobile devices, such as laptops, and sometimes handheld devices, such as tablets or e-readers. As a result, by 2012, many students no longer had to move to separate computer labs, school libraries or specific locations within the classroom to access computers; rather, computers could be available everywhere, anytime, thus expanding the range of activities and situations in which they could be used.

Between 2009 and 2012, the share of students using laptop computers increased, on average across OECD countries, while the overall share of students using computers remained stable, and the share of students using desktop computers declined. This evolution was particularly strong in Australia and Sweden. In both countries, laptop computers were used by only a minority of students in 2009, but by 2012 these devices had surpassed desktop computers as the most commonly used computers in schools (Table 2.3).

A comparison between students who use desktop computers only and students who use laptops and tablet computers at school, sometimes in addition to desktop computers, shows that computer use at school is significantly more frequent and more varied among the latter group. There is a significant difference in the percentage of students who use the Internet at school or regularly (i.e. at least once a week) engage in any of the activities examined in the PISA ICT questionnaire, depending on what device is available. For instance, while 27% of laptop or tablet users download, upload or browse material from the school's website at least once or twice a week, only 18% of desktop users do (Figure 2.16).

■ Figure 2.16 ■

Use of computers at school among desktop and laptop or tablet users

Percentage of students who reported engaging in each activity (OECD average)

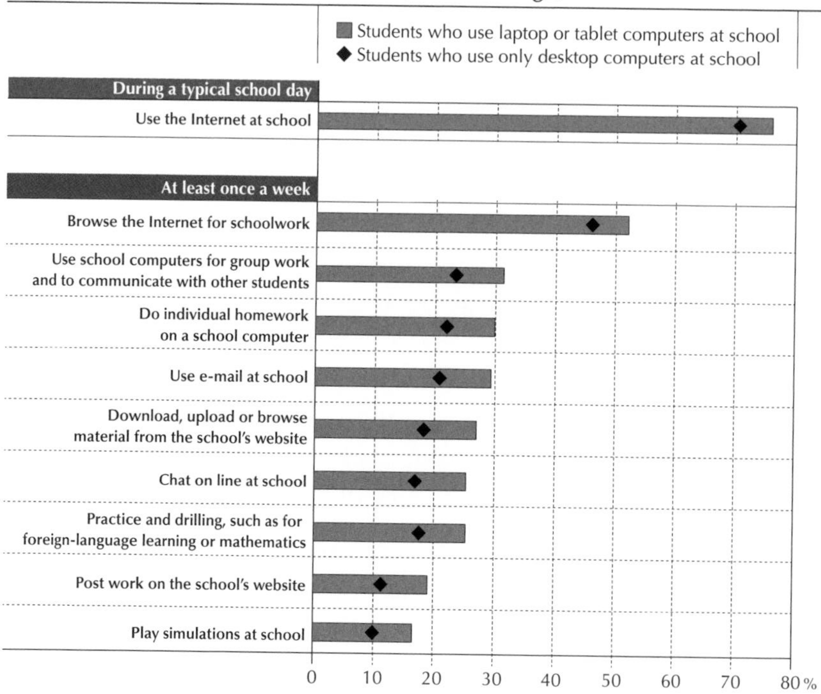
Students who use laptop or tablet computers at school
Students who use only desktop computers at school
During a typical school day
Use the Internet at school
At least once a week
Browse the Internet for schoolwork
Use school computers for group work and to communicate with other students
Do individual homework on a school computer
Use e-mail at school
Download, upload or browse material from the school's website
Chat on line at school
Practice and drilling, such as for foreign-language learning or mathematics
Post work on the school's website
Play simulations at school
0
10
20
30
40
50
60
70
80 %

Source: OECD, PISA 2012 Database, Table 2.12.
StatLink http://dx.doi.org/10.1787/888933252838

At the system level, countries and economies with the largest increases in the share of frequent users are often those that implemented laptop- or tablet-expansion programmes (Figure 2.17). For instance, the share of students who frequently do their individual homework on school computers grew by more than 10 percentage points in Australia, Greece, the Netherlands and New Zealand – all countries where the share of students who have access to laptop computers at school increased by a similar degree.

■ Figure 2.17 ■

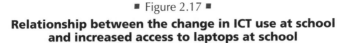

Relationship between the change in ICT use at school and increased access to laptops at school

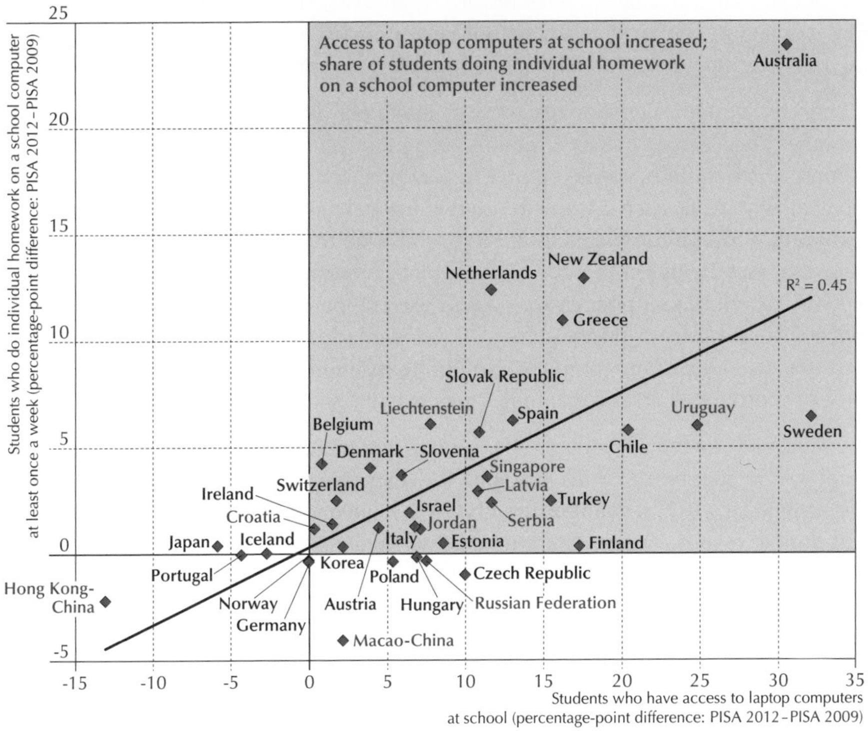
Access to laptop computers at school increased; share of students doing individual homework on a school computer increased
Students who do individual homework on a school computer at least once a week (percentage-point difference: PISA 2012 - PISA 2009)
Students who have access to laptop computers at school (percentage-point difference: PISA 2012 - PISA 2009)
R^2 = 0.45
25
20
15
10
5
0
-5
-15
-10
-5
0
5
10
15
20
25
30
35
Australia
New Zealand
Netherlands
Greece
Slovak Republic
Liechtenstein
Spain
Uruguay
Sweden
Belgium
Chile
Denmark
Slovenia
Singapore
Latvia
Switzerland
Ireland
Turkey
Israel
Croatia
Serbia
Jordan
Japan
Iceland
Italy
Estonia
Finland
Korea
Portugal
Poland
Czech Republic
Hong Kong-China
Norway
Austria
Hungary
Russian Federation
Germany
Macao-China

Source: OECD, PISA 2012 Database, Tables 2.1 and 2.9.
StatLink http://dx.doi.org/10.1787/888933252847

However, PISA data also show that greater use of ICT at school did not always coincide with hardware-expansion programmes. In fact, previous studies show that the uptake of new technologies in schools is largely dependent on whether teachers are offered professional development activities to help them integrate new tools into their classroom practice (Hennessy and London, 2013). It is also the case that teachers with more experience in integrating ICT in instruction sometimes spend less time using computers than novice users. Quantity does not always coincide with quality.

Curricula and the use of ICT at school for instruction

Teachers may find guidance and support in integrating ICT into teaching practice in official curriculum documents or in school policies. PISA asked school principals whether their school had a policy on how to use computers in mathematics classes, e.g. to guide teachers on the extent to which computers should be used in mathematics lessons or on what specific mathematics computer programme to use. On average across OECD countries, 32% of students attend schools whose principal reported that such a policy exists. This share ranges from 93% of students in Slovenia to less than 5% of students in Sweden (Table 2.14).

Within countries, the degree of computer use during mathematics instruction seems only weakly related to the existence of such school policies. Indeed, most of the variation in computer use during mathematics instruction lies within schools, as opposed to between schools (Table 2.14). The use of computers in mathematics lessons, it appears, depends on teacher and (perhaps) student-level factors, rather than on school-level policies, to a greater extent than for more general uses of computers at school (such as browsing the Internet for schoolwork).

In fact, only 11 countries/economies show a significant difference in the *index of computer use in mathematics lessons* between schools where a policy on ICT use for mathematics exists, and schools where there is no such policy. It may be that school policies are more concerned with qualitative aspects, such as how to use existing software, rather than quantitative aspects, such as whether to use computers at all. It may also be that school policies are occasionally introduced to limit the use of ICT during mathematics instruction, rather than to support it. The only country where school policies on how to use computers in mathematics classes make a large difference in students' use of computers is Denmark. Interestingly, in Denmark the large between-schools variation in computer use during mathematics instruction also indicates the existence of coordinated practices among teachers in the same school (Table 2.14).

Other policies not directly related to ICT, such as the national curriculum, may play a more important role in supporting or discouraging the integration of ICT into teaching. Figure 2.18 shows whether using ICT in mathematics classes is related to the content to which students are exposed during lessons. This is determined using students' answers about how often, during their mathematics lessons, they have encountered four types of tasks: word problems, formal mathematics problems, applied tasks set in a mathematical context, and applied tasks where – as in most PISA problems – students have to apply their knowledge of mathematics to real-world contexts (see Box 2.1).

Box 2.1. **PISA measures of exposure to different mathematics tasks**

Four questions from the PISA student questionnaire were used to measure students' exposure to different types of content during mathematics lessons. Each question presented students with two examples of mathematics tasks and asked students not to solve them, but to report whether they had encountered similar types of problems "frequently", "sometimes", "rarely" or "never" during their mathematics lessons. The example tasks are shown below.

Question 1 – Word problems

Below are examples of tasks that require you to understand a problem written in text and perform the appropriate calculations. Usually the problem talks about practical situations, but the numbers and people and places mentioned are made up. All the information you need is given.

1. <Ann> is two years older than <Betty> and <Betty> is four times as old as <Sam>. When <Betty> is 30, how old is <Sam>?

2. Mr <Smith> bought a television and a bed. The television cost <$625> but he got a 10% discount. The bed cost <$200>. He paid <$20> for delivery. How much money did Mr <Smith> spend?

...

Question 2 – Formal mathematics tasks

Below are examples of another set of mathematical skills.

1) Solve 2x + 3 = 7.

2) Find the volume of a box with sides 3m, 4m and 5m.

Question 3 – Applied mathematics tasks – mathematics contexts

In the next type of problem, you have to use mathematical knowledge and draw conclusions. There is no practical application provided. Here are two examples.

1) Here you need to use geometrical theorems:

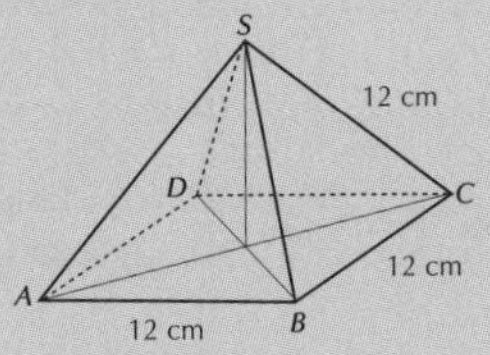
S
12 cm
D
C
12 cm
A
12 cm
B

Determine the height of the pyramid.

2) Here you have to know what a prime number is:

If n is any number: can $(n+1)^2$ be a prime number?

Question 4 – Applied mathematics tasks – real-world contexts

In this type of problem, you have to apply suitable mathematical knowledge to find a useful answer to a problem that arises in everyday life or work. The data and information are about real situations. Here are two examples.

Example 1

A TV reporter says "This graph shows that there is a huge increase in the number of robberies from 1998 to 1999."

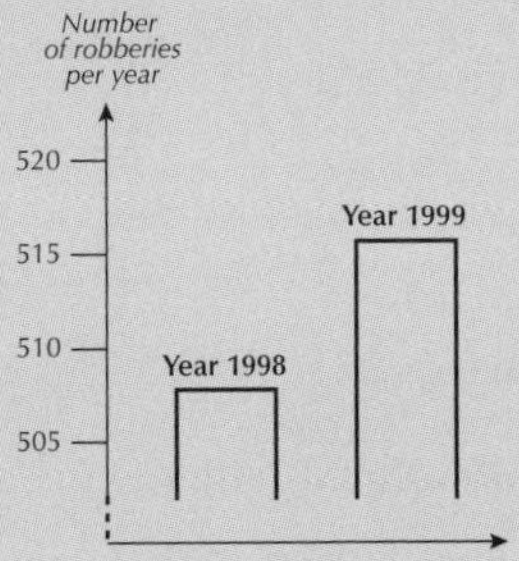
Number
of robberies
per year
520
515
510
505
Year 1999
Year 1998

Do you consider the reporter's statement to be a reasonable interpretation of the graph?

Give an explanation to support your answer.

Example 2

For years the relationship between a person's recommended maximum heart rate and the person's age was described by the following formula:

Recommended maximum heart rate = 220 – age

Recent research showed that this formula should be modified slightly. The new formula is as follows:

Recommended maximum heart rate = 208 – (0.7 × age)

From which age onwards does the recommended maximum heart rate increase as a result of the introduction of the new formula? Show your work.

■ Figure 2.18 ■

Relationship between computer use in mathematics lessons and students' exposure to various mathematics tasks

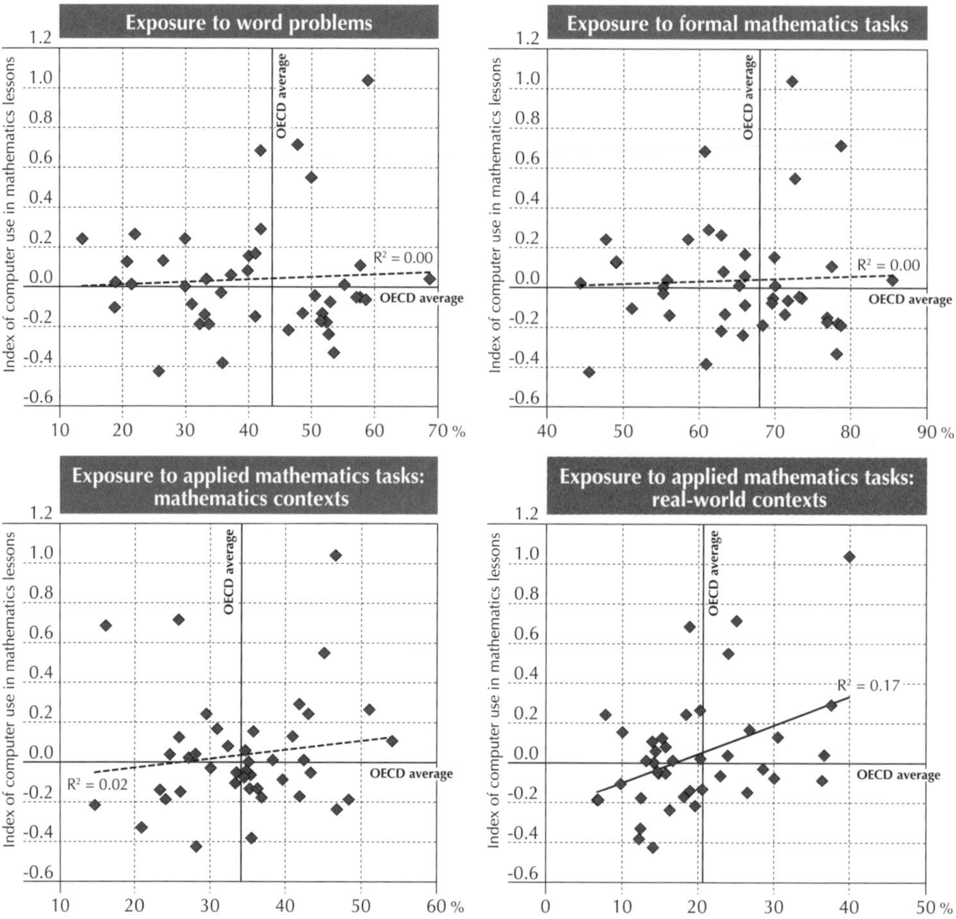
Exposure to word problems
Index of computer use in mathematics lessons
OECD average
R² = 0.00
OECD average
1.2
1.0
0.8
0.6
0.4
0.2
0.0
-0.2
-0.4
-0.6
10
20
30
40
50
60
70 %
Exposure to formal mathematics tasks
Index of computer use in mathematics lessons
OECD average
R² = 0.00
OECD average
40
50
60
70
80
90 %
Exposure to applied mathematics tasks: mathematics contexts
Index of computer use in mathematics lessons
OECD average
R² = 0.02
OECD average
10
20
30
40
50
60 %
Exposure to applied mathematics tasks: real-world contexts
Index of computer use in mathematics lessons
OECD average
R² = 0.17
OECD average
0
10
20
30
40
50 %

Notes: The dotted lines indicate non-significant relationships. The solid line indicates a correlation higher than 0.4 (R^2 higher than 0.16).

For each chart, the horizontal axis represents the percentage of students who reported that they encounter the corresponding type of tasks "frequently" during mathematics lessons.

Each diamond represents the mean values of a country/economy.

Source: OECD, PISA 2012 Database, Table 2.15.

StatLink http://dx.doi.org/10.1787/888933252859

Across countries, greater exposure to formal mathematics or word problems is not strongly related to differences in computer use during mathematics lessons. In contrast, countries where computers are used more during mathematics instruction tend to be those where students have greater-than-average exposure to applied mathematics tasks – particularly to tasks in which they can practice their mathematics skills in real-world contexts. This shows that the content of the curriculum can influence the desirability, and use, of computers for instruction (Figure 2.18).

HOW ICT USE IS RELATED TO PEDAGOGICAL PRACTICES IN MATHEMATICS

According to the literature on educational effectiveness, a number of classroom variables appear to be related to better learning outcomes, particularly classroom climate and instructional quality. How is computer use during mathematics lessons linked to student discipline and the quality of instruction?

Instructional quality is difficult to measure, as existing evidence suggests that there is no single best way of teaching. Close monitoring, adequate pacing and classroom management as well as clarity of presentation, well-structured lessons and informative and encouraging feedback – which are good instructional practices – have generally been shown to have a positive impact on student achievement, as they help to create an orderly classroom environment and maximise learning time (OECD, 2013c).

This is not enough, however. Teachers provide learning opportunities; but to be effective, those opportunities must be recognised and seized by the student. This is particularly important if students are to go beyond rote learning and to develop the skills that they can confidently apply in new contexts. For these reasons, teaching that fosters deep conceptual understanding involves more than "direct instruction". Based on results from the Trends in International Mathematics and Science Study (TIMSS) video study, Klieme, Pauli and Reusser (2009) proposed three pillars for quality teaching: clear and well-structured classroom management; student orientation; and cognitive activation with challenging content. The PISA measures of mathematics teaching, which distinguish structure (teacher-directed instruction), student orientation, formative assessment and cognitive activation in mathematics lessons, are grounded in this framework (see Box 2.2) (OECD, 2013c).

Box 2.2. **PISA 2012 indices of mathematics teaching practices**

Two questions were used to gauge mathematics teachers' classroom practices in PISA 2012. In each of them, the question stem was "how often do these things happen in your mathematics lessons?", followed by a series of items describing teacher behaviours. Students were asked to report on the frequency with which they observed these behaviours on a four-point scale (from "every lesson" to "never or hardly ever" in question ST79; from "always or almost always" to "rarely" in question ST80).

These behaviours were grouped to form the four indices of teacher behaviour (structuring practices, student-oriented practices, formative assessment practices and cognitive activation practices), as follows:

Structuring practices (teacher-directed instruction):

ST79Q01	The teacher sets clear goals for our learning
ST79Q02	The teacher asks me or my classmates to present our thinking or reasoning at some length
ST79Q06	The teacher asks questions to check whether we have understood what was taught
ST79Q08	At the beginning of a lesson, the teacher presents a short summary of the previous lesson
ST79Q15	The teacher tells us what we have to learn

...

Student-oriented practices:

ST79Q03	The teacher gives different work to classmates who have difficulties learning and/or to those who can advance faster
ST79Q04	The teacher assigns projects that require at least one week to complete
ST79Q07	The teacher has us work in small groups to come up with joint solutions to a problem or task
ST79Q10	The teacher asks us to help plan classroom activities or topics

Formative assessment practices:

ST79Q03	The teacher tells me about how well I am doing in my mathematics class
ST79Q04	The teacher gives me feedback on my strengths and weaknesses in mathematics
ST79Q07	The teacher tells us what is expected of us when we get a test, quiz or assignment
ST79Q10	The teacher tells me what I need to do to become better in mathematics

Cognitive activation practices:

ST80Q01	The teacher asks questions that make us reflect on the problem
ST80Q04	The teacher gives problems that require us to think for an extended time
ST80Q05	The teacher asks us to decide on our own procedures for solving complex problems
ST80Q06	The teacher presents problems for which there is no immediately obvious method of solution
ST80Q07	The teacher presents problems in different contexts so that students know whether they have understood the concepts
ST80Q08	The teacher helps us to learn from mistakes we have made
ST80Q09	The teacher asks us to explain how we have solved a problem
ST80Q10	The teacher presents problems that require students to apply what they have learned to new contexts
ST80Q11	The teacher gives problems that can be solved in several different ways

Several features of ICT support teachers in giving adaptive feedback to students and, more generally, individualising instruction; in other words, they support student-oriented and formative assessment behaviours in teachers' classroom practice. They also facilitate collaborative projects and enable teachers to extend the spatial and temporal boundaries of their lessons, thus creating the potential for cognitively challenging and engaging activities. In contrast, teachers cannot expect computers to be much help in managing the classroom or in certain structuring practices, such as presenting a short summary of the previous lesson at the beginning of each new lesson.

Is there a relationship, in PISA, between the degree of integration of technology in mathematics instruction and the quality of teachers' pedagogical practices? Figure 2.19 shows that, in general, students who use ICT during mathematics lessons more often describe their teachers as frequently using effective instructional strategies and behaviours, such as structuring practices (e.g. setting clear goals, asking questions to verify understanding), student-oriented practices (e.g. giving different work to students who have difficulties or who can advance faster, having students work in small groups), formative assessment (e.g. giving feedback on strengths and weaknesses), and cognitive activation (e.g. giving problems that require students to apply what they have learned to new contexts and/or giving problems that can be solved in several different ways).

■ Figure 2.19 ■

Teaching practices and disciplinary climate, by computer use in mathematics lessons

Mean indices (OECD average)

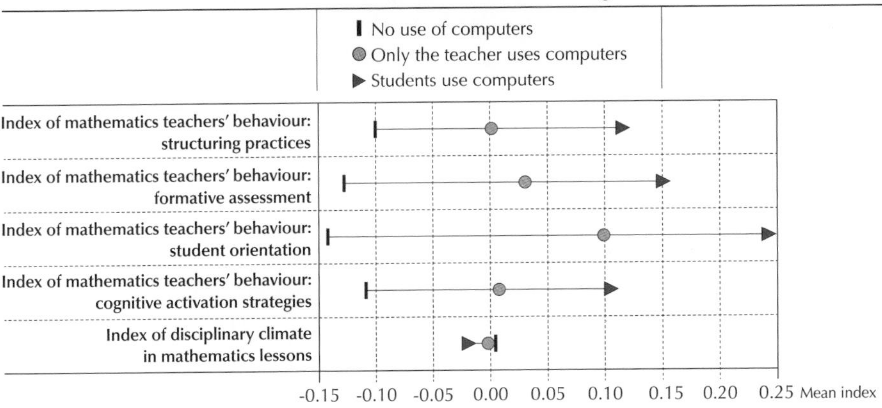
No use of computers
Only the teacher uses computers
Students use computers
Index of mathematics teachers' behaviour: structuring practices
Index of mathematics teachers' behaviour: formative assessment
Index of mathematics teachers' behaviour: student orientation
Index of mathematics teachers' behaviour: cognitive activation strategies
Index of disciplinary climate in mathematics lessons
-0.15 -0.10 -0.05 0.00 0.05 0.10 0.15 0.20 0.25 Mean index

Note: All differences between students who reported using computers during mathematics lessons and students who reported computers are not used are statistically significant.

Source: OECD, PISA 2012 Database, Tables 2.13b, c, d, e and f.

StatLink http://dx.doi.org/10.1787/888933252861

The strongest association between ICT use and teachers' classroom practices, by a large margin, is with student-oriented practices and formative assessment practices. Uniformly positive associations may raise the suspicion that the relation between ICT use and teacher behaviour is not direct and specific, but hinges on another factor that is associated with both variables, such as class time, teacher experience, or student response style. In contrast, the strong association with student-oriented practices, which include individualised pacing, collaborative learning and project-based learning, suggests a specific association: these are precisely the kinds of practices that can benefit from ICT. Computers are also extremely efficient at giving individualised feedback (formative assessment) to users in well-designed learning situations.

The evidence from PISA supports the conclusion that teachers who are more inclined and better prepared for student-oriented teaching practices, such as group work, individualised learning, and project work, are more willing to integrate computers into their lessons, when the required resources are available. Indeed, a specific association between teachers' use of student-oriented teaching practices and the use of ICT in mathematics lessons is observed not only within countries and economies, but also at the system level. When countries and economies are compared against each other, the relationship between the average frequency of student-oriented teaching practices and the extent to which ICT is used in mathematics classes is strong and significant (Figures 2.20 and 2.21).

PISA also shows that in most countries and economies there is no association between the disciplinary climate in mathematics classes and computer use by students (disciplinary climate refers to students' perceptions that mathematics lessons are orderly, with minimal loss of instruction time due to noise or indiscipline). However, some countries show positive or negative associations between the two. While in Australia, Denmark, Macao-China, Norway and Switzerland students who use computers during mathematics instruction reported better disciplinary climate in their classroom than students who do not use computers, in eleven countries/economies (the Czech Republic, Greece, Hungary, Israel, Mexico, Portugal, Serbia, the Slovak Republic, Slovenia, Turkey and Uruguay), the disciplinary climate is significantly worse when students reported greater use of computers (Figure 2.20).

■ Figure 2.20 ■

Student-oriented teaching and disciplinary climate, by computer use in mathematics lessons

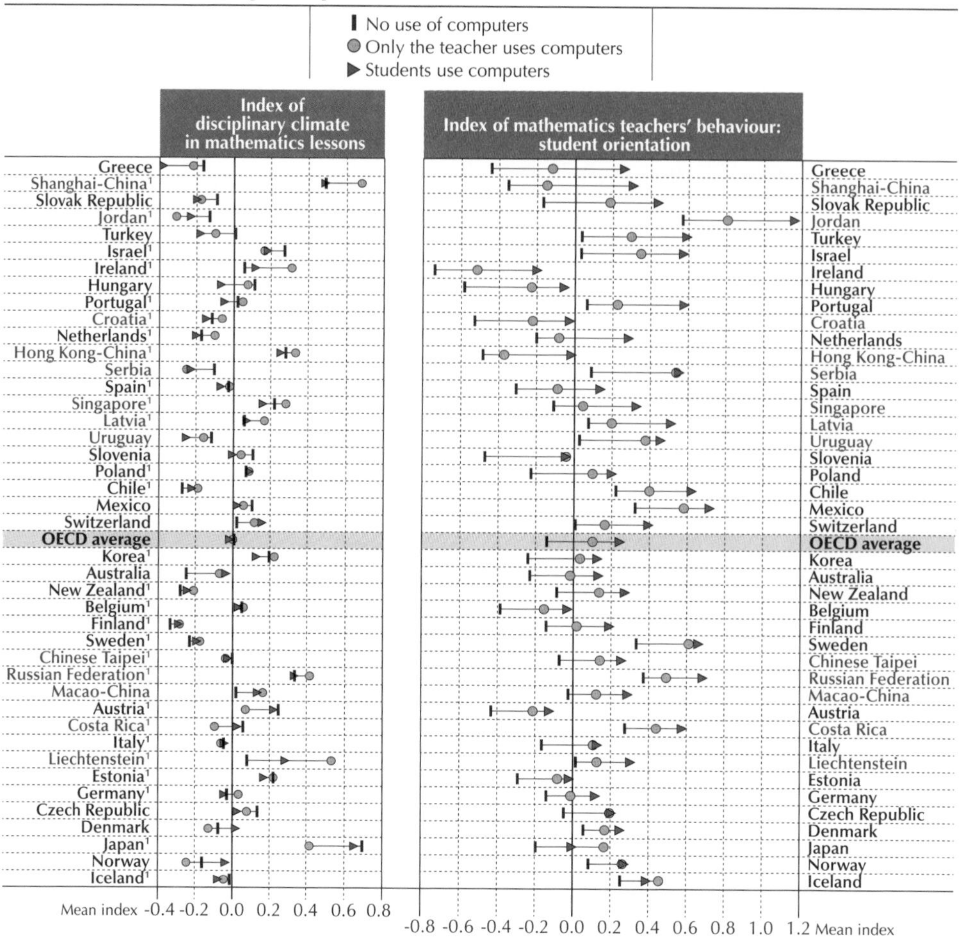
No use of computers
Only the teacher uses computers
Students use computers
Index of disciplinary climate in mathematics lessons
Index of mathematics teachers' behaviour: student orientation
Greece
Shanghai-China
Slovak Republic
Jordan
Turkey
Israel
Ireland
Hungary
Portugal
Croatia
Netherlands
Hong Kong-China
Serbia
Spain
Singapore
Latvia
Uruguay
Slovenia
Poland
Chile
Mexico
Switzerland
OECD average
Korea
Australia
New Zealand
Belgium
Finland
Sweden
Chinese Taipei
Russian Federation
Macao-China
Austria
Costa Rica
Italy
Liechtenstein
Estonia
Germany
Czech Republic
Denmark
Japan
Norway
Iceland
Mean index -0.4 -0.2 0.0 0.2 0.4 0.6 0.8
-0.8 -0.6 -0.4 -0.2 0.0 0.2 0.4 0.6 0.8 1.0 1.2 Mean index

1. Countries and economies in which differences are not statistically significant between students who reported using computers in mathematics lessons and students who reported computers are not used.

Countries and economies are ranked in descending order of the difference in the mean index of mathematics teachers' behaviour (student orientation) *between students who reported using computers during mathematics lessons and students who reported computers are not used.*

Source: OECD, PISA 2012 Database, Tables 2.13b and 2.13e.

StatLink http://dx.doi.org/10.1787/888933252876

■ Figure 2.21 ■

Relationship between computer use in mathematics lessons and teachers' behaviour

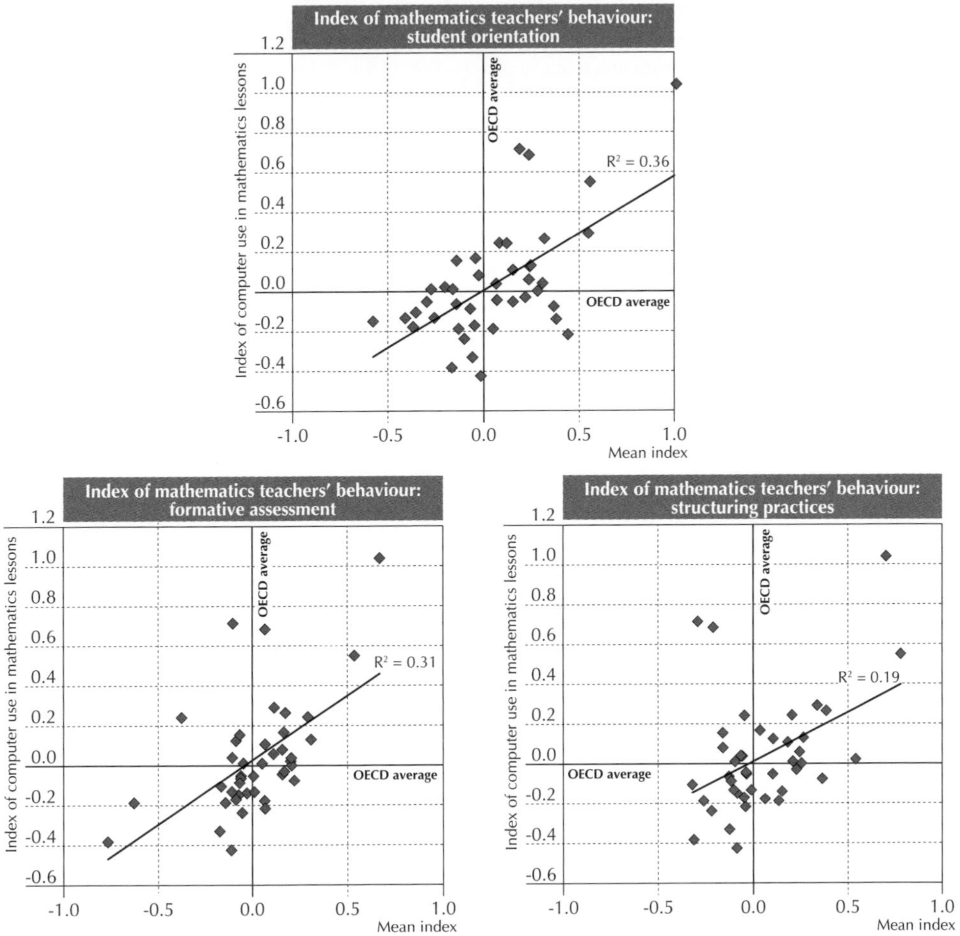
Index of mathematics teachers' behaviour: student orientation
Index of mathematics teachers' behaviour: formative assessment
Index of mathematics teachers' behaviour: structuring practices
Index of computer use in mathematics lessons
Mean index
OECD average
R² = 0.36
R² = 0.31
R² = 0.19
1.2
1.0
0.8
0.6
0.4
0.2
0.0
-0.2
-0.4
-0.6
-1.0
-0.5
0.0
0.5
1.0

Note: Each diamond represents the mean values of a country/economy.
Source: OECD, PISA 2012 Database, Table 2.15.
StatLink http://dx.doi.org/10.1787/888933252886

One possible reason for the difference is that in the former group of countries/economies, teachers have more experience integrating technology in teaching, while in the latter group, this process is only starting. As a result, teachers' low level of confidence in using ICT, and possibly a lack of professional development activities to help teachers learn how to use new tools in their teaching, may lead to disorder in the classroom when computers are used. In all systems participating in the TALIS survey, teachers cited improving their ICT skills as one of the most important priorities for their professional development (OECD, 2014a).[6] Integrating technology into teaching should always be done in the service of pedagogy (OECD, 2010).

Notes

1. The *Technical Report* (OECD, 2014b) provides details on how indices derived from the ICT familiarity questionnaire were scaled.

2. Values for the *index of ICT use at school* cannot be directly compared to the corresponding 2009 index. The response categories for items included in the construction of this index changed between the 2009 and 2012 surveys. Nevertheless, it is possible to compare relative rankings. A comparison of rankings relative to the OECD average shows that, in some countries and economies, such as Australia, Greece, Spain and Uruguay, the frequency and variety of ICT use in schools increased more than the average increase, while in other countries and economies, notably Hong Kong-China, Hungary, Iceland and Portugal, all of which were at or above the OECD average in 2009, the frequency and variety of ICT use at school fell below the OECD average by 2012.

3. In this context, "computers" include desktop, laptop and tablet computers, but do not include other ICT devices, such as smartphones.

4. For results based on the Teaching and Learning International Survey (TALIS), see OECD, 2014a and OECD, 2015.

5. Tablet computers became popular only after 2010, when the first Apple iPad® was released. Although no question about tablets was asked in PISA 2009, it can be safely assumed that no student had access to tablet computers during that survey.

6. In Brazil, France, Iceland, Italy, Japan, Malaysia and Sweden, over one in four teachers reported that they have a high level of need for professional development in the area of ICT skills for teaching.

Chapter 2 tables are available on line at http://dx.doi.org/10.1787/edu-data-en.

Note regarding Israel

The statistical data for Israel are supplied by and under the responsibility of the relevant Israeli authorities. The use of such data by the OECD is without prejudice to the status of the Golan Heights, East Jerusalem and Israeli settlements in the West Bank under the terms of international law.

References

Avvisati, F., S. Hennessy, R.B. Kozma and **S. Vincent-Lancrin** (2013), "Review of the Italian strategy for digital schools", *OECD Education Working Papers*, No. 90, OECD Publishing, Paris, http://dx.doi.org/10.1787/5k487ntdbr44-en.

Frost, D. and **J. Durrant** (2003), "Teacher leadership: Rationale, strategy and impact", *School Leadership & Management*, Vol. 23/2, pp.173-186.

Harris, A. (2005), "Teacher leadership: More than just a feel-good factor?", *Leadership and Policy in Schools, Vol.* 4/3, pp. 201-219.

Hennessy, S. and **L. London** (2013), "Learning from international experiences with interactive whiteboards: The role of professional development in integrating the technology", *OECD Education Working Papers*, No. 89, OECD Publishing, Paris, http://dx.doi.org/10.1787/5k49chbsnmls-en.

Horn, I. S. and **J.W. Little** (2010), "Attending to problems of practice: Routines and resources for professional learning in teachers' workplace interactions," *American Educational Research Journal*, Vol. 47/1, pp. 181-217.

Klieme, E., C. Pauli and **K. Reusser** (2009), "The Pythagoras study: Investigating effects of teaching and learning in Swiss and German mathematics classrooms", in Tomáš, J. and T. Seidel (eds.), *The Power of Video Studies in Investigating Teaching and Learning in the Classroom*, pp. 137-160, Waxmann Verlag GmbH, Münster, Germany.

Little, J.W. (1982), "Norms of collegiality and experimentation: Workplace conditions of school success", *American Educational Research Journal, Vol.* 19/2, pp. 325-340.

Livingstone, S. (2011), "Critical reflections on the benefits of ICT in education", *Oxford Review of Education*, Vol. 38/1, pp. 9-24.

OECD (2015), "Embedding professional development in schools for teacher success", *Teaching in Focus*, No. 10, OECD Publishing, Paris, http://dx.doi.org/10.1787/5js4rv7s7snt-en.

OECD (2014a), "Developing and supporting teachers", in OECD, *TALIS 2013 Results: An International Perspective on Teaching and Learning*, OECD Publishing, Paris, http://dx.doi.org/10.1787/9789264196261-7-en.

OECD (2014b), *PISA 2012 Technical Report*, PISA, OECD, Paris, www.oecd.org/pisa/pisaproducts/pisa2012technicalreport.htm.

OECD (2013a), *OECD Skills Outlook 2013: First Results from the Survey of Adult Skills*, OECD Publishing, Paris, http://dx.doi.org/10.1787/9789264204256-en.

OECD (2013b), *PISA 2012 Results: What Makes Schools Successful (Volume IV): Resources, Policies and Practices*, PISA, OECD Publishing, Paris, http://dx.doi.org/10.1787/9789264201156-en.

OECD (2013c), *PISA 2012 Assessment and Analytical Framework: Mathematics, Reading, Science, Problem Solving and Financial Literacy*, PISA, OECD Publishing, Paris, http://dx.doi.org/10.1787/9789264190511-en.

OECD (2012), *The Protection of Children Online: Recommendation of the OECD Council: Report on Risks Faced by Children Online and Policies to Protect Them*, OECD, Paris, www.oecd.org/sti/ieconomy/childrenonline_with_cover.pdf.

OECD (2011), *PISA 2009 Results: Students On Line: Digital Technologies and Performance (Volume VI)*, PISA, OECD Publishing, Paris, http://dx.doi.org/10.1787/9789264112995-en.

OECD (2010), *Inspired by Technology, Driven by Pedagogy: A Systemic Approach to Technology-Based School Innovations*, Educational Research and Innovation, OECD Publishing, Paris, http://dx.doi.org/10.1787/9789264094437-en.

Resnick, L.B., J.P. Spillane, P. Goldman and **E.S. Rangel** (2010), "Implementing innovation: From visionary models to everyday practice", in Dumont, H., D. Instance and F. Benavides (eds.), *The Nature of Learning. Using Research to Inspire Practice*, pp. 285-315. OECD Publishing, Paris, http://dx.doi.org/10.1787/9789264086487-en.

Tondeur, J., J. van Braak, G. Sang, J. Voogt, P. Fisser and **A. Ottenbreit-Leftwich** (2012), "Preparing pre-service teachers to integrate technology in education: A synthesis of qualitative evidence", *Computers & Education*, Vol. 59/1, pp. 134-44.

3

Main Results from the PISA 2012 Computer-Based Assessments

Computer-based tests expand the range of situations in which students' ability to apply their knowledge can be measured. Students in 32 countries and economies that participated in the PISA 2012 pencil-and-paper assessment were invited to take a test of reading and mathematics on computers. This chapter discusses the results of those computer-based assessments.

In 32 countries and economies, students who participated in the PISA 2012 pencil-and-paper assessment were also invited to take a test of reading and mathematics on computers.[1] This latter assessment included 18 reading questions originally developed for use in the 2009 assessment of digital reading, and 41 specially designed mathematics questions. This chapter reports results from the PISA 2012 computer-based assessments.

What the data tell us

- Singapore, followed by Korea, Hong Kong-China, Japan, Canada and Shanghai-China were the top-performing countries/economies in digital reading in 2012; Singapore and Shanghai-China, followed by Korea, Hong Kong-China, Macao-China, Japan and Chinese Taipei were top performers in the 2012 computer-based mathematics assessment.
- In Korea and Singapore, students score more than 20 points higher on the digital reading scale, on average, than students in other countries with similar skills in print reading.
- Students in Australia, Austria, Canada, Japan, Slovenia and the United States, as well as students in partner countries/economies Macao-China and the United Arab Emirates, perform better on mathematics tasks that require the use of computers to solve problems compared to their success on traditional tasks. By contrast, students in Belgium, Chile, France, Ireland, Poland and Spain perform worse than expected on such tasks, given their performance on traditional mathematics tasks.

While both reading and mathematics tasks in the computer-based assessment were developed within the same framework as their corresponding paper-based tasks, the results of the former assessment are reported on separate scales. Indeed, computer-based tests expand the range of situations in which reading and mathematics are assessed in PISA. A key feature of digital reading tasks is that they use the typical text formats encountered on line; as a result, many of them require students to navigate through and across texts by using such tools as hyperlinks, browser button or scrolling, in order to access the information. The design of mathematics tasks, on the other hand, ensured that mathematical reasoning and processes take precedence over mastery of using the computer as a tool. Several tasks, however, also involve typical situations in which information and communication tools, such as using spreadsheets to collect data or create a chart, help to solve mathematics problems.

Demands for general knowledge and skills related to computers were kept to a minimum. They included using a keyboard and mouse, and knowing common conventions, such as arrows to move forward. A short introduction to the test provided all students with the opportunity to practice using the tools through which they could interact with the test items, as well as response formats.

SIMILARITIES AND DIFFERENCES BETWEEN PAPER-BASED AND COMPUTER-BASED ASSESSMENTS

This section highlights what is particular about the computer-based assessments of reading and mathematics in PISA 2012. The discussion starts by highlighting differences with paper-based assessments in what is assessed, and ends by looking at how proficiency is assessed. More details about the framework for these assessments can be found in the framework publication (OECD, 2013); details about the test design and operational characteristics can be found in the technical report (OECD, 2014a).

Items from units *SERAING*, *SPORTS CLUB* and *LANGUAGE LEARNING* – three digital reading units used in the PISA 2012 assessment – can be seen, and tested, on the website of the Australian Consortium for Educational Research (http://cbasq.acer.edu.au/index.php?cmd=toEra2012). Items from three computer-based mathematics units used in the PISA 2012 main survey (*CD PRODUCTION*, *STAR POINTS* and *BODY MASS INDEX*), as well as items from four field-trial units, can also be found on the same website (http://cbasq.acer.edu.au/index.php?cmd=toMaths). All main survey items are available in 91 languages.

Differences between digital and print reading

The framework for reading treats digital and print reading as a single domain, while acknowledging the differences between reading on paper and reading on digital platforms. These differences are reflected in the assessment tasks used to assess reading in the two media.

First, in a typical Internet reading situation, the reader is generally unable to see the physical amount of text available; at the same time, he can access multiple sources more easily than in a print environment. While there are offline situations where readers need to consult several printed documents, the PISA assessment makes minimal use of such situations. All stimulus material fits onto a single page in the PISA assessment of print reading, and this limits the extent to which texts from multiple sources can be used. By contrast, because reading on the Internet usually involves referring to several pages, and often to several texts from different sources, composed by different authors and appearing in different formats, it was important that the computer-based assessment allowed for the possibility of using multiple texts simultaneously.

Another distinction between digital and print reading is the text types that are typical of each medium. Much reading in the digital medium involves personal communications and exchanges that aim to achieve a specific purpose (transactions), as in e-mails and text messages that set the date of a meeting or ask a friend for a suggestion. Narrative texts, in contrast, are more common in print reading. As a consequence, there are no assessment tasks in the digital reading assessment that are based on narrative texts, whereas transaction texts are absent from the print reading assessment in PISA.

Finally, while the major cognitive processes involved in print and digital reading are the same, performing tasks that demand these processes may pose a greater challenge in the digital medium than on paper, because navigation is required (see Chapter 4). *Access and retrieve* tasks, for instance, involve locating information: on line, readers need to search for information in a more abstract space than in printed books or documents, without seeing the full text. Search tools are also specific to each medium: search engines and menus on line, tables of contents and indices in printed documents. *Integrate and interpret* tasks require readers to contrast or compare information from different locations. In digital reading, such tasks often involve multiple texts and diverse text formats; and because the texts are usually not visible simultaneously, readers must rely on their short-term memory to perform these tasks. *Reflection and evaluation* processes tend to be required only for the most difficult tasks on paper. In contrast, when reading on line, readers must often assess the credibility of the content even when solving simple tasks, given that there are fewer filters between the author and the reader to decide what is published.

Knowledge of some techniques of navigation and some navigation tools (e.g. hyperlinks, tabs, menus, the "back" button) are part of being literate in the digital medium. Such skills and knowledge should be regarded as ICT skills that are measured, together with the mastery of reading processes, in the assessment of digital reading.

Differences between computer-based and paper-based mathematics

The computer-based assessment of mathematics recognises that mathematical competency in the 21st century includes usage of computers. Indeed, computers offer tools to describe, explain, or predict phenomena by employing mathematical concepts, facts, procedures and reasoning. Students' ability to use these tools is an aspect of mathematical literacy that could not be assessed on paper, and was only assessed in the computer-based assessment. Conversely, the mathematical competencies that are tested on paper are all represented in the computer-based assessment of mathematics (although the small number of tasks means that not all of them could be covered well).

Thus, the main difference between the paper-based and computer-based mathematics assessment is that only in the latter are skills related to using ICT tools for mathematics tasks assessed. These skills include using computers to make a chart from data, produce graphs of functions, sort data sets, use on-screen calculators, use virtual instruments, or use a mouse or a dialog box to rotate, translate, or reflect a geometrical figure.

Differences in test design and operational characteristics of computer- and paper-based assessments

In addition to differences in the constructs of the reading and mathematics assessments, there are differences in how tests were administered. The obvious difference is that the paper-based assessments were completed with pen and paper as part of a two-hour test session. By contrast, computer-based assessments were completed with a keyboard and mouse, while looking at questions on a screen, and lasted only 40 minutes.

A consequence of the difference in testing time is that more items were used in the print reading and paper-based mathematics assessments than in the digital reading and computer-based mathematics assessments. For this reason, the uncertainty associated with the measurement of performance is greater in the computer-based tests, particularly at very high or very low levels of proficiency. In addition, results are only reported on a single, global scale, not on subscales.

Not all students who sat the paper-based assessments completed the computer-based assessment; nor did they necessarily encounter questions from the digital reading assessment or the computer-based mathematics assessment in their test forms. In fact, in the 32 countries that participated in the optional computer-based assessments of reading and mathematics, only about half of all students who were sampled for PISA within each participating school were also invited to take a computer-based test. And because three domains (digital reading, computer-based mathematics and problem solving) were assessed on computers, of all students who were sampled for the computer-based test, only two out of three encountered questions from a particular domain in their forms.

STUDENT PERFORMANCE IN DIGITAL READING

PISA outcomes are reported in a variety of ways. This section gives the country results and shows how performance varies within and across countries. In addition, it shows trends in the digital reading performance of countries/economies that participated in both the PISA 2009 and PISA 2012 assessments.

When digital reading was assessed for the first time in 2009, the scale was fixed so that the average mean score and standard deviation for OECD countries would match those of the print reading scale for the same year and the same countries (OECD, 2011). In 2012, results were reported on the same scale as in 2009.

Average performance in digital reading

When comparing countries and economies on the basis of their average digital reading score, it is important to remember that not all performance differences observed between countries are statistically significant. In other words, because the PISA survey is based on a sample of students and a limited number of items, some small differences may be observed by chance, even when there are no differences in the true proficiency of students on average. When interpreting mean performance, only those differences among countries and economies that are statistically significant should be taken into account. These are differences that are large enough – so large in fact as to make it highly unlikely that the difference observed among samples of students does not reflect a true difference in the populations from which these students are drawn.

Figure 3.1 lists each participating country and economy in descending order of its mean digital-reading score (left column). The values range from a high of 567 points for partner country Singapore to a low of 396 points for partner country Colombia. Countries and economies are also divided into three broad groups: those whose mean scores are not statistically different from the mean for the 23 OECD countries participating in the assessment (highlighted in dark blue), those whose mean scores are significantly above the OECD mean (highlighted in pale blue), and those whose mean scores are significantly below the OECD mean. The best-performing OECD country is Korea, followed by Japan. Partner country Singapore performs better than all other countries and economies, including Korea, while the performance of Hong Kong-China is not statistically different from that of Korea or Japan. Canada, Shanghai-China, Estonia, Australia, Ireland, Chinese Taipei, Macao-China, the United States, France and Belgium (in decreasing order of mean performance) also perform above the OECD average, but below the four best-performing countries and economies.

Because the figures are derived from samples, it is not possible to determine a country's precise rank among the participating countries/economies. However, it is possible to determine, with confidence, a range of ranks in which the performance of the country/economy lies (Figure 3.2).

■ Figure 3.1 ■

Comparing countries' and economies' performance in digital reading

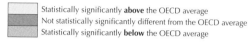

- Statistically significantly **above** the OECD average
- Not statistically significantly different from the OECD average
- Statistically significantly **below** the OECD average

Mean score	Comparison country/economy	Countries/economies whose mean score is NOT statistically significantly different from that of the comparison country/economy
567	Singapore	
555	Korea	Hong Kong-China
550	Hong Kong-China	Korea, Japan
545	Japan	Hong Kong-China
532	Canada	Shanghai-China
531	Shanghai-China	Canada, Estonia
523	Estonia	Shanghai-China, Australia, Ireland, Chinese Taipei
521	Australia	Estonia, Ireland, Chinese Taipei, United States
520	Ireland	Estonia, Australia, Chinese Taipei, Macao-China, United States, France
519	Chinese Taipei	Estonia, Australia, Ireland, Macao-China, United States, France
515	Macao-China	Ireland, Chinese Taipei, United States, France
511	United States	Australia, Ireland, Chinese Taipei, Macao-China, France, Italy, Belgium
511	France	Ireland, Chinese Taipei, Macao-China, United States, Italy, Belgium
504	Italy	United States, France, Belgium, Norway, Sweden, Denmark
502	Belgium	United States, France, Italy, Norway, Sweden
500	Norway	Italy, Belgium, Sweden, Denmark
498	Sweden	Italy, Belgium, Norway, Denmark
495	Denmark	Italy, Norway, Sweden, Portugal
486	Portugal	Denmark, Austria, Poland
480	Austria	Portugal, Poland, Slovak Republic
477	Poland	Portugal, Austria, Slovak Republic, Slovenia, Spain, Russian Federation
474	Slovak Republic	Austria, Poland, Slovenia, Spain, Russian Federation
471	Slovenia	Poland, Slovak Republic, Spain, Russian Federation
466	Spain	Poland, Slovak Republic, Slovenia, Russian Federation, Israel
466	Russian Federation	Poland, Slovak Republic, Slovenia, Spain, Israel
461	Israel	Spain, Russian Federation, Chile, Hungary
452	Chile	Israel, Hungary
450	Hungary	Israel, Chile
436	Brazil	
407	United Arab Emirates	
396	Colombia	

Source: OECD, PISA 2012 Database.
StatLink http://dx.doi.org/10.1787/888933252891

■ Figure 3.2 ■

Where countries and economies rank in digital reading performance

	Digital reading scale					
			Range of ranks			
			OECD countries		All countries/economies	
	Mean score	S.E.	Upper rank	Lower rank	Upper rank	Lower rank
Singapore	567	(1.2)			1	1
Korea	555	(3.6)	1	1	2	3
Hong Kong-China	550	(3.6)			2	4
Japan	545	(3.3)	2	2	3	4
Canada	532	(2.3)	3	3	5	6
Shanghai-China	531	(3.7)			5	6
Estonia	523	(2.8)	4	6	7	10
Australia	521	(1.7)	4	6	7	10
Ireland	520	(3.0)	4	7	7	11
Chinese Taipei	519	(3.0)			7	11
Macao-China	515	(0.9)			10	12
United States	511	(4.5)	6	10	10	15
France	511	(3.6)	7	9	10	14
Italy	504	(4.3)	7	12	12	17
Belgium	502	(2.6)	9	12	14	17
Norway	500	(3.5)	9	13	14	18
Sweden	498	(3.4)	9	13	14	18
Denmark	495	(2.9)	11	14	16	19
Portugal	486	(4.4)	13	16	18	21
Austria	480	(3.9)	14	17	19	22
Poland	477	(4.5)	14	18	19	23
Slovak Republic	474	(3.5)	15	19	20	24
Slovenia	471	(1.3)	17	19	22	24
Spain	466	(3.9)	17	20	23	26
Russian Federation	466	(3.9)			23	26
Israel	461	(5.1)	19	22	24	28
Chile	452	(3.6)	20	22	26	28
Hungary	450	(4.4)	21	22	26	28
Brazil	436	(4.9)			29	29
United Arab Emirates	407	(3.3)			30	30
Colombia	396	(4.0)			31	31

Source: OECD, PISA 2012 Database.
StatLink http://dx.doi.org/10.1787/888933252903

Trends in average digital reading performance

PISA 2012 marks the second time digital reading was assessed in PISA, with tasks that are built around the typical text formats encountered on line. Of the 19 countries and economies that participated in the digital reading assessment in 2009, 17 renewed their participation in 2012 (Iceland and New Zealand are the exceptions). Because the PISA 2012 assessment of digital reading uses a subset of the items developed and used in PISA 2009, results from the two assessments can be compared over time.

Among the 16 countries and economies for which results can be compared over time,[2] four show a decline in the mean performance of their students, four show no change, and eight countries and economies show a significant improvement in performance (Figure 3.3).

■ Figure 3.3 ■
Digital reading performance in 2009 and 2012

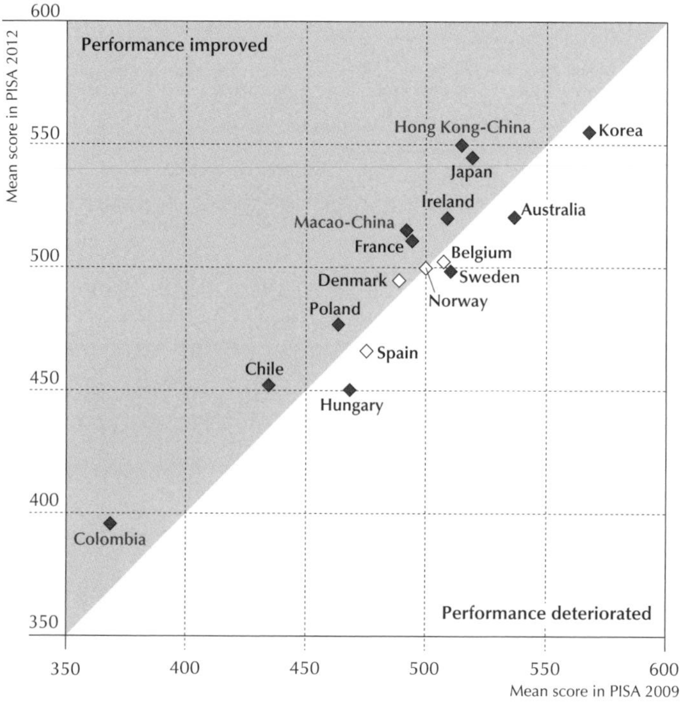
Mean score in PISA 2012
600
550
500
450
400
350
Performance improved
Hong Kong-China
Korea
Japan
Ireland
Australia
Macao-China
France
Belgium
Sweden
Denmark
Norway
Poland
Spain
Chile
Hungary
Colombia
Performance deteriorated
350
400
450
500
550
600
Mean score in PISA 2009

Note: Statistically significant score-point changes between PISA 2012 and PISA 2009 are marked in a darker tone.
Source: OECD, PISA 2012 Database, Table 3.2.
StatLink http://dx.doi.org/10.1787/888933252910

The largest improvement in average performance is observed in Hong Kong-China, where students scored 35 score points higher, on average, than they did in 2009. Significant improvements in average performance are also observed in Colombia, Japan, Macao-China, Chile, France, Poland and Ireland, in decreasing order of their magnitude. A stable mean performance is found in Belgium, Denmark, Norway and Spain. In Australia, Hungary, Korea and Sweden, students in 2012 performed more than ten points below the level achieved by students in 2009. Korea was the top-performing country in 2009, with a mean score of 568 points, almost 50 points above Hong Kong-China and Japan. By 2012, students in Korea performed on par with students in Hong Kong-China (Figure 3.3).

In general, trends in digital reading performance are highly correlated to trends in print reading performance. Figure 3.4 shows that most countries where digital reading performance improved also saw similar gains in their print reading performance. The most notable exceptions are Chile and Colombia, where digital reading performance improved significantly, but performance on the print reading assessment remained stable. These trends are examined further below.

■ Figure 3.4 ■

Change in digital and print reading performance between 2009 and 2012

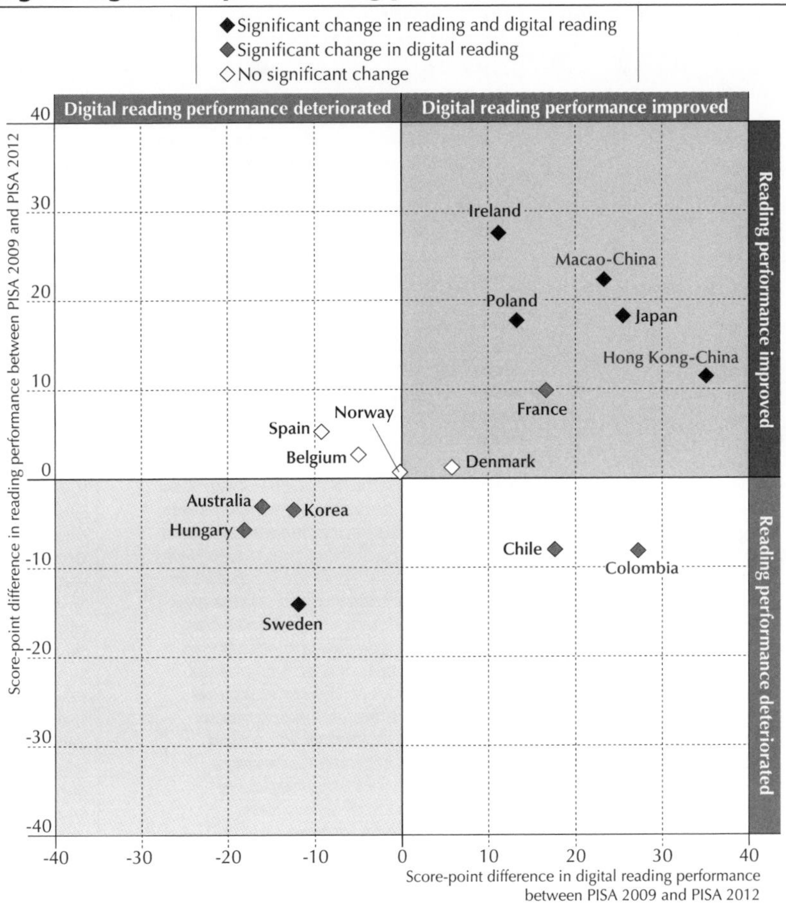
◆Significant change in reading and digital reading
◆Significant change in digital reading
◇No significant change
Digital reading performance deteriorated
Digital reading performance improved
Reading performance improved
Reading performance deteriorated
Score-point difference in reading performance between PISA 2009 and PISA 2012
Score-point difference in digital reading performance between PISA 2009 and PISA 2012
40
30
20
10
0
-10
-20
-30
-40
Ireland
Macao-China
Poland
Japan
Hong Kong-China
France
Norway
Spain
Belgium
Denmark
Australia
Korea
Hungary
Chile
Colombia
Sweden

Source: OECD, PISA 2012 Database, Table 3.2.
StatLink http://dx.doi.org/10.1787/888933252926

Students at the different levels of proficiency in digital reading

This section describes performance in terms of the levels of proficiency that were constructed for reporting the PISA 2009 digital reading scale. Because the PISA digital reading assessment is a short test based on a limited number of tasks, only four proficiency levels could be described, rather than the usual six. The lowest described level of proficiency is equivalent to Level 2 on the reading scale, and corresponds to a baseline level of proficiency in digital reading. The highest described level of proficiency is equivalent to Level 5 on the reading scale.

The distribution of student performance across these proficiency levels in each participating country is shown in Figure 3.5. A detailed description of proficiency levels can be found in *PISA 2009 Results: Students On Line* (OECD, 2011).

■ Figure 3.5 ■

Proficiency in digital reading

Percentage of students at the different levels of digital reading proficiency

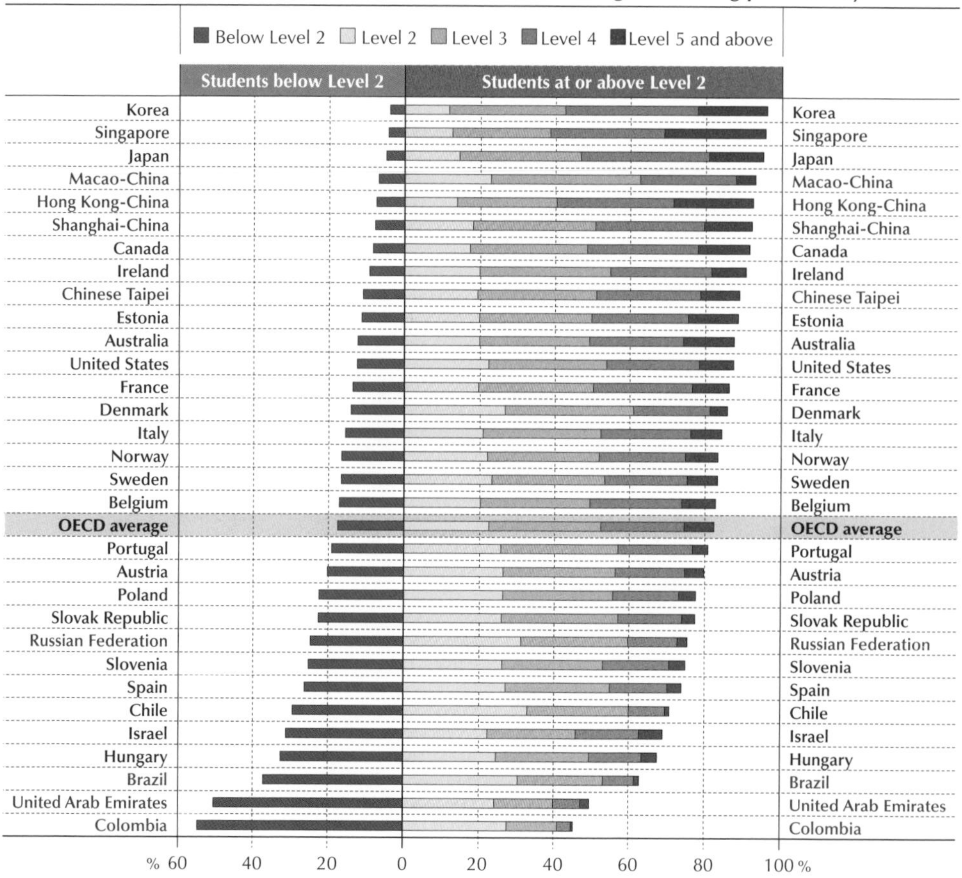
Below Level 2
Level 2
Level 3
Level 4
Level 5 and above
Students below Level 2
Students at or above Level 2
Korea
Singapore
Japan
Macao-China
Hong Kong-China
Shanghai-China
Canada
Ireland
Chinese Taipei
Estonia
Australia
United States
France
Denmark
Italy
Norway
Sweden
Belgium
OECD average
Portugal
Austria
Poland
Slovak Republic
Russian Federation
Slovenia
Spain
Chile
Israel
Hungary
Brazil
United Arab Emirates
Colombia
% 60
40
20
0
20
40
60
80
100 %

Countries and economies are ranked in descending order of the percentage of students at or above Level 2 in digital reading.
Source: OECD, PISA 2012 Database, Table 3.3.
StatLink http://dx.doi.org/10.1787/888933252935

Top performers in digital reading

Students proficient at Level 5 or above are skilled online readers. Top performers in digital reading are able to evaluate information from several sources, assessing the credibility and utility of what they read using criteria that they have generated themselves. They are also able to solve tasks that require the reader to locate information, related to an unfamiliar context, in the presence of ambiguity and without explicit directions. In short, they are able to navigate autonomously and efficiently. Critical evaluation and expertise in locating relevant information are the key skills in online reading, given the virtually unlimited number of texts that can be accessed on line, and the variation in their credibility and trustworthiness. Students performing at Level 5 or above are able to deal with more technical material as well as with more popular and idiomatic texts.

They notice fine distinctions in the detail of the text, allowing them to draw inferences and form plausible hypotheses.

Across the 23 OECD countries that participated in the digital reading assessment in 2012, 8% of students performed at this level and can be considered top performers in digital reading. In Singapore, more than one in four students (27%) perform at Level 5 or above. So do about one in five students in Hong Kong-China (21%) and Korea (18%).

In general, a ranking of countries and economies by the proportion of top-performing students (students at Level 5 or above) matches the ranking of countries/economies by mean performance, but there are a number of exceptions. Mean performance in Israel is below the OECD average, but the share of top-performing students in Israel is similar to the share found across the OECD on average. By contrast, students in Macao-China perform above students in Belgium, Italy and Norway, but these countries all have larger proportions of top-performing students than Macao-China.

Low performers in digital reading

At the lower end of the scale, students performing below Level 2 are able to complete only the easiest digital reading tasks in the PISA 2012 assessment, if any. They have difficulties using conventional navigation tools and features, and locating links or information that are not prominently placed. Some of these students can scroll and navigate across web pages, and can locate simple pieces of information in a short text, if given explicit directions. These students are referred to as low performers in digital reading because they perform at levels that are not likely to allow them full access to education, employment and social opportunities afforded by digital devices.

Some 18% of students are considered low performers in digital reading, on average across the 23 participating OECD countries. In partner countries Colombia and the United Arab Emirates, more than half of all 15-year-old students perform at this low level. Large proportions of low-performing students are also found in Brazil (37%), Hungary (32%), Israel (31%), Chile (29%) and Spain (26%). By contrast, less than 5% of students perform below Level 2 in Japan, Korea and Singapore. These countries are close to ensuring that all students have the basic knowledge and skills required to access and use information that can be found on the Internet.

Progressions in digital reading proficiency

As students progress from the lower levels of proficiency to ever greater skill in digital reading, they become more autonomous in their navigation and better able to deal with a range of online text formats and text types, including unfamiliar ones. At Level 2 on the digital reading scale, students can successfully follow explicit instructions to locate information on line, form generalisations, such as recognising the intended audience of a website, and use typical online order forms that include drop-down menus or open text fields. At Level 3, in addition to mastering Level 2 tasks, students can cope with more complex digital reading tasks, including tasks that require integrating information from across different websites. At Level 4, students complete even more challenging tasks: they can assess the authority and relevance of sources when provided with support, and can explain the criteria on which their judgements are based.

They can also synthesise information across several sites (as is required, for instance, in the sample unit *SERAING*, Task 3: see Chapter 7) and understand texts written in technical language.

Box 3.1. **The International Computer and Information Literacy Study (2013) and its relation to digital reading in PISA**

In 2013, 21 education systems around the world participated in the first International Computer and Information Literacy Study (ICILS), organised by the International Association for the Evaluation of Educational Achievement (IEA). Computer and information literacy is defined as "an individual's ability to use computers to investigate, create and communicate in order to participate effectively at home, at school, in the workplace and in society". The framework highlights two strands of digital competence: "collecting and managing information", which also involves locating and evaluating information, and "producing and exchanging information", of which an understanding of online safety and security issues are part.

While some aspects highlighted by the PISA digital reading framework are covered, in particular, by the first strand of the ICILS framework, the concept of computer and information literacy is clearly distinct from digital reading.

The test was administered to eighth-grade students. Among the 12 countries that met the sampling requirements for ICILS, the Czech Republic obtained the highest mean score, followed by a group of four countries (Australia, Korea, Norway [grade 9] and Poland) with similar mean scores. While the target population differs, it is notable that the mean performance of Poland was clearly above that of countries, such as the Russian Federation, the Slovak Republic and Slovenia, whose mean scores in the PISA digital reading assessment was similar.

Source: Fraillon et al., 2014.

Trends at the top and bottom of the performance distribution in digital reading

Changes in a country's/economy's average performance can result from improvements or deterioration in performance at different points in the performance distribution. Trends in the proportion of low- and top-performing students indicate, in particular, what students can do better in 2012 than in 2009 (Figure 3.6).

Between 2009 and 2012, two countries, Chile and Colombia, significantly reduced the share of students performing below Level 2 in digital reading. Both countries still have large proportions of students performing at the lowest levels, but they were able to reduce underperformance significantly within only three years. The fact that no reduction was observed in these countries in the share of low achievers in print reading suggests that improvements in digital reading performance are related to improved ICT skills and better dispositions towards the use of computers among students. In the past, lack of familiarity with ICT tools and online text formats may have been a major obstacle for some students to complete even the easiest digital reading tasks.

■ Figure 3.6 ■

Percentage of low achievers and top performers in digital reading in 2009 and 2012

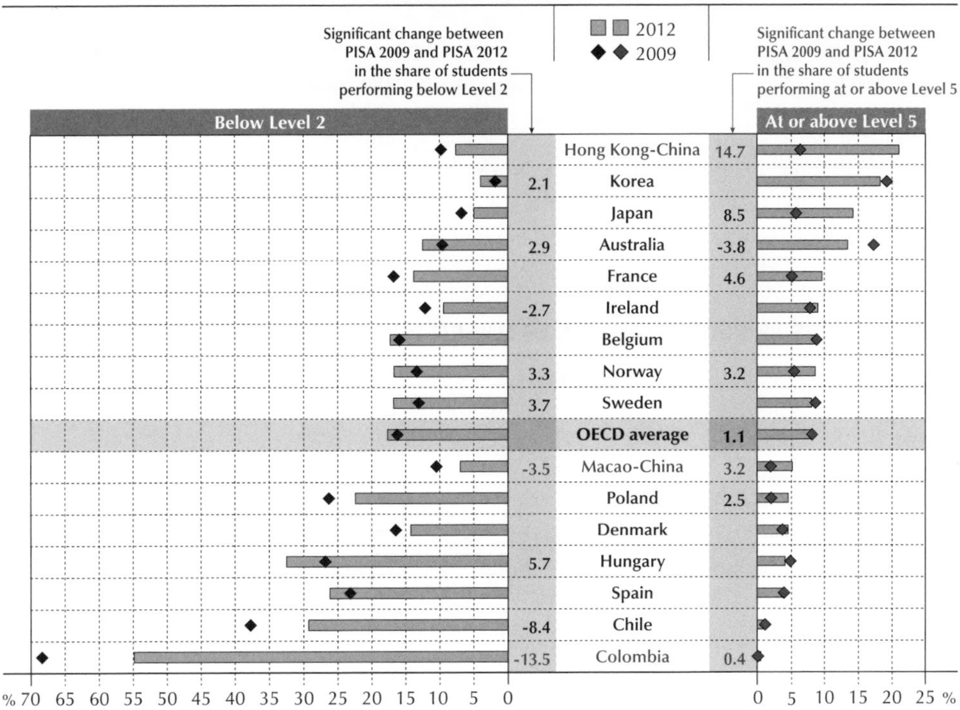
Significant change between PISA 2009 and PISA 2012 in the share of students performing below Level 2
2012
2009
Significant change between PISA 2009 and PISA 2012 in the share of students performing at or above Level 5
Below Level 2
At or above Level 5
Hong Kong-China 14.7
Korea 2.1
Japan 8.5
Australia 2.9 -3.8
France 4.6
Ireland -2.7
Belgium
Norway 3.3 3.2
Sweden 3.7
OECD average 1.1
Macao-China -3.5 3.2
Poland 2.5
Denmark
Hungary 5.7
Spain
Chile -8.4
Colombia -13.5 0.4
% 70 65 60 55 50 45 40 35 30 25 20 15 10 5 0
0 5 10 15 20 25 %

Notes: This figure includes only countries/economies that participated in both the PISA 2009 and PISA 2012 assessments of digital reading.
Changes that are statistically significant are reported next to the country/economy name.
For the OECD average, the diamonds denote all OECD countries that participated in the PISA 2009 assessment, the bars denote all OECD countries that participated in the PISA 2012 assessment, and the reported change applies only to OECD countries that participated in both assessments of digital reading.
Countries and economies are ranked in descending order of the percentage of students at or above Level 5 in digital reading in 2012.
Source: OECD, PISA 2012 Database, Table 3.4.
StatLink http://dx.doi.org/10.1787/888933252943

In Hong Kong-China and Japan, the share of top-performing students increased significantly between 2009 and 2012. In both, a similar, though smaller, increase in the share of top performers was observed in print reading as well (OECD, 2014b, Table I.4.1b). This may indicate that Hong Kong-China and Japan achieved gains at higher levels of proficiency by improving students' ability to master difficult reading tasks across both printed and online texts.

It is also possible to assess whether these changes in performance occurred among the countries'/economies' strongest or weakest students by looking at trends in percentiles. Eight countries/economies improved their average performance between 2009 and 2012. In Chile, improvements were largest among the lowest-performing students. By contrast, Colombia, Hong Kong-China and Japan were able to raise performance in digital reading mainly among their best-performing students. France, Ireland, Macao-China and Poland showed similar improvements among students at the top and bottom of the performance distribution (Table 3.5).

Among countries with deteriorating performance in digital reading, Hungary, Korea and Sweden show the biggest declines in performance among their weakest students. In Australia, performance declined to a similar extent across the distribution (Table 3.5).

Four countries, namely Belgium, Denmark, Norway and Spain, showed stable mean performance. However, in Norway, the lack of change in mean performance masks a significant widening of performance differences, with the lowest-achieving students performing even lower, and the highest-achieving students even higher, in 2012 compared to 2009 (Table 3.5).

DIFFERENCES IN PERFORMANCE BETWEEN PRINT AND DIGITAL READING

Overall, the correlation between the digital and print reading performance of students is 0.81, about the same correlation as observed between digital reading and (paper-based) mathematics scores (0.78) (Table 3.9).[3]

While, in general, strong readers will perform well both in print and digital reading, there is significant variation in digital reading performance at all levels of performance in print reading. The variation in digital reading performance that is not explained by differences in print reading skills is referred to as residual variation. Some of this residual variation contributes to differences in performance observed across countries/economies. It is then referred to as the relative performance of countries/economies in digital reading (Figure 3.7). This relative performance may be related to skills that are used, to a greater extent, when reading on line (see Chapter 4). It may also be related to students' dispositions towards the medium and the variation in students' familiarity with basic ICT skills, such as operating a mouse and keyboard to use hyperlinks, browser buttons, drop-down menus and text-entry fields.

In 11 countries and economies, students perform significantly better in digital reading, on average, than students in other countries with similar skills in print reading. A large, positive difference in digital reading performance, after accounting for print reading performance, is observed in Singapore (32 score points) and Korea (24 score points). Students in Australia, Canada, Estonia, Hong Kong-China, Italy, Japan, Macao-China, Sweden and the United States also perform better than would be expected, based on their performance in print reading (Figure 3.7).

In 15 countries and economies, students perform below par in digital reading, on average, when compared to students in other participating countries and economies who display the same level of proficiency in print reading. Large gaps in relative performance in digital reading are found in the United Arab Emirates (50 score points), Hungary (43 score points), Poland (40 score points), Israel (31 score points), Colombia (30 score points), Shanghai-China (26 score points) and Spain (25 score points). Students in Austria, Belgium, Denmark, the Russian Federation, Portugal and Slovenia also perform worse in digital reading, on average, than would be expected, based on their performance in print reading (Figure 3.7).

■ Figure 3.7 ■

Relative performance in digital reading

Score-point difference between actual and expected performance

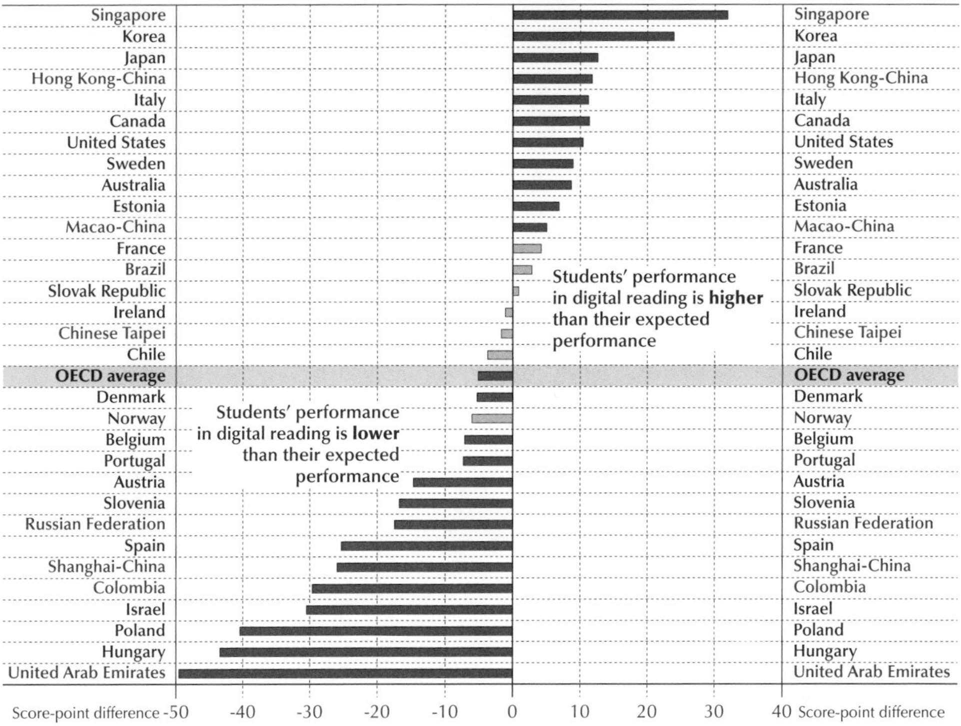
Singapore
Korea
Japan
Hong Kong-China
Italy
Canada
United States
Sweden
Australia
Estonia
Macao-China
France
Brazil
Slovak Republic
Ireland
Chinese Taipei
Chile
OECD average
Denmark
Norway
Belgium
Portugal
Austria
Slovenia
Russian Federation
Spain
Shanghai-China
Colombia
Israel
Poland
Hungary
United Arab Emirates
Students' performance in digital reading is higher than their expected performance
Students' performance in digital reading is lower than their expected performance
Score-point difference
-50
-40
-30
-20
-10
0
10
20
30
40

Notes: Statistically significant differences are shown in a darker tone.

Each student's expected performance is estimated, using a regression model, as the predicted performance in digital reading given his or her score in print reading.

Countries and economies are ranked in descending order of the score-point difference between actual and expected performance.

Source: OECD, PISA 2012 Database, Table 3.6.

StatLink http://dx.doi.org/10.1787/888933252959

Top performers in digital and print reading

Figure 3.8 shows the proportion of top performers across countries and economies participating in the digital reading assessment, highlighting the extent to which those students who demonstrate high proficiency in print reading can perform at similar levels in digital reading as well. On average across OECD countries, 8% of students perform at Level 5 or above in digital reading. Of these, about half (4%) also perform at this level in print reading.

Conversely, in many countries and economies, about half of the top performers in print reading also perform at the top in digital reading. In Australia, Estonia and Singapore, more than two in three top performers in print reading also perform at the top in digital reading. In these countries, good readers usually are able to perform at similar levels regardless of the medium.

■ Figure 3.8 ■

Overlapping of top performers in digital and print reading

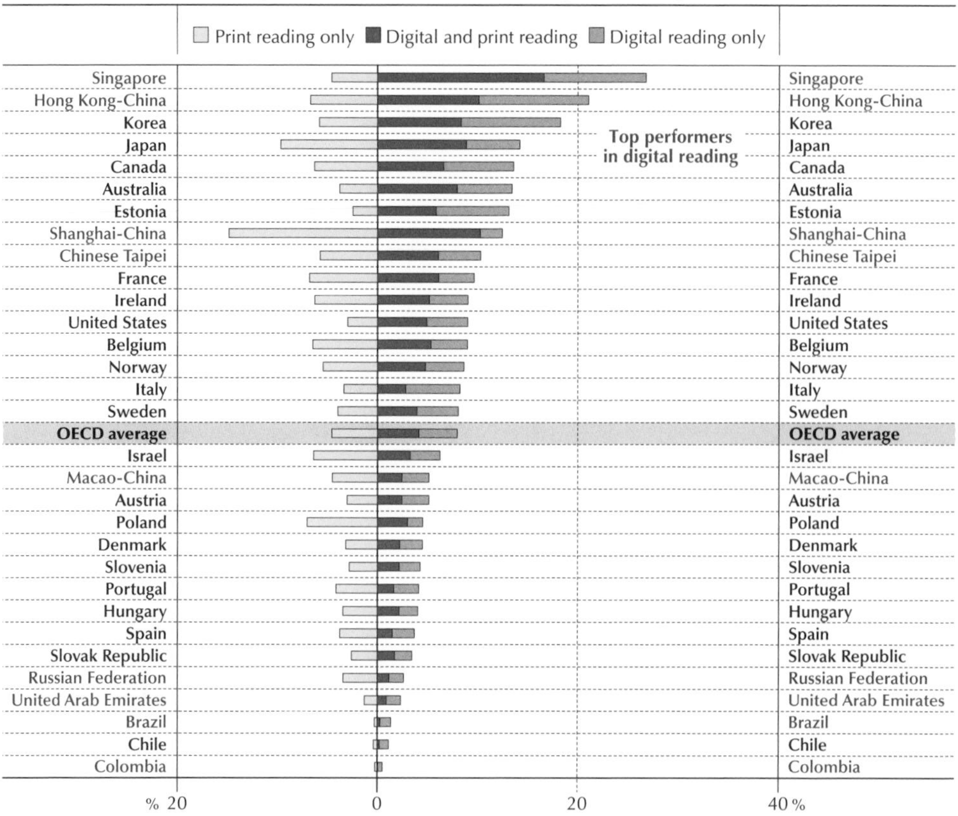
Print reading only
Digital and print reading
Digital reading only
Top performers in digital reading
Singapore
Hong Kong-China
Korea
Japan
Canada
Australia
Estonia
Shanghai-China
Chinese Taipei
France
Ireland
United States
Belgium
Norway
Italy
Sweden
OECD average
Israel
Macao-China
Austria
Poland
Denmark
Slovenia
Portugal
Hungary
Spain
Slovak Republic
Russian Federation
United Arab Emirates
Brazil
Chile
Colombia
% 20
0
20
40 %

Countries and economies are ranked in descending order of the percentage of top performers in digital reading.
Source: OECD, PISA 2012 Database, Table 3.7.
StatLink http://dx.doi.org/10.1787/888933252962

In Poland, however, fewer than one in three top performers in print reading also performs at the top in digital reading. This may indicate that, more often than in other countries, in Poland, good readers of print documents lack the evaluation and navigation skills that would make them skilled online readers.

Low performers in digital and print reading

Figure 3.9 shows the proportion of low performers across OECD countries, highlighting the extent to which low-performing students in digital reading also encounter difficulties when reading print documents. In general, there is a greater overlap among low-performers than among top-performers across the two media.

At the same time, several countries and economies have significant proportions of student who, despite being able to read at Level 2 or above when assessed on paper, perform below Level 2 when assessed on computer. In Colombia, Hungary, Israel, Poland, the Russian Federation, Spain and the United Arab Emirates, more than one in ten students is a low performer in digital reading but not in print reading (Figure 3.9). In these countries, many students may have difficulties with the generic ICT skills and conventions required to interact with the test platform, and thus perform poorly in digital reading despite their relatively good reading skills.

■ Figure 3.9 ■

Overlapping of low performers in digital and print reading

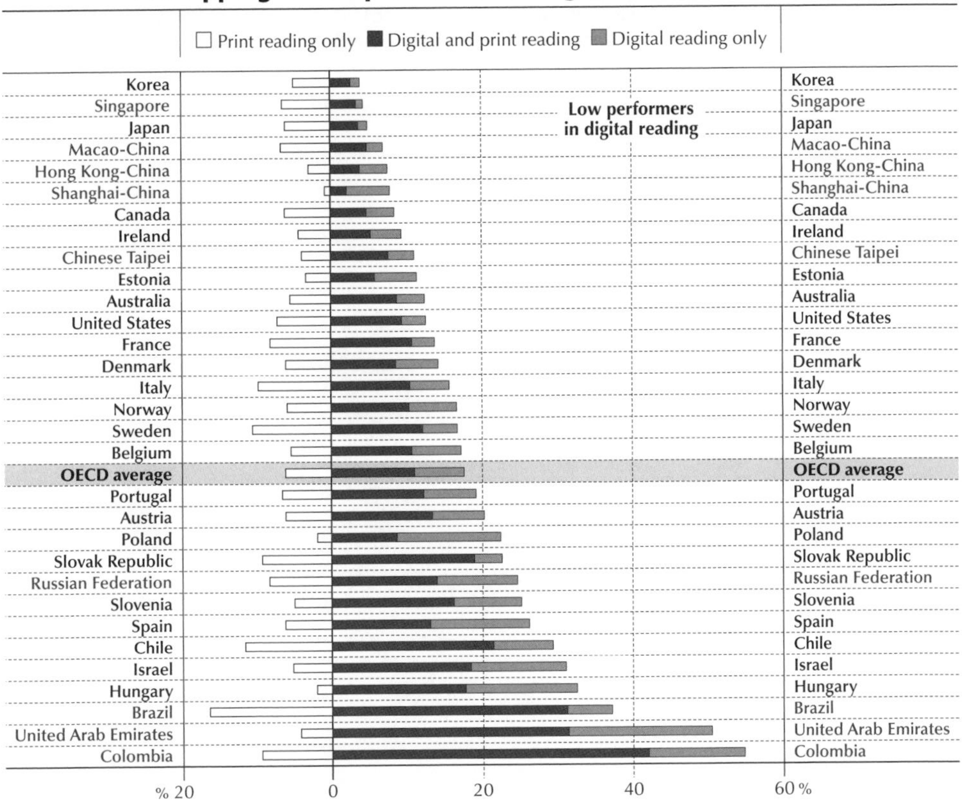
Print reading only
Digital and print reading
Digital reading only
Low performers in digital reading
Korea
Singapore
Japan
Macao-China
Hong Kong-China
Shanghai-China
Canada
Ireland
Chinese Taipei
Estonia
Australia
United States
France
Denmark
Italy
Norway
Sweden
Belgium
OECD average
Portugal
Austria
Poland
Slovak Republic
Russian Federation
Slovenia
Spain
Chile
Israel
Hungary
Brazil
United Arab Emirates
Colombia
% 20
0
20
40
60 %

Countries and economies are ranked in ascending order of the percentage of low performers in digital reading.

Source: OECD, PISA 2012 Database, Table 3.7.

StatLink http://dx.doi.org/10.1787/888933252976

STUDENT PERFORMANCE IN THE COMPUTER-BASED ASSESSMENT OF MATHEMATICS

Mathematics was the focus of the PISA 2012 assessment, meaning that booklets in the paper-based test contained questions measuring students' capacity to formulate, employ and interpret mathematics to a larger extent than questions for reading and science, the other domains assessed on paper. For the first time, mathematics was also assessed on computers in 2012. This section reports the results from the computer-based assessment of mathematics.

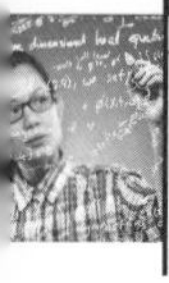

Average performance in the computer-based assessment of mathematics

The same 32 countries/economies that participated in the optional assessment of digital reading also participated in the computer-based assessment of mathematics. The scale for reporting performance on the computer-based test of mathematics was fixed so that the average mean score and standard deviation for OECD countries would match those of the paper-based mathematics scale for the same year and the same countries.

■ Figure 3.10 ■

Comparing countries' and economies' performance in the computer-based assessment of mathematics

Statistically significantly **above** the OECD average
Not statistically significantly different from the OECD average
Statistically significantly **below** the OECD average

Mean score	Comparison country/economy	Countries/economies whose mean score is NOT statistically significantly different from that of the comparison country/economy
566	Singapore	Shanghai-China
562	Shanghai-China	Singapore, Korea
553	Korea	Shanghai-China, Hong Kong-China
550	Hong Kong-China	Korea, Macao-China
543	Macao-China	Hong Kong-China, Japan, Chinese Taipei
539	Japan	Macao-China, Chinese Taipei
537	Chinese Taipei	Macao-China, Japan
523	Canada	
516	Estonia	Belgium
512	Belgium	Estonia, France, Australia, Austria
508	France	Belgium, Australia, Austria, Italy, United States
508	Australia	Belgium, France, Austria
507	Austria	Belgium, France, Australia, Italy, United States
499	Italy	France, Austria, United States, Norway, Slovak Republic, Denmark, Ireland, Sweden, Russian Federation, Poland, Portugal
498	United States	France, Austria, Italy, Norway, Slovak Republic, Denmark, Ireland, Sweden, Russian Federation, Poland, Portugal
498	Norway	Italy, United States, Slovak Republic, Denmark, Ireland, Sweden, Poland
497	Slovak Republic	Italy, United States, Norway, Denmark, Ireland, Sweden, Russian Federation, Poland, Portugal
496	Denmark	Italy, United States, Norway, Slovak Republic, Ireland, Sweden, Russian Federation, Poland, Portugal
493	Ireland	Italy, United States, Norway, Slovak Republic, Denmark, Sweden, Russian Federation, Poland, Portugal
490	Sweden	Italy, United States, Norway, Slovak Republic, Denmark, Ireland, Russian Federation, Poland, Portugal, Slovenia
489	Russian Federation	Italy, United States, Slovak Republic, Denmark, Ireland, Sweden, Poland, Portugal, Slovenia
489	Poland	Italy, United States, Norway, Slovak Republic, Denmark, Ireland, Sweden, Russian Federation, Portugal, Slovenia
489	Portugal	Italy, United States, Slovak Republic, Denmark, Ireland, Sweden, Russian Federation, Poland, Slovenia
487	Slovenia	Sweden, Russian Federation, Poland, Portugal
475	Spain	Hungary
470	Hungary	Spain
447	Israel	
434	United Arab Emirates	Chile
432	Chile	United Arab Emirates
421	Brazil	
397	Colombia	

Source: OECD, PISA 2012 Database.
StatLink http://dx.doi.org/10.1787/888933252985

Figure 3.10 lists each participating country and economy in descending order of its mean score in the computer-based mathematics test (left column). The values range from a high of 566 points for partner country Singapore to a low of 397 points for partner country Colombia. Shanghai-China (562 points) performs at the same level as Singapore. Students in Korea, Hong Kong-China,

Macao-China, Japan and Chinese Taipei (in descending order of mean performance) score lower than students in Singapore, on average, but significantly higher than the mean performance of students in any other country/economy participating in the assessment.

Differences between countries' mean scores on the computer-based and paper-based mathematics assessment are smaller than those observed between the digital and print-reading assessments. Indeed, the correlation between students' results on the paper- and computer-based mathematics scale is higher (0.86) than the correlation between the digital and print-reading scores (0.81), when considering the pooled sample of students from all participating countries (Table 3.9). Table 3.10 reports differences in mean scores between the computer-based and the paper-based assessment of mathematics, by country.

Figure 3.11 shows where each country/economy ranks in its mean performance in the computer-based mathematics test. A range of ranks is presented to reflect the uncertainty associated with this estimate.

■ Figure 3.11 ■

Where countries and economies rank in computer-based mathematics performance

	Computer-based mathematics scale					
			Range of ranks			
			OECD countries		All countries/economies	
	Mean score	S.E.	Upper rank	Lower rank	Upper rank	Lower rank
Singapore	566	(1.3)			1	2
Shanghai-China	562	(3.4)			1	2
Korea	553	(4.5)	1	1	2	4
Hong Kong-China	550	(3.4)			3	4
Macao-China	543	(1.1)			5	6
Japan	539	(3.3)	2	2	5	7
Chinese Taipei	537	(2.8)			6	7
Canada	523	(2.2)	3	3	8	8
Estonia	516	(2.2)	4	5	9	10
Belgium	512	(2.5)	4	7	9	12
France	508	(3.3)	5	9	10	14
Australia	508	(1.6)	6	8	11	13
Austria	507	(3.5)	5	9	10	14
Italy	499	(4.2)	8	15	13	20
United States	498	(4.1)	8	15	13	20
Norway	498	(2.8)	9	14	14	19
Slovak Republic	497	(3.5)	9	15	13	20
Denmark	496	(2.7)	9	15	14	20
Ireland	493	(2.9)	11	17	15	22
Sweden	490	(2.9)	13	18	18	24
Russian Federation	489	(2.6)			19	24
Poland	489	(4.0)	12	18	17	24
Portugal	489	(3.1)	13	18	18	24
Slovenia	487	(1.2)	16	18	21	24
Spain	475	(3.2)	19	20	25	26
Hungary	470	(3.9)	19	20	25	26
Israel	447	(5.6)	21	21	27	27
United Arab Emirates	434	(2.2)			28	29
Chile	432	(3.3)	22	22	28	29
Brazil	421	(4.7)			30	30
Colombia	397	(3.2)			31	31

Source: OECD, PISA 2012 Database.
StatLink http://dx.doi.org/10.1787/888933252992

DIFFERENCES IN PERFORMANCE RELATED TO THE USE OF ICT TOOLS FOR SOLVING MATHEMATICS PROBLEMS

Computers provide a range of opportunities for developing tests that are more interactive, authentic and engaging (Stacey and Wiliam, 2012); they are also increasingly used in the workplace and in everyday life to deal with problems involving numbers, quantities, two or three-dimensional figures, and data. While the assessment framework for the PISA computer-based mathematics assessment is the same as for the paper-based test, some of the computer-based tasks could not exist in a paper test because of their response format (e.g. "drag and drop"), or because they require students to use the computer as a mathematical tool, by interacting with the stimulus to solve a mathematics problem.

■ Figure 3.12 ■

Success on mathematics tasks that require/do not require the use of computers to solve problems

Average percentage of full-credit responses across countries and economies

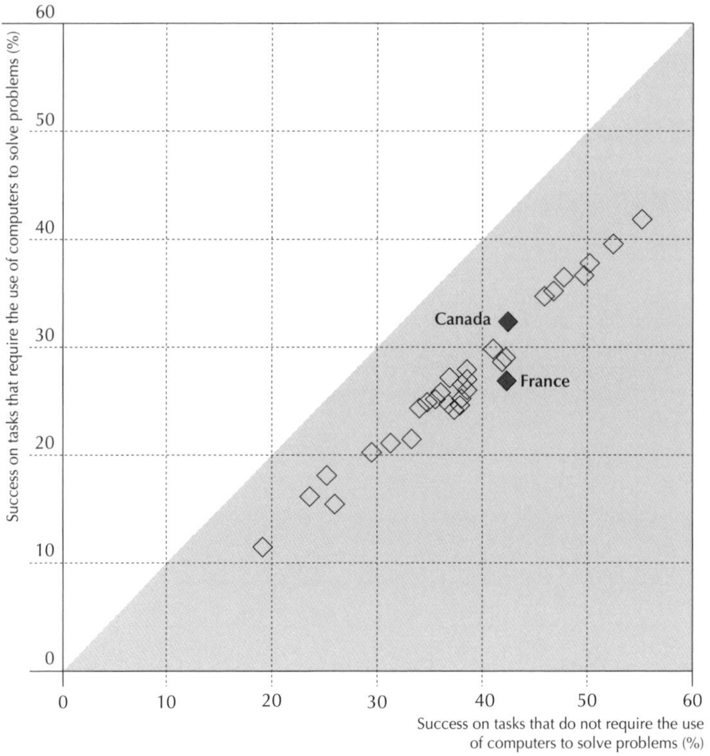
Success on tasks that require the use of computers to solve problems (%)
60
50
40
30
20
10
0
Canada
France
0
10
20
30
40
50
60
Success on tasks that do not require the use of computers to solve problems (%)

Notes: Each diamond represents the mean values of a country/economy.
In the computer-based assessment of mathematics, Canada and France share similar levels of performance on tasks that do not require the use of computers to solve mathematics problems, but differ in their students' performance on tasks that do require such use; this example is discussed in the text.
Source: OECD, PISA 2012 Database, Table 3.11.
StatLink http://dx.doi.org/10.1787/888933253005

Such tasks require students to build and rotate a three-dimensional figure using a mouse, to find out how the graphical representation of a function changes depending on its parameters, to use an on-screen calculator, to sort a data set, or to produce a chart from data.

By design, not all computer-based tasks involved the use of the computer as a mathematical tool. This variation makes it possible to analyse the impact of these kinds of demands on performance. While task formats that involve the use of computers as mathematical tools may appear more engaging, not all students may react similarly to them. These types of tasks also typically require greater familiarity with computers and their application to mathematics.

Figure 3.12 plots average success rates for tasks that require the use of computers to solve mathematics problems against average success rates for more traditional mathematics tasks.[4] While both types of tasks were presented on screen, only in the former set of tasks did the solution require the use of computer tools, or was made easier if the computer was used as a tool. Tasks in unit *CD PRODUCTION*, for instance, require students to use an on-screen calculator. Tasks in units *STAR POINTS* and *BODY MASS INDEX*, in contrast, are examples of "traditional" items. The fact that students use keyboard and mouse, instead of pens and pencils, to answer these items does not make them easier than their corresponding paper versions would be.[5]

In general, country rankings are similar across the two types of tasks. However, as Figure 3.12 shows, performance is not perfectly aligned. Countries that share similar levels of success on tasks that do not require the use of computers to solve problems do not necessarily perform similarly on tasks that require students to use mathematics-specific ICT tools in order to solve the task. Often, when considering two countries with similar performance on the first set of tasks, one country is significantly stronger than the other on the second set of tasks.

Students in Canada, for instance, have similar success rates as students in France on tasks where the use of computers as tools for solving mathematics problems is not required. In both countries, students answer around 42% of these tasks correctly. Students in Canada, however, have significantly greater success than students in France (32% vs. 27%) on tasks where the solution is only possible, or is made easier, by using computers as mathematical tools.

Figure 3.13 ranks countries and economies according to whether their students had greater success on tasks that require the use of computers to solve problems, or on the remaining tasks, relative to their overall success. This analysis accounts for differences in the difficulty of tasks across the two sets by comparing success on both types of tasks in each country/economy to the average success rate across OECD countries.

According to these adjusted figures, students in Australia, Austria, Canada, Japan, Slovenia and the United States as well as those in partner countries/economies Macao-China and the United Arab Emirates perform better on tasks that require the use of computers to solve problems, compared to their success on traditional tasks. By contrast, relative success is only 0.86 in France (significantly below par), indicating weaker-than-expected performance when students are confronted with tasks that require the use of computer-based tools to arrive at the solution. Students in Belgium, Chile, Ireland, Poland and Spain also perform worse than expected on such tasks.

■ Figure 3.13 ■

Relative success on mathematics tasks that require the use of computers to solve problems

Compared to the OECD average

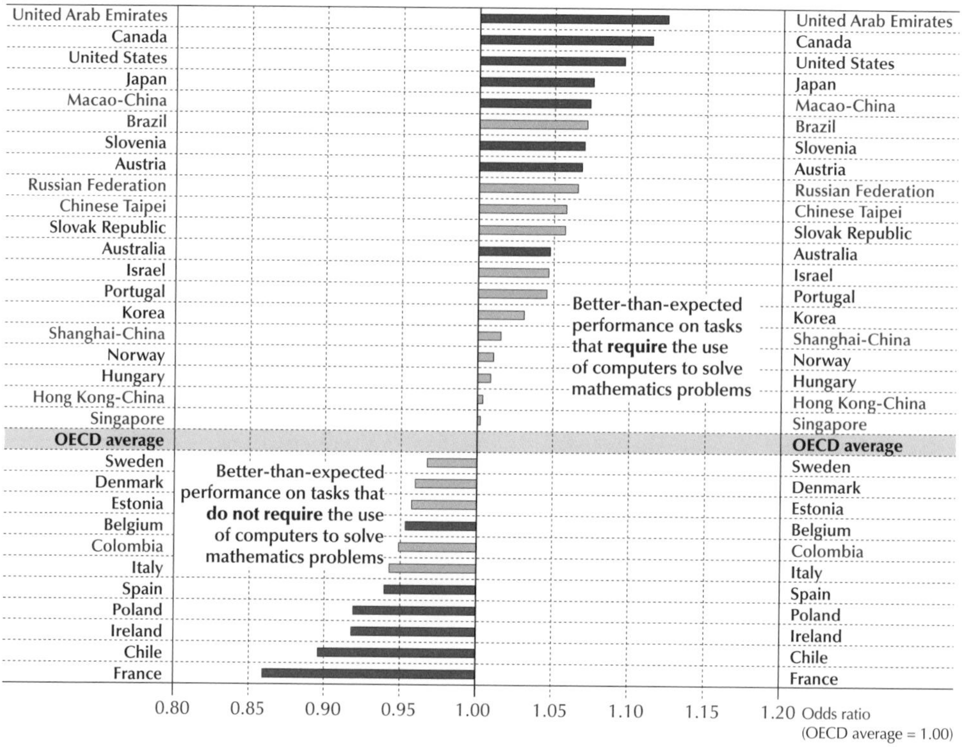
United Arab Emirates
Canada
United States
Japan
Macao-China
Brazil
Slovenia
Austria
Russian Federation
Chinese Taipei
Slovak Republic
Australia
Israel
Portugal
Korea
Shanghai-China
Norway
Hungary
Hong Kong-China
Singapore
OECD average
Sweden
Denmark
Estonia
Belgium
Colombia
Italy
Spain
Poland
Ireland
Chile
France
Better-than-expected performance on tasks that **require** the use of computers to solve mathematics problems
Better-than-expected performance on tasks that **do not require** the use of computers to solve mathematics problems
0.80
0.85
0.90
0.95
1.00
1.05
1.10
1.15
1.20
Odds ratio (OECD average = 1.00)

Notes: Values that are statistically significant are marked in a darker tone.

This figure shows that students in Canada are 1.11 times more likely than students across OECD countries, on average, to succeed on tasks in the computer-based mathematics assessment that require the use of computers to solve problems, given their success on other tasks in the assessment.

Countries and economies are ranked in descending order of their relative success on tasks involving the use of computers to solve problems.

Source: OECD, PISA 2012 Database, Table 3.11.

StatLink http://dx.doi.org/10.1787/888933253011

Notes

1. Germany participated in the assessments of digital reading and computer-based mathematics as a research project. Results for Germany are not reported.

2. Although Austria did participate in both assessments, the comparability of the 2009 data with data from PISA 2012 cannot be assured. A negative atmosphere surrounding educational assessment affected the conditions under which the assessment was administered in 2009, and could have adversely affected student motivation to respond to the PISA tasks.

3. Both figures refer to the latent correlation in the pooled sample of students from all countries/economies participating in computer-based assessments. Student observations are weighted with final student weights.

4. Some of the items classified as "traditional", because they do not require the use of computers to solve problems, may, however, have response formats that are only possible on screen, such as drag and drop, or may involve animated stimulus information. This classification is therefore meant to capture the difference in item demands, rather than a difference merely related to item presentation.

5. The examples refer to released computer-based mathematics items, which can be tried out on the website of the Australian Consortium for Educational Research (http://cbasq.acer.edu.au/index.php?cmd=toMaths).

Chapter 3 tables are available on line at http://dx.doi.org/10.1787/edu-data-en.

Note regarding Israel

The statistical data for Israel are supplied by and under the responsibility of the relevant Israeli authorities. The use of such data by the OECD is without prejudice to the status of the Golan Heights, East Jerusalem and Israeli settlements in the West Bank under the terms of international law.

References

Fraillon, J., J. Ainley, W. Schulz, T. Friedman and **E. Gebhardt** (2014), "Executive summary", in Fraillon, J., J. Ainley, W. Schulz, T. Friedman and E. Gebhardt (eds.), *Preparing for Life in a Digital Age*, pp. 15-25, Springer International Publishing.

OECD (2014a), *PISA 2012 Technical Report*, PISA, OECD, Paris, www.oecd.org/pisa/pisaproducts/pisa2012technicalreport.htm.

OECD (2014b), *PISA 2012 Results: What Students Know and Can Do (Volume I, Revised edition, February 2014): Student Performance in Mathematics, Reading and Science*, PISA, OECD Publishing, Paris, http://dx.doi.org/10.1787/9789264208780-en.

OECD (2013), *PISA 2012 Assessment and Analytical Framework: Mathematics, Reading, Science, Problem Solving and Financial Literacy*, PISA, OECD Publishing, Paris, http://dx.doi.org/10.1787/9789264190511-en.

OECD (2011), *PISA 2009 Results: Students On Line (Volume VI): Digital Technologies and Performance*, PISA, OECD Publishing, Paris, http://dx.doi.org/10.1787/9789264112995-en.

Stacey, K. and **D. Wiliam** (2012), "Technology and assessment in mathematics", in Clements, M.A.K., A.J. Bishop, C. Keitel, J. Kilpatrick and F.K.S. Leung (eds.), *Third International Handbook of Mathematics Education*, Springer International Handbooks of Education, Vol. 27, Springer New York, pp. 721-751.

4

The Importance of Navigation in Online Reading: Think, then Click

Not only are certain text-processing skills particularly important when reading on line, readers must also be able to navigate through and among different texts. This chapter describes students' digital navigation abilities and examines the relationship between navigation skills and performance in digital reading.

While some similar skills are required to read both online and printed documents, online texts often pose greater challenges to readers than printed texts. In both types of documents, readers need to locate key pieces of information, interpret nuances of language, integrate different elements of the text, draw upon prior knowledge of textual and linguistic structures and features, and reflect on the arguments used or the appropriateness of the style, based on their own experience and knowledge of the world. Among these skills, *evaluative skills* can be particularly important for the typical text forms encountered on line. Students who read on line use their prior experience (e.g. about the authority of a certain source) and hints, such as layout, poor grammar and spelling, to assess the trustworthiness and relevance of the information and draw correct inferences from their reading.

In contrast to typical print documents, however, typical online documents are characterised by multi-modality (the combination of text, static images, animations, embedded videos including sound, etc.) and by the presence of hyper-links that create non-sequential page structures. Thus, not only are certain *text-processing* skills particularly important when reading on line, readers must also *navigate* through and among different texts.

What the data tell us

- One in ten students in OECD countries demonstrated limited or no web-browsing activity during the digital reading assessment, signalling a lack of basic computer skills, a lack of familiarity with web browsing or a lack of motivation. By contrast, most students in Korea, Macao-China, Shanghai-China and Chinese Taipei navigated through a high number of pages to arrive at their answer.
- Students in Singapore, Australia, Korea, Canada, the United States and Ireland rank the highest for the average quality of their web browsing (task-oriented browsing). More often than in other countries, these students carefully select links to follow before clicking on them, and follow relevant links for as long as is needed to answer the question.
- There is a strong association between countries' digital reading performance and the quality of students' navigation (task-oriented browsing), even after accounting for performance in print reading.

The skills required to master navigation include good evaluation: assessing the credibility of sources and predicting the likely content of a series of unseen screens, based on hints such as the explicit name assigned to a link, the surrounding text, and the URL that appears by hovering over the link with a mouse. They also include organisational and spatial skills, such as the ability to construct a mental representation of the structure of a website in order to move confidently across the different pages of which it is composed. While related skills are required in print reading as well, the greater uniformity of document types (such as books) and the physical existence of printed documents help readers to meet these demands (Noyes and Garland, 2003; Mangen et al., 2013).

Moreover, students' navigation behaviour and skills cannot be assessed in print reading, but can be measured, in online text, by tracking students' clicking and scrolling behaviour.

PISA digital reading tasks, which were originally developed for use in the PISA 2009 assessment, were constructed to vary in the level of text-processing skills required as well as in the complexity of the required navigation. Box 4.1 describes the main factors that determine the difficulty of navigation.

Box 4.1. **What accounts for the difficulty of navigation?**

The main source of navigation complexity is the number of pages that need to be viewed in order to complete the task. A simple digital reading task may focus on information that is immediately visible on the starting page of the task. It may require scrolling on that page, or it may require the reader to visit several pages or sites. A task becomes more difficult when the information needed to complete it is not immediately visible.

Complexity of navigation also depends on the quantity, prominence, consistency and familiarity of navigation tools and structures on the available pages. When moving between pages is required, if there are many hyperlinks or menu items to choose from, the reader is likely to find the task more difficult than if there are only one or two hyperlinks to choose from. A task is easier if there are prominently placed links in a conventional location on the screen; a task is more difficult if links are embedded in the text or are in an otherwise unconventional or inconspicuous part of the screen. Cluttered web pages and the presence of advertisements or visuals that deflect the readers' attention from the relevant links contribute to the difficulty of navigation.

Explicit instructions about the navigation required also reduce task difficulty. Even when the reader needs to consult several pages, explicit directions about the pages that must be visited and the navigation structures to use can make the task relatively easy. A familiar organisation of a website, such as a hierarchical structure, may function as an implicit hint and can facilitate navigation.

Figure 4.1 shows how demands for navigation and text processing contribute to the difficulty of tasks used in the PISA 2012 assessment of digital reading competence. These tasks are a subset of those used in 2009.

As the figure shows, navigation demands and requirements for text-processing skills both contribute to the overall difficulty of each task. The most difficult tasks combine high demands for navigation and advanced text-processing skills. Sometimes, tasks with similar demands for these two sets of skills may still vary in difficulty. Other factors also contribute to task difficulty, such as whether students are asked to construct a response or simply to select a response from a list of suggested answers.

■ Figure 4.1 ■

Relationship between text processing and navigation in digital reading tasks

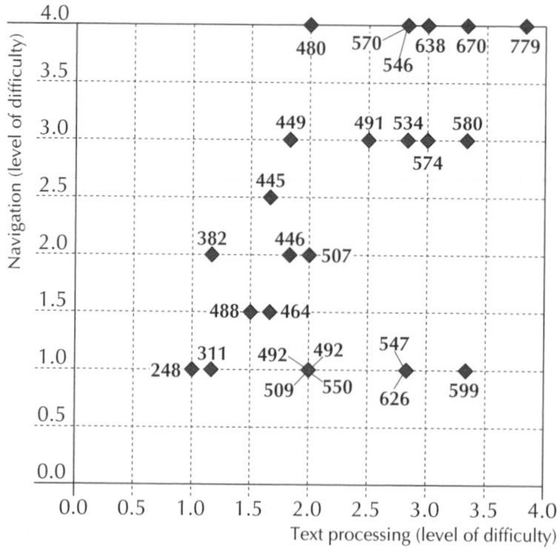
Navigation (level of difficulty)
4.0
3.5
3.0
2.5
2.0
1.5
1.0
0.5
0.0
480
570
546
638
670
779
449
491
534
580
574
445
382
446
507
488
464
311
248
492
492
509
550
547
626
599
0.0
0.5
1.0
1.5
2.0
2.5
3.0
3.5
4.0
Text processing (level of difficulty)

Notes: The horizontal axis shows the average of experts' ratings of text-processing demands; the vertical axis shows the average of experts' ratings of navigation demands (both ratings are expressed on a 1-4 scale, with 4 corresponding to the most difficult). Each task is represented by a diamond labelled with its overall difficulty, expressed in PISA score points. Several tasks may have the same level of text processing / navigation difficulty.

Source: OECD (2011), *PISA 2009 Results: Students on Line: Digital Technologies and Performance (Volume VI)*, p.43, http://dx.doi.org/10.1787/9789264112995-en.

StatLink http://dx.doi.org/10.1787/888933253022

SUCCESSFUL AND UNSUCCESSFUL NAVIGATION

How do students master navigation demands? What constitutes good navigation?

Clearly, good navigation behaviour cannot be defined in the abstract; the purpose of each task must be taken into account. Reading, including online reading, is always performed with particular goals in mind. Good navigation can be characterised as navigation behaviour that is consistent with these goals. This alignment of behaviour and goals requires both cognitive resources, e.g. understanding the goal of each task, and meta-cognitive regulation, e.g. ensuring that navigation is guided by task demands and not by personal interests.

In order to describe students' navigation behaviour, the sequence of pages visited by students in the process of solving each task was extracted from the log files recorded by the test administration platform. A first measure of students' navigation activity is the length of navigation sequences, which corresponds to the number of movements between different pages (steps) recorded in log files. The number of movements can be expected to be positively related to performance in digital reading for three reasons. First, because by being active on the task, students generate information that they can use to solve the task. Second, longer sequences are often required to solve the more complex tasks. Finally, because short navigation sequences may indicate a lack of motivation and persistence or lack of basic computer skills and familiarity with the typical text formats encountered on line.

To further identify task-adaptive navigation, pages were classified as relevant and non-relevant to the task, and each step (movement between pages) in the full sequence was classified as a task-relevant step (from and to a relevant page), a misstep (movement from a relevant to a non-relevant page), a correction (from a non-relevant to a relevant page), or a task-irrelevant step (from and to non-relevant pages). Relevant pages meet at least one of the following criteria (OECD, 2011; Naumann, forthcoming):

- the page contains information that is necessary in order to complete the task;
- the page contains information that could be assumed to be helpful in completing the task;
- it is necessary to transit through the page in order to reach a page that meets one of the two previous criteria (the starting page of each item, for instance, is always coded as relevant).[1]

While it is possible to follow different paths in order to collect the information required to solve a task, the most effective and efficient paths typically remain on relevant pages only. It is therefore expected that performance in digital reading is positively related to the number of task-relevant steps, and negatively related to movements that stray from the expected path, particularly if students do not revert to the expected path at a later stage. Task-irrelevant movements between non-relevant pages are also expected to signal lower performance.

How navigation is related to success in digital reading tasks

To identify effective navigation behaviours, success on each digital reading task was related, in regression models, to variables describing students' navigation sequence. In a first model, the navigation sequence was described only in terms of its length (the number of movements between pages, or steps, that made up the sequence). In a second, more detailed model, the quality of these steps was inspected, with the sequence decomposed into the four types of steps described above: task-relevant steps, task-irrelevant steps, and missteps, which were separated into those for which a further navigation step later on provided a correction, and those that remained uncorrected (see Annex A.3 for details about the estimation).

In general, longer navigation sequences were associated with greater success. It can be estimated that students who visited one additional page per task scored 11 points higher on the PISA scale, on average across countries (Figure 4.2). However, as expected, not all navigation steps signal better performance. Only task-relevant steps – from relevant to relevant pages – are positively associated with performance. Movements from relevant to non-relevant pages are associated with lower performance, in general, and particularly if they are not corrected later on by returning to a relevant page.

The relation between navigation behaviour and success in digital reading tasks varies, too, depending on the difficulty of navigation required. Actively generating information by visiting a high number of pages is important only where this is required to solve the problem. In simple tasks, a high level of browsing activity may signal unfocused behaviour, and is therefore negatively associated with performance (Figure 4.3). This negative association is particularly evident in high-income countries where students are familiar with computers and with online texts (see Table 4.5b for estimates about individual countries/economies).

■ Figure 4.2 ■

Relationship between success in digital reading tasks and the quantity and quality of navigation steps

Score-point difference associated with a one-unit increase in the average number of navigation steps across tasks (OECD average)

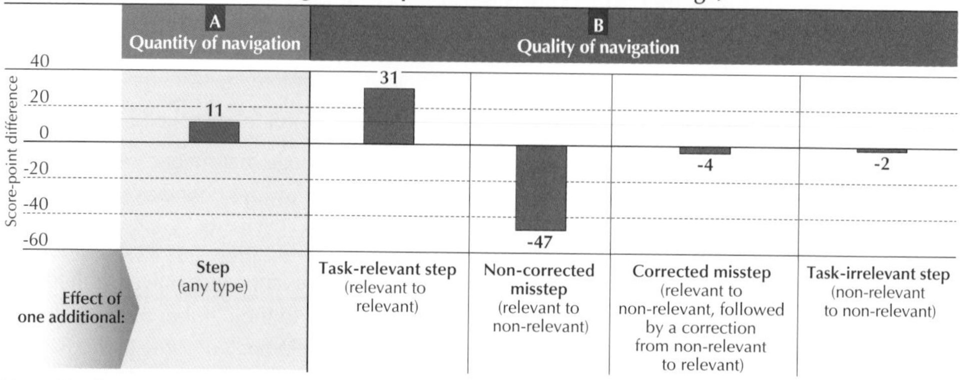
A
Quantity of navigation
B
Quality of navigation
Score-point difference
40
20
0
-20
-40
-60
11
31
-47
-4
-2
Effect of one additional:
Step (any type)
Task-relevant step (relevant to relevant)
Non-corrected misstep (relevant to non-relevant)
Corrected misstep (relevant to non-relevant, followed by a correction from non-relevant to relevant)
Task-irrelevant step (non-relevant to non-relevant)

Notes: The figure reports estimates from two separate logit models (A and B). Logit coefficients are converted into PISA score-point equivalents (see Annex A.3).
All estimates are statistically significant.
The figure shows that, across the OECD on average, one additional step in each task's navigation sequence is associated with a gain of 11 score points on the digital reading scale. One additional task-relevant step is associated with a gain of 31 score points on the digital reading scale.
Source: OECD, PISA 2012 Database, Tables 4.5a and b.
StatLink http://dx.doi.org/10.1787/888933253039

■ Figure 4.3 ■

Relationship between success in digital reading tasks and the quantity of navigation steps, by difficulty of tasks

Score-point difference associated with a one-unit increase in the average number of navigation steps across tasks (OECD average)

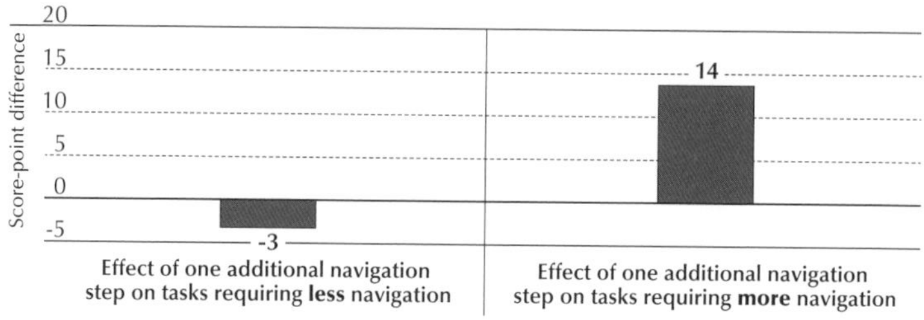
Score-point difference
20
15
10
5
0
-5
-3
14
Effect of one additional navigation step on tasks requiring less navigation
Effect of one additional navigation step on tasks requiring more navigation

Notes: The figure reports estimates from a logit model where the dependent variable has been interacted with a binary indicator of demands for navigation. Logit coefficients are converted into PISA score-point equivalents (see Annex A.3).
All estimates are statistically significant.
The figure shows that, in tasks requiring less navigation, sequences that become longer by one step, on average, are associated with a decline of 3 points on the digital reading scale. In contrast, in tasks requiring more navigation (where the number of required steps is higher), a one-unit increase in the average number of steps observed is associated with a gain of 14 points on the digital reading scale.
Tasks requiring less navigation are defined as those tasks where the average of experts' ratings of navigation demands (see Figure 4.1) is not greater than 1.5 on a scale of 1 to 4.
Source: OECD, PISA 2012 Database, Table 4.5a.
StatLink http://dx.doi.org/10.1787/888933253040

Furthermore, in tasks where demands for navigation are minimal (as in *SERAING*, Task 1[2]), e.g. because the relevant information is on the starting page or can be clearly accessed from it, the most important predictor of success is whether the student performed the few relevant steps that were required.[3] Indeed, when the relevant information is only one or two steps away, any task-relevant sequence is a big step towards the solution. Deviations from the task-relevant path may signal curiosity, more than difficulties with navigation, and are rare; they are associated with relatively small penalties in terms of performance.[4]

In contrast, in tasks demanding complex navigation, many steps are required to locate the relevant information, which itself is often dispersed, so that students need to integrate information from several pages to reach a solution. This is the case in the second and third tasks within the unit *SERAING*. In these and similar tasks, each step along the task-relevant path is a small step towards the solution. Steps away from the task-relevant path that are not followed by a correction can reduce the likelihood that all relevant information to solve the task will be collected. Thus they are associated with a significant penalty. On average, students whose navigation sequences end on non-relevant pages in tasks demanding complex navigation score an estimated 77 points lower on the PISA digital reading scale than students whose navigation ends on a relevant page. Figure 4.4 shows how the relationship between performance in digital reading, on the one hand, and task-relevant and task-irrelevant steps, on the other, varies across tasks requiring simple or complex navigation.

■ Figure 4.4 ■

Relationship between success in digital reading tasks and the quality of navigation, by difficulty of tasks

Score-point difference associated with a one-unit increase in the average number of navigation steps across tasks (OECD average)

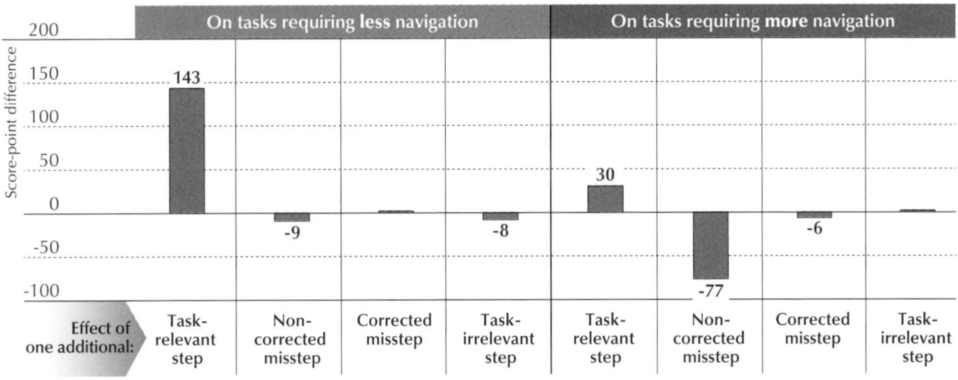
On tasks requiring less navigation
On tasks requiring more navigation
Score-point difference
200
150
100
50
0
-50
-100
143
-9
-8
30
-77
-6
Effect of one additional:
Task-relevant step
Non-corrected misstep
Corrected misstep
Task-irrelevant step
Task-relevant step
Non-corrected misstep
Corrected misstep
Task-irrelevant step

Notes: The figure reports estimates from a logit model where dependent variables have been interacted with a binary indicator of demands for navigation. Logit coefficients are converted into PISA score-point equivalents (see Annex A.3).
Statistically significant estimates are reported above/below the columns.
The figure shows that, in tasks requiring less navigation, one additional task-relevant step is associated with a gain of 143 points on the digital reading scale. In tasks requiring more navigation (where the number of required steps is higher), one additional task-relevant step is associated with a gain of 30 points on the digital reading scale.
Tasks requiring less navigation are defined as those tasks where the average of experts' ratings of navigation demands (see Figure 4.1) is not greater than 1.5 on a scale of 1 to 4.
Source: OECD, PISA 2012 Database, Table 4.5b.
StatLink http://dx.doi.org/10.1787/888933253054

In sum, navigation behaviour predicts success in digital reading tasks. More precisely, effective navigation is characterised by a task-oriented selection of what to read, and can thus be measured by observing whether readers access the relevant nodes within a hypertext, e.g. by counting the number of steps in the navigation sequence that involve only relevant pages. Effective navigation is further characterised by sequences that always end on relevant pages. Movements away from the expected navigation path must be corrected to succeed in complex digital reading tasks.

THE NAVIGATION BEHAVIOUR OF STUDENTS IN THE PISA ASSESSMENT OF DIGITAL READING

Based on the analysis of what constitutes effective and ineffective navigation, two indices were computed to describe how students navigate websites when performing typical online reading tasks. The first index captures the quantity of navigation; the second index, the quality of navigation.

Student-level indices used to describe navigation behaviour

First, as a rough measure of the amount of students' overall activity, the total number of tabs and links visited, beyond the starting page, is examined. The *index of overall browsing activity* varies between 0 and 100, with 0 indicating no activity and 100 indicating maximum activity.[5] Very low scores on this index may indicate either lack of motivation, great difficulties in basic text-processing skills (e.g. understanding the purpose of a task) or lack of familiarity with the typical forms of hypertext encountered on line or with basic computer skills, such as using a mouse to navigate a webpage or scroll down a list.

Second, an *index of task-oriented browsing* is formed by examining the sequence of page views and distinguishing between task-relevant steps, missteps, and task-irrelevant steps within the navigation sequence.[6] This index captures whether students carefully select the links they follow, according to the demands of each task. Students who navigate websites by staying on the task-relevant track, and who persist in doing so until they reach the solution, score the highest on this index. Those who navigate in an unstructured way, and are easily distracted by task-irrelevant content, score the lowest on this index, followed by students with insufficient navigation activity.

The typical navigation behaviour of students across countries/economies

There is considerable variation in the navigation behaviour of students across the countries and economies that participated in the PISA assessment of digital reading.

Overall browsing activity

Figure 4.5 shows students' average rank among all students who sat the PISA test, based on their amount of browsing activity. Students with the highest number of page visits score a value of 100 on this index, while students with the lowest number of page visits score a value of 0. This measure is related to the willingness of students to engage in reading, their familiarity with basic computer skills, their ability to read fast, and their persistence in solving difficult tasks.

By this simple measure, East Asian countries and economies (Korea, Chinese Taipei, Macao-China, Shanghai-China, Hong Kong-China, Singapore and Japan, in decreasing order of their mean value on this index) stand out for having the highest average values.

■ Figure 4.5 ■

Overall browsing activity

Average rank of students in the international comparison of students taking the same test form

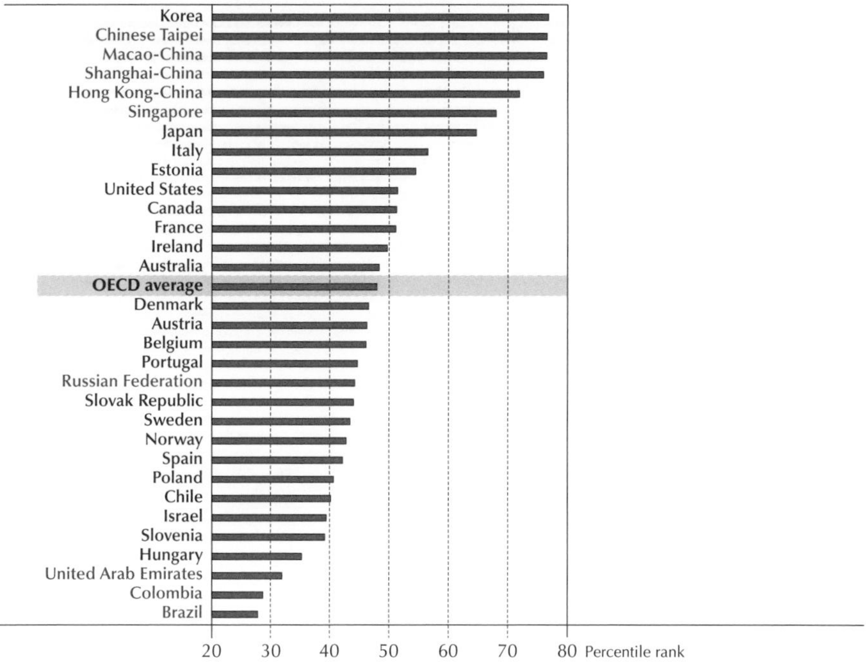
Korea
Chinese Taipei
Macao-China
Shanghai-China
Hong Kong-China
Singapore
Japan
Italy
Estonia
United States
Canada
France
Ireland
Australia
OECD average
Denmark
Austria
Belgium
Portugal
Russian Federation
Slovak Republic
Sweden
Norway
Spain
Poland
Chile
Israel
Slovenia
Hungary
United Arab Emirates
Colombia
Brazil
20
30
40
50
60
70
80
Percentile rank

Note: The *index of overall browsing activity* varies from 0 to 100, with 0 indicating no browsing activity (no page visits beyond the starting page) and 100 indicating the highest recorded level of browsing activity (page visits) for each test form.
Countries and economies are ranked in descending order of the index of overall browsing activity.
Source: OECD, PISA 2012 Database, Table 4.1.
StatLink http://dx.doi.org/10.1787/888933253068

Within each country/economy, however, students' navigation behaviour varies. To characterise this variation in students' browsing activity, four categories of students were constructed (Figure 4.6): students with no browsing activity, students with some but limited browsing activity, and students with intensive browsing activity. The fourth middle category groups students with moderate browsing activity.

At the bottom are students for whom no browsing activity at all was recorded in log files. Most likely, these students lack basic computer skills, such as operating a mouse, or lack basic familiarity with web browsing, such as knowledge of links and tabs. In a few cases, a technical failure in the hardware or software used to administer the test may have resulted in no activity being recorded. On average across OECD countries, 3% of students are in this category. In Israel (9%) and Hungary (7%), as well as in partner countries Colombia (15%), the United Arab Emirates (11%) and Brazil (8%), the share is much larger (Figure 4.6).

■ Figure 4.6 ■

Classification of students based on their overall browsing activity

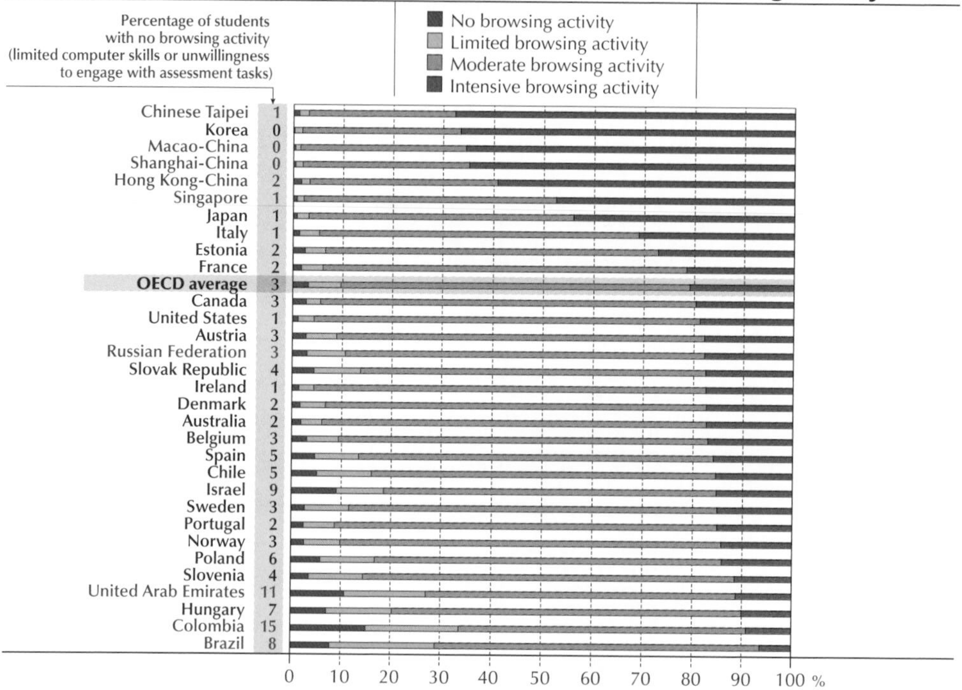
Percentage of students with no browsing activity (limited computer skills or unwillingness to engage with assessment tasks)
No browsing activity
Limited browsing activity
Moderate browsing activity
Intensive browsing activity
Chinese Taipei 1
Korea 0
Macao-China 0
Shanghai-China 0
Hong Kong-China 2
Singapore 1
Japan 1
Italy 1
Estonia 2
France 2
OECD average 3
Canada 3
United States 1
Austria 3
Russian Federation 3
Slovak Republic 4
Ireland 1
Denmark 2
Australia 2
Belgium 3
Spain 5
Chile 5
Israel 9
Sweden 3
Portugal 2
Norway 3
Poland 6
Slovenia 4
United Arab Emirates 11
Hungary 7
Colombia 15
Brazil 8
0 10 20 30 40 50 60 70 80 90 100 %

Note: The four categories in this figure are defined as follows. No browsing activity: students with no navigation steps recorded in log files; Limited browsing activity: some navigation steps recorded, but *index of overall browsing activity* equal to 10 or lower; Moderate browsing activity: *index of overall browsing activity* between 10 and 75; Intensive browsing activity: *index of overall browsing activity* higher than 75.
Countries and economies are ranked in descending order of the share of students who browse intensively.
Source: OECD, PISA 2012 Database, Table 4.2.
StatLink http://dx.doi.org/10.1787/888933253075

The next group shows some, but only limited activity. Their level of activity places these students in the bottom decile among all students who were given the same digital reading questions. Combined with the no-activity group described above, these groups represent 10% of students, on average across OECD countries. In East Asian countries and economies participating in PISA, however, fewer than 4% of all students show no, or only limited, activity. One reason for these countries'/economies' good performance on the test, therefore, may be their students' willingness to try to answer questions.

At the other extreme are students with high levels of activity (those with the longest navigation sequences). For better or worse, these students are persistent in their navigation behaviour. They rank in the top quarter of all students who sat the PISA test internationally, based on the amount of navigation recorded. About two in three students in Hong Kong-China, Korea, Macao-China, Shanghai-China and Chinese Taipei belong to this category – significantly more than in any other country/economy participating in PISA. Students in Estonia, Italy, Japan and Singapore are also more frequently found in this group than students across OECD countries, on average (Figure 4.6).

Task-oriented browsing

Reading a lot and fast is not always desired or efficient. It can be the sign of reading that is unfocused, oblivious to the specific purposes of the task. What's more, online readers who access non-relevant links may expose themselves or their hardware to significant threats, such as illegal or fraudulent content, spyware, viruses or worms. To avoid such threats, students need to exert self-control while reading on line.

The second measure used to characterise students' navigation proficiency thus assesses whether or not students' navigation conforms to expectations, given the demands of the task. Students score high on this index if they select the links that they follow based on the purpose of each task ("think, then click"). Students who are less selective, and only think whether the link is relevant after having clicked on it (if at all), score low on this index, as do students who do not persist in their navigation for as long as the task demands.

Figure 4.7 shows that, on average, students in Singapore, followed by students in Australia, Korea, Canada, the United States and Ireland, rank the highest for the average quality of their browsing.

■ Figure 4.7 ■

Task-oriented browsing

Average rank of students in the international comparison of students taking the same test form

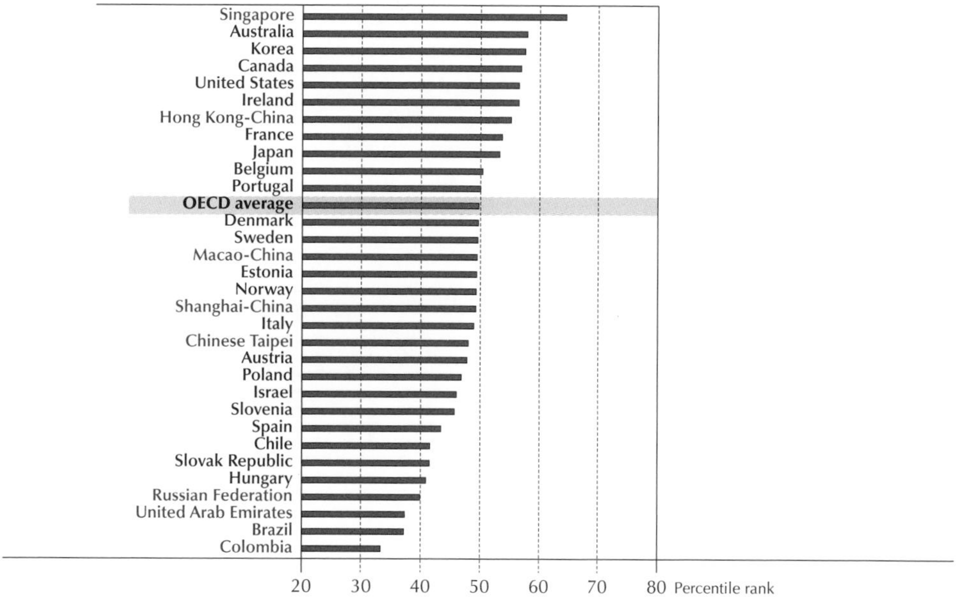
Singapore
Australia
Korea
Canada
United States
Ireland
Hong Kong-China
France
Japan
Belgium
Portugal
OECD average
Denmark
Sweden
Macao-China
Estonia
Norway
Shanghai-China
Italy
Chinese Taipei
Austria
Poland
Israel
Slovenia
Spain
Chile
Slovak Republic
Hungary
Russian Federation
United Arab Emirates
Brazil
Colombia
20
30
40
50
60
70
80
Percentile rank

Note: The *index of task-oriented browsing* varies from 0 to 100. High values on this index reflect long navigation sequences that contain a high number of task-relevant steps and few or no missteps or task-irrelevant steps.
Countries and economies are ranked in descending order of the index of task-oriented browsing activity.
Source: OECD, PISA 2012 Database, Table 4.1.
StatLink http://dx.doi.org/10.1787/888933253082

Students in these countries tend to be the most selective in their online navigation behaviour, carefully selecting links to follow before clicking on them, and following relevant links for as long as is needed to solve the task.

There are large differences in the rankings of countries, depending on whether the quality of students' browsing (Figure 4.7) or the quantity of students' browsing (Figure 4.5) is considered. While students in Macao-China, Shanghai-China and Chinese Taipei have among the highest levels of activity, they rank much lower in terms of the quality of their browsing activity.

Indeed, some students know how to browse and are willing to engage with a task, but are "digitally adrift", in that they do not navigate as if they were guided by a clear direction. Figure 4.8 shows that more than one in five students in Macao-China, Shanghai-China and Chinese Taipei belong to the group of students with mostly unfocused browsing activity. In contrast, in Australia, Canada, France, Ireland, Poland, Singapore, Sweden and the United States, less than 10% of all students belong to this group.

■ Figure 4.8 ■

Classification of students based on the quality of their browsing activity

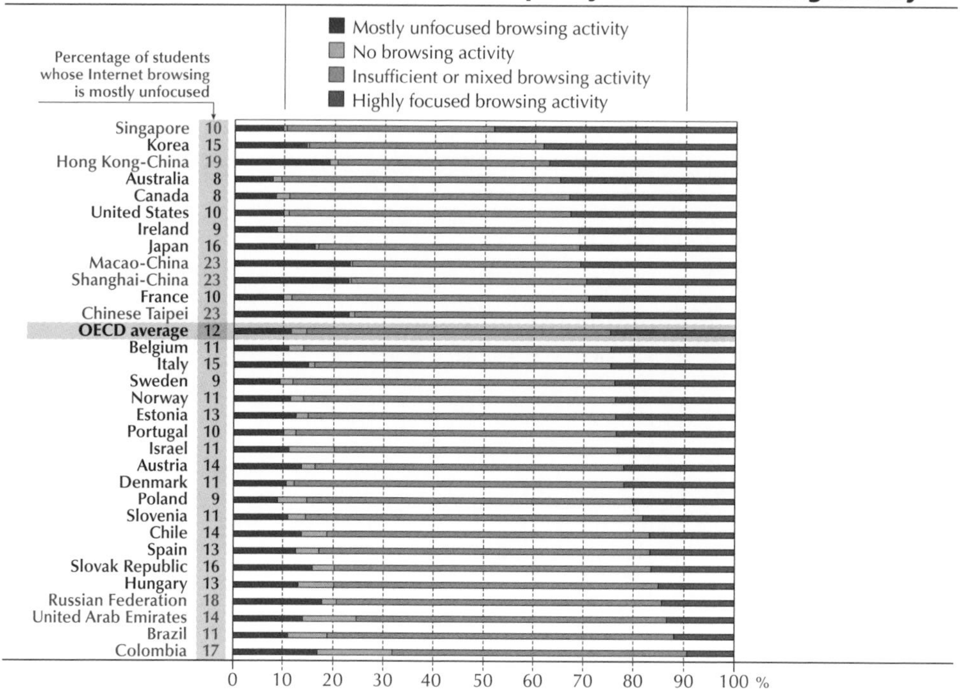
Mostly unfocused browsing activity
No browsing activity
Insufficient or mixed browsing activity
Highly focused browsing activity
Percentage of students whose Internet browsing is mostly unfocused
Singapore 10
Korea 15
Hong Kong-China 19
Australia 8
Canada 8
United States 10
Ireland 9
Japan 16
Macao-China 23
Shanghai-China 23
France 10
Chinese Taipei 23
OECD average 12
Belgium 11
Italy 15
Sweden 9
Norway 11
Estonia 13
Portugal 10
Israel 11
Austria 14
Denmark 11
Poland 9
Slovenia 11
Chile 14
Spain 13
Slovak Republic 16
Hungary 13
Russian Federation 18
United Arab Emirates 14
Brazil 11
Colombia 17
0 10 20 30 40 50 60 70 80 90 100 %

Note: The four categories in this figure are defined as follows. Mostly unfocused browsing activity: students for whom the sum of navigation missteps and task-irrelevant steps is higher than the number of task-relevant steps; No browsing activity: no navigation steps recorded in log files; Insufficient or mixed browsing activity: the sum of navigation missteps and task-irrelevant steps is equal to the number of task-relevant steps or lower, and the *index of task-oriented browsing* is equal to 75 or lower. Highly focused browsing activity: *index of task-oriented browsing* higher than 75.

Countries and economies are ranked in descending order of the share of students with highly focused browsing activity.

Source: OECD, PISA 2012 Database, Table 4.3.

StatLink http://dx.doi.org/10.1787/888933253097

At the same time, the group of students whose navigation behaviour best conforms to task demands – those who rank in the top quarter for the quality of their browsing among all students who sat the PISA digital reading test – is largest in Singapore (48%), Korea (38%), Hong Kong-China (37%), Australia (35%), Canada (33%) and the United States (33%) (Figure 4.8 and Table 4.3).

The difference between rankings based on quantity and rankings based on quality may be related to the behaviour of students who make missteps when navigating a website. Box 4.2 explores cross-country differences in how students react to such missteps.

In sum, students in Australia, Canada, Korea, Singapore and the United States have, on average, the most task-driven, and thus better, navigation sequences. Students in East Asian countries and economies tend to have long navigation sequences. More often than in other countries, however, these sequences occasionally deviate from the expected path. A possible reason for this is that in these countries and economies, even the students who are most likely to make mistakes are willing to try. In the confined space of a simulated web environment, this behaviour occasionally leads them to the right cues to solve PISA tasks. It may have more negative consequences if applied to the unconfined World Wide Web.

Box 4.2. **How students react when they deviate from the expected navigation path**

A third measure used to describe students' typical browsing activity focuses on students' missteps. Leaving students with no or only limited browsing activity aside, it groups students into three classes: those who never deviate from the task-relevant path (no missteps); those who occasionally deviate and visit task-irrelevant pages, but always correct such mistakes by returning to the expected path (in which case, the number of corrections is equal to the number of missteps); and those who make missteps and do not always correct them (e.g. because they do not realise their misstep or do not know how to return on the task-relevant path). Figure 4.a presents the share of students in each category across countries and economies participating in the digital reading assessment.

It is relatively common for students to have missteps in their navigation sequences. On average across OECD countries, only 7% of students never deviate from the task-relevant navigation path (this excludes students with no or limited navigation). In those countries and economies where students have the longest navigation sequences, on average, less than 5% of students do not make any mistakes when navigating on line. This includes all East Asian countries and economies (Hong Kong-China, Japan, Korea, Macao-China, Shanghai-China, Singapore and Chinese Taipei) as well as Estonia and Italy. What students do after committing a misstep, however, differs widely across countries.

In Italy, Korea, Macao-China, Shanghai-China and Chinese Taipei, more than three out of five students visit task-irrelevant pages, and do not correct such missteps by returning to the task-relevant path. Furthermore, because students in these countries/economies who

...

commit a misstep often do not give up on solving the task, they tend to have long navigation sequences (see Figure 4.5 in this chapter). In contrast, in Australia, Canada, Ireland and the United States (all countries with a high average quality of navigation; see Figure 4.7 in this chapter), there are both more students with clean navigation sequences than on average across OECD countries, and more students who return to the navigation path that is relevant to solve the task after making a misstep.

■ Figure 4.a ■

Classification of students based on their reaction to navigation missteps

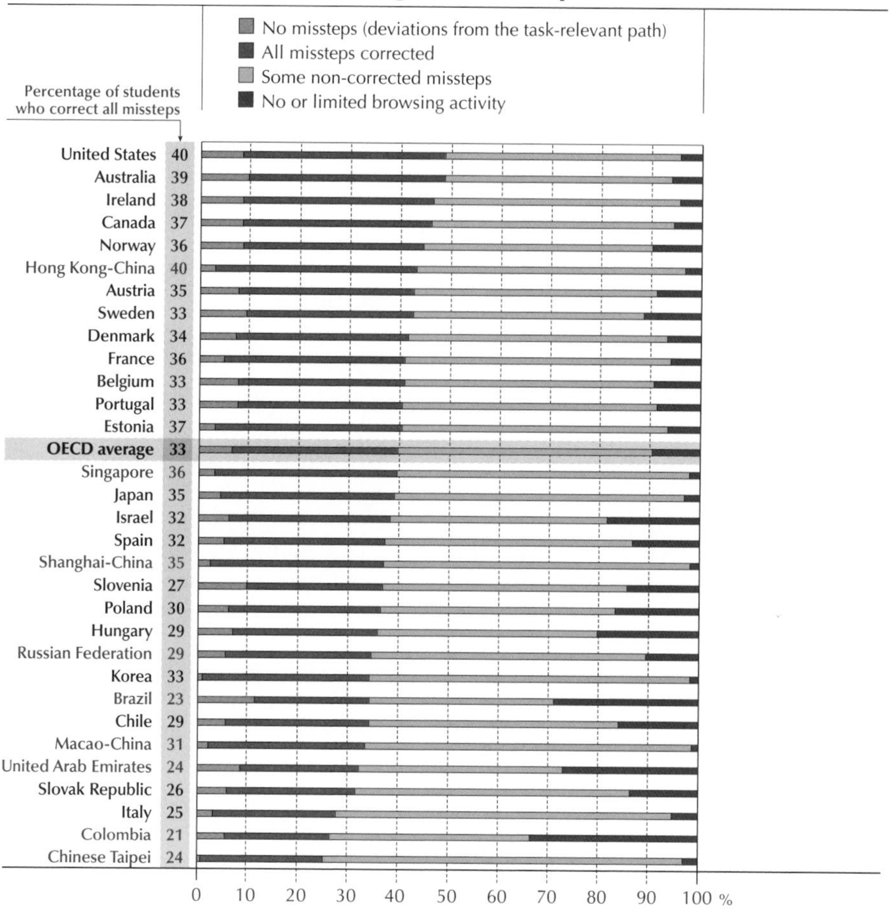
No missteps (deviations from the task-relevant path)
All missteps corrected
Some non-corrected missteps
No or limited browsing activity
Percentage of students who correct all missteps
United States 40
Australia 39
Ireland 38
Canada 37
Norway 36
Hong Kong-China 40
Austria 35
Sweden 33
Denmark 34
France 36
Belgium 33
Portugal 33
Estonia 37
OECD average 33
Singapore 36
Japan 35
Israel 32
Spain 32
Shanghai-China 35
Slovenia 27
Poland 30
Hungary 29
Russian Federation 29
Korea 33
Brazil 23
Chile 29
Macao-China 31
United Arab Emirates 24
Slovak Republic 26
Italy 25
Colombia 21
Chinese Taipei 24
0 10 20 30 40 50 60 70 80 90 100 %

Countries and economies are ranked in descending order of the share of students who either make no missteps or correct all missteps.

Source: OECD, PISA 2012 Database, Table 4.4.

StatLink http://dx.doi.org/10.1787/888933253101

THE RELATIONSHIP BETWEEN PERFORMANCE IN DIGITAL READING AND STUDENTS' NAVIGATION BEHAVIOUR

Students' performance in digital reading is not perfectly aligned with their performance in print reading. This is true at aggregate levels too. In some countries/economies, average performance lies above or below the level that could be expected, given their students' performance in print reading. Are such differences related to students' navigation behaviour?

Figure 4.9 shows that students' average navigation behaviour – quantified by the indices of overall navigation activity and task-oriented navigation activity – explains a significant part of the differences in digital reading performance between countries/economies that is not accounted for by differences in print-reading performance. Of the 20% of unexplained variation, only about one-fourth (5%) is not associated with between-country differences in students' average navigation behaviour.

More precisely, after controlling for differences in print reading, the quantity of navigation (as measured through the *index of overall browsing activity*) accounts for about one-fifth of the remaining between-country differences in digital reading performance (or 4.4% of the overall variation in reading performance). The quality of students' navigation (as measured through the *index of task-oriented browsing*) explains more than half of the residual variation (an additional 10.4% of the overall variation).

■ Figure 4.9 ■

Explained variation in the digital reading performance of countries and economies

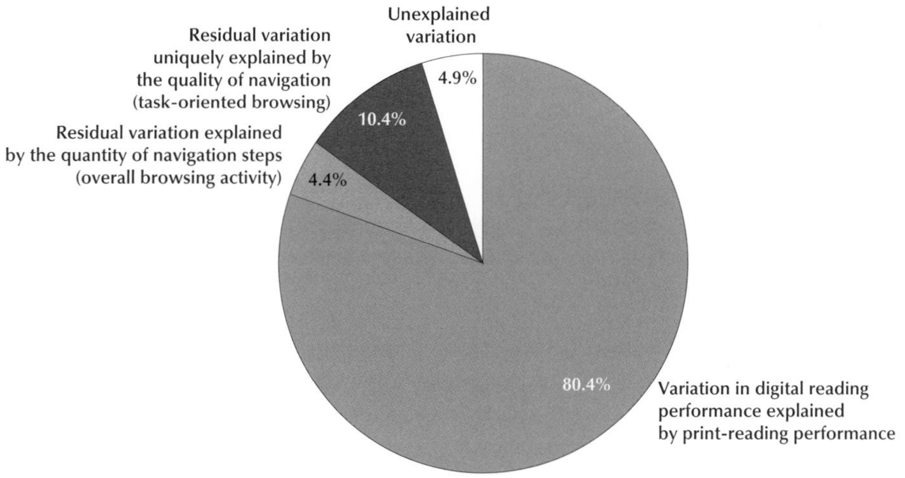
Unexplained variation
4.9%
Residual variation uniquely explained by the quality of navigation (task-oriented browsing)
10.4%
Residual variation explained by the quantity of navigation steps (overall browsing activity)
4.4%
80.4%
Variation in digital reading performance explained by print-reading performance

Notes: Percentages may not total 100% due to rounding.
The figure is based on results from regressions of countries' and economies' mean performance in digital reading on mean performance in print reading and average values for the two indices of navigation.
Source: OECD, PISA 2012 Database, Table 4.6b.
StatLink http://dx.doi.org/10.1787/888933253119

Figure 4.10 illustrates how the association between digital reading performance and navigation works in practice. The charts in the top row show that students' average navigation behaviour is strongly related to mean performance in digital reading. However, much of students' navigation behaviour can be predicted by whether they are good readers – i.e. by their performance in print reading. This is because, to a large extent, good navigation relies on the same cognitive skills and motivational aspects that are prerequisites for success in the paper-based assessment of reading as well.

■ Figure 4.10 ■

Relationship between digital reading performance and navigation behaviour in digital reading

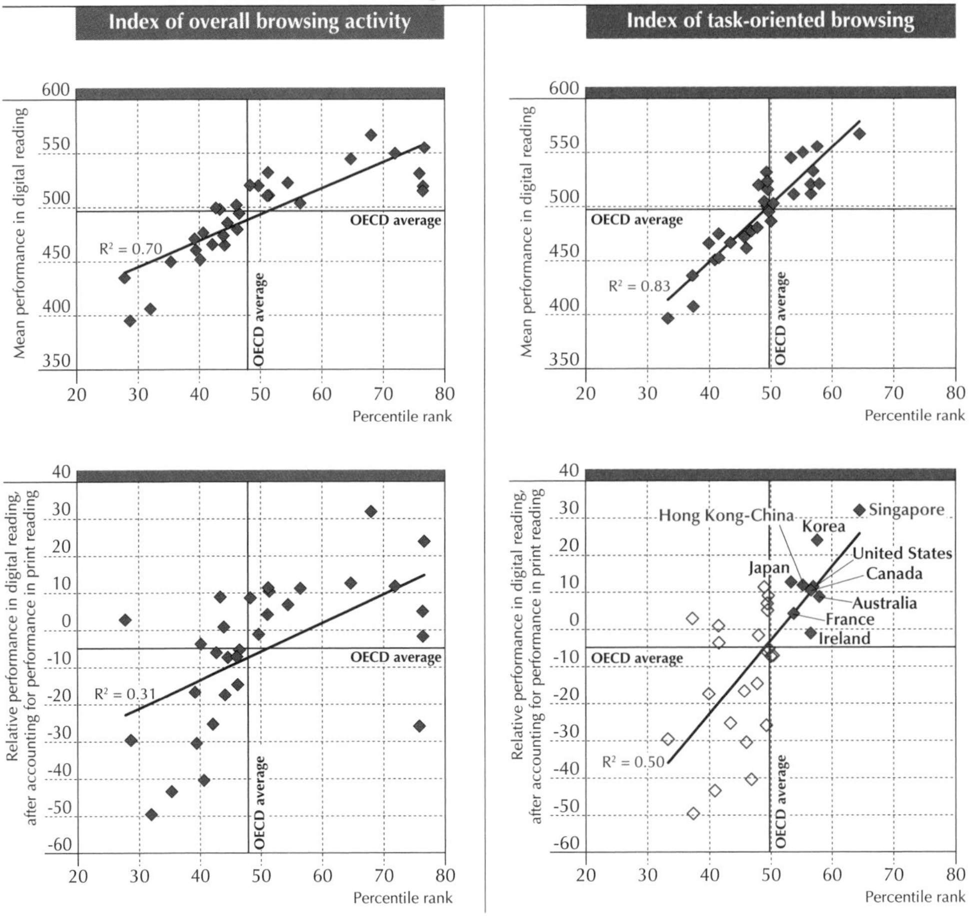
Index of overall browsing activity
Index of task-oriented browsing
Mean performance in digital reading
Relative performance in digital reading, after accounting for performance in print reading
Percentile rank
OECD average
$R^2 = 0.70$
$R^2 = 0.83$
$R^2 = 0.31$
$R^2 = 0.50$
Hong Kong-China
Singapore
Korea
United States
Japan
Canada
Australia
France
Ireland

Notes: The relative performance of countries/economies in digital reading is the average difference between students' observed and expected performance. Each student's expected performance is estimated, using a regression model, as the predicted performance in digital reading given his or her score in print reading.
Each diamond represents the mean values of a country/economy.
Source: OECD, PISA 2012 Database, Tables 3.6 and 4.1.
StatLink http://dx.doi.org/10.1787/888933253123

Does good navigation require more than good reading? And if so, can good navigation explain differences in performance across countries, after accounting for reading performance?

The bottom row in Figure 4.10 shows that there is a strong association between digital reading and the quality of navigation (task-oriented browsing), even after accounting for performance in print reading. Performance is often better in digital reading than would be expected, based on print-reading performance, in countries/economies where students' navigation is of better-than-average quality, namely in Australia, Canada, France, Hong Kong-China, Ireland, Japan, Korea, Singapore and the United States.

A similar relationship exists within countries, among students (Table 4.6a). Across all countries/economies, the variation in digital reading performance observed among students, within countries, who perform at the same level in print reading can be largely accounted for by differences in their navigation behaviour. An estimated 9% of the total variation in digital reading performance, on average, is uniquely explained by students' navigation behaviour.[7]

If navigation skills are so critically important, how can they be developed? Statistical analyses show that students' reading skills in print documents strongly predict their navigation behaviour in a digital environment (Tables 4.6b and 4.7a). This indicates that the development of print-reading skills is likely to contribute to better navigation skills as well. Indeed, the quantity of navigation may be linked to reading engagement, in general, while the quality of navigation depends on the kinds of skills, such as drawing inferences, that can be practiced just as well in print as in electronic texts.

Problem-solving skills are also important. Among student with similar reading skills, those with higher scores in the PISA assessment of problem solving tend to be more persistent in their navigation (as indicated by higher values on the *index of overall browsing activity*). Often, these students navigate better too (as indicated by higher values on the *index of task-oriented browsing activity*). This suggests that to navigate on line, students use generic problem-solving skills and dispositions, such as the ability to think, autonomously, about unfamiliar problems and how to solve them, and their willingness to engage with such situations in the first place (OECD, 2014).

Good navigation therefore requires good problem-solving skills. But even among students of similar skill in both reading and problem solving, differences in navigation remain strongly associated with differences in digital reading proficiency. In fact, the skills measured in the PISA assessment of problem solving only marginally reduce the strength of the relationship between the navigation indices and performance in digital reading (Table 4.8). For the most part, the problem-solving skills that students demonstrate when navigating complex online texts are specific, and are likely best learned in the context of reading from the Internet.

Notes

1. The coding of pages and navigation steps in sample task *SERAING*, presented in Chapter 7, illustrates how even within the same unit (i.e. the same website), the relevant pages may vary depending on the purpose of each task.

2. Items from unit *SERAING* can be seen, and tested, on the website of the Australian Consortium for Education Research (http://cbasq.acer.edu.au/index.php? cmd=toEra2012).

3. Tasks with minimal navigation demands are defined as those where the average of experts' ratings of navigation demands (see Figure 4.1) is not greater than 1.5, on a 1 to 4 scale.

4. In tasks where little navigation is required, many of these "non-corrected missteps" are observed after students have found the information they need (which is sometimes presented on the starting page itself).

5. The number of steps (clicks on tabs or links leading to a different page) that are contained in the navigation sequence for each task is summed across tasks. To convert this number into an *index of overall browsing activity*, a percentile score reflecting the rank of the student among all students who were administered the same digital reading questions is computed. The unweighted, pooled distribution of students from all participating countries is used.

6. To compute this index, the number of steps that start and end on relevant pages is computed first (task-relevant steps), then the number of steps that end on a non-relevant page (missteps and task-irrelevant steps) is subtracted from this sum. The result is then transformed into a percentile score reflecting the rank of the student among all students who were administered the same digital reading questions, in order to make fair comparisons between students who were given different questions.

7. Because navigation indices were not used in the conditioning model for generating plausible values of digital reading performance, the percentage of variation explained by navigation indices may be underestimated.

Chapter 4 tables are available on line at http://dx.doi.org/10.1787/edu-data-en.

Note regarding Israel

The statistical data for Israel are supplied by and under the responsibility of the relevant Israeli authorities. The use of such data by the OECD is without prejudice to the status of the Golan Heights, East Jerusalem and Israeli settlements in the West Bank under the terms of international law.

References

Mangen, A., B.R. Walgermo and **K. Brønnick** (2013), "Reading linear texts on paper versus computer screen: Effects on reading comprehension", *International Journal of Educational Research*, Vol. 58, pp. 61-68.

Naumann, J. (forthcoming), "A model of online reading engagement: Linking engagement, navigation and performance in digital reading", *Computers in Human Behavior.*

Noyes, J.M. and **K.J. Garland** (2003), "VDT versus paper-based text: Reply to Mayes, Sims and Koonce", *International Journal of Industrial Ergonomics*, Vol. 31/6, pp. 411-423.

OECD (2014), *PISA 2012 Results: Creative Problem Solving (Volume V): Students' Skills in Tackling Real-Life Problems*, PISA, OECD Publishing, Paris, http://dx.doi.org/10.1787/9789264208070-en.

OECD (2011), *PISA 2009 Results: Students On Line: Digital Technologies and Performance (Volume VI)*, PISA, OECD Publishing, Paris, http://dx.doi.org/10.1787/9789264112995-en.

5

Inequalities in Digital Proficiency: Bridging the Divide

Digital inequality refers to differences in the material, cultural and cognitive resources required to make good use of information and communication technology (ICT). This chapter examines differences in access to and use of ICT that are related to students' socio-economic status, gender, geographic location, and the school a child attends. It also investigates whether performance on computer-based tests is related to students' socio-economic status and their familiarity with computers.

Disparities in access to and proficiency in information and communication technology (ICT), particularly between socio-economically advantaged and disadvantaged children, and between rural and urban residents, have long been a focus of public policy. The expression "digital divide" was coined to underline the fact that such disparities may threaten social and national cohesion, as they impede full participation in work and reduce political efficacy for population groups that are left behind on the analogue side of the divide (OECD, 2001). Indeed, given the many opportunities that technology makes available for civic participation, networking or improving one's productivity at work, the unequal distribution of material, cultural and cognitive resources to tap into these opportunities may perpetuate and even exacerbate existing status differences.

What the data tell us

- In most countries, differences in computer access between advantaged and disadvantaged students shrank between 2009 and 2012; in no country did the gap increase.
- In countries/economies where the socio-economic gap in access to the Internet is small, the amount of time that students spend on line does not differ widely across socio-economic groups; but what students do with computers, from using e-mail to reading news on the Internet, is related to students' socio-economic background.
- In mathematics, the relationship between socio-economic status and performance on the computer-based assessment reflects differences observed in performance on the paper-based assessment, not differences in the ability to use computers; in digital reading, this relationship also reflects differences in navigation and evaluation skills across socio-economic groups.

ONE DIVIDE OR MANY DIVIDES? DIGITAL ACCESS, DIGITAL USE AND DIGITAL PRODUCTION

Digital inequality refers to differences in the material, cultural and cognitive resources required to make good use of ICT. Traditionally, research on digital inequality has focused on differences in physical access to and possession of ICT tools, while emphasising that access is only one of the many factors required to make good use of technology. The greater attention given to material resources is certainly related to the relative abundance of data measuring these factors, as compared to data on differences in cultural and cognitive resources, such as the norms of use of ICT in the community or individuals' digital knowledge and skills (Hargittai and Hsieh, 2013).

A first, core "digital divide" thus concerns issues of physical access: are computers accessible, available and up-to-date? Is there an Internet connection that allows access to the most recently developed content? Comparisons of PISA data from different years confirm an observation already made about the United States in the early 2000s (Compaine, 2001): with time, information and communication technologies that were once exclusively available to the most wealthy fraction of the population, tend to become universally available. As a consequence, many gaps in access close. Yet while older technologies become available to more and more people, new digital technologies, tools and services are almost invariably marketed only to the most wealthy, thus reinforcing, at least initially, the privilege of more advantaged populations (Hargittai and Hsieh, 2013).

Equal access, however, does not imply equal opportunities (equity). Indeed, even when opportunities to learn about the world, practice new skills, participate in online communities or develop a career plan are only a few clicks away, students from socio-economically disadvantaged backgrounds may not be aware of how technology can help to raise one's social status. They may not have the knowledge and skills required to engage with massively open online courses (MOOCs), e-government websites, open educational resources, etc.

To refer to the non-material resources that condition students' ability to take full advantage of ICT tools, the terms "second" or "second-order" digital divide have been used (Attewell, 2001; Dimaggio et al., 2004). More recently, "proficiency" and "opportunity" gaps have been distinguished, referring to differences in what people can do, and what they actually do, when using computers and other digital tools (Stern et al., 2009). PISA data are a unique source of evidence to determine the width of such divides, and to analyse how effective education systems and schools are in narrowing them.

ACCESS AND EXPERIENCE GAPS RELATED TO SOCIO-ECONOMIC STATUS

By 2012, in most countries and economies that participate in PISA, socio-economic differences were no longer associated with large divides in access to computers (the so-called "first digital divide"). However, gaps previously observed in the quantity, variety and quality of ICT tools available, as well as in the mastery of them, persisted.

Socio-economic differences in access to computers and the Internet

In a majority of countries and economies participating in PISA, over 90% of students – even among the most disadvantaged students – have at least one computer at home. Some middle- and low-income countries and economies, nevertheless, still show large differences in basic measures of access between disadvantaged and advantaged students. In fact, the digital divide between advantaged and disadvantaged students within countries is sometimes larger than the divide observed between PISA-participating countries and economies (Figure 5.1).

Figure 5.1 shows the relationship between students' socio-economic background and the availability of a computer at home. Students in the top quarter of the *PISA index of economic, social and cultural status* (ESCS) in their country were categorised as being relatively advantaged, and those in the bottom quarter were categorised as being relatively disadvantaged.

Figure 5.1 shows that in all but three countries and economies (Indonesia, Peru and Viet Nam), at least 90% of advantaged students have access to computers. But while in some countries and economies – namely Denmark, Finland, Hong Kong-China, the Netherlands, Slovenia and Sweden – more than 99% of disadvantaged students have access to a computer at home, in 12 other countries fewer than half of the disadvantaged students do. In other words, across countries and economies, access to ICT is more similar among students from well-off families than among students from poorer families. Meanwhile, in almost all countries and economies, fewer disadvantaged students than advantaged students have access to a computer at home. A gap of at least 75 percentage points between the two groups is observed in Mexico, Peru, Tunisia and Viet Nam.

■ Figure 5.1 ■

Access to computers at home and students' socio-economic status

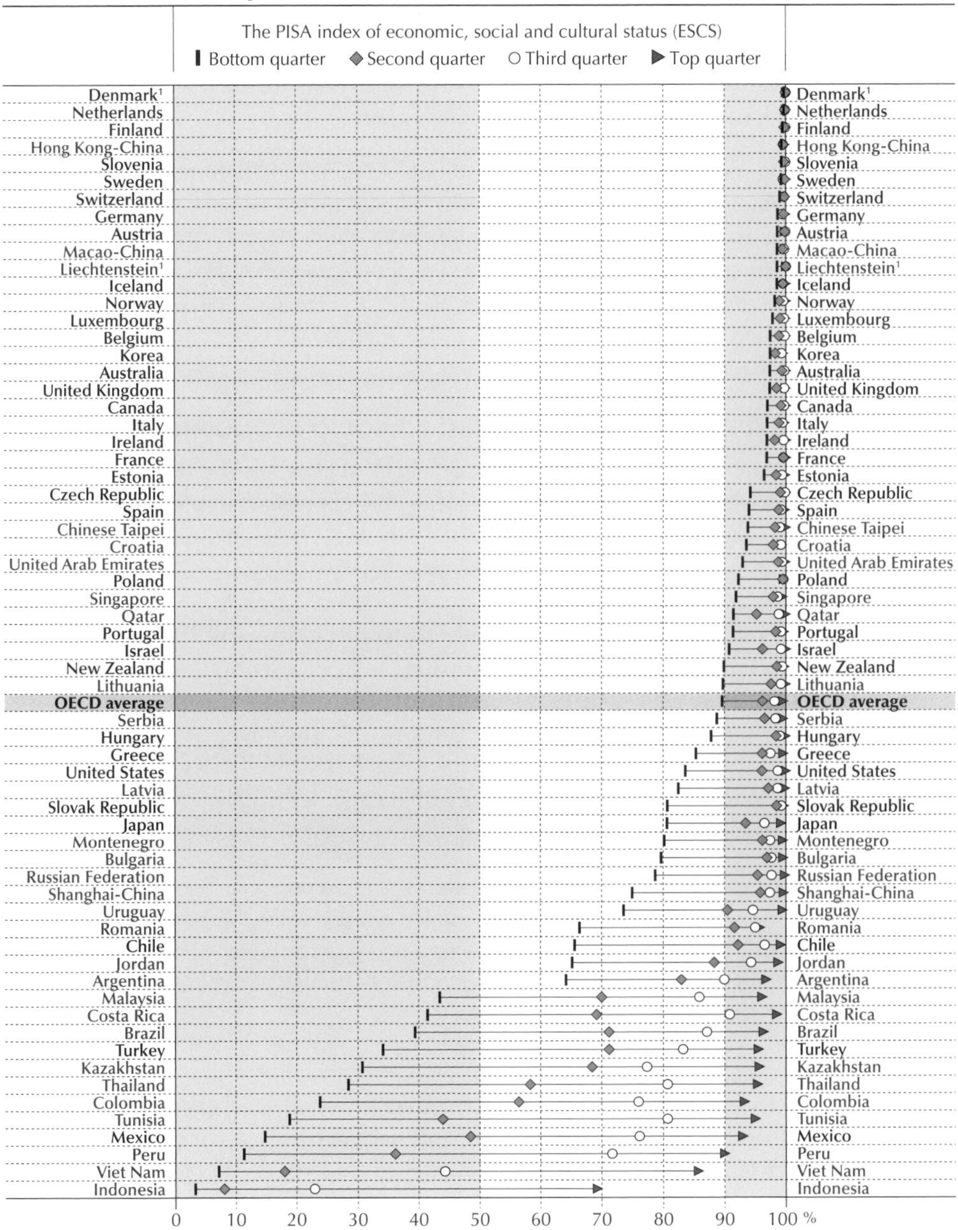
The PISA index of economic, social and cultural status (ESCS)
Bottom quarter
Second quarter
Third quarter
Top quarter
Denmark[1]
Netherlands
Finland
Hong Kong-China
Slovenia
Sweden
Switzerland
Germany
Austria
Macao-China
Liechtenstein[1]
Iceland
Norway
Luxembourg
Belgium
Korea
Australia
United Kingdom
Canada
Italy
Ireland
France
Estonia
Czech Republic
Spain
Chinese Taipei
Croatia
United Arab Emirates
Poland
Singapore
Qatar
Portugal
Israel
New Zealand
Lithuania
OECD average
Serbia
Hungary
Greece
United States
Latvia
Slovak Republic
Japan
Montenegro
Bulgaria
Russian Federation
Shanghai-China
Uruguay
Romania
Chile
Jordan
Argentina
Malaysia
Costa Rica
Brazil
Turkey
Kazakhstan
Thailand
Colombia
Tunisia
Mexico
Peru
Viet Nam
Indonesia
0
10
20
30
40
50
60
70
80
90
100 %

1. The difference between the top and the bottom quarter of ESCS is not statistically significant.

Countries and economies are ranked in descending order of the percentage of students in the bottom quarter of ESCS who have a computer at home.

Source: OECD, PISA 2012 Database, Table 5.1a.

StatLink http://dx.doi.org/10.1787/888933253134

■ Figure 5.2 ■

Access to the Internet at home and students' socio-economic status

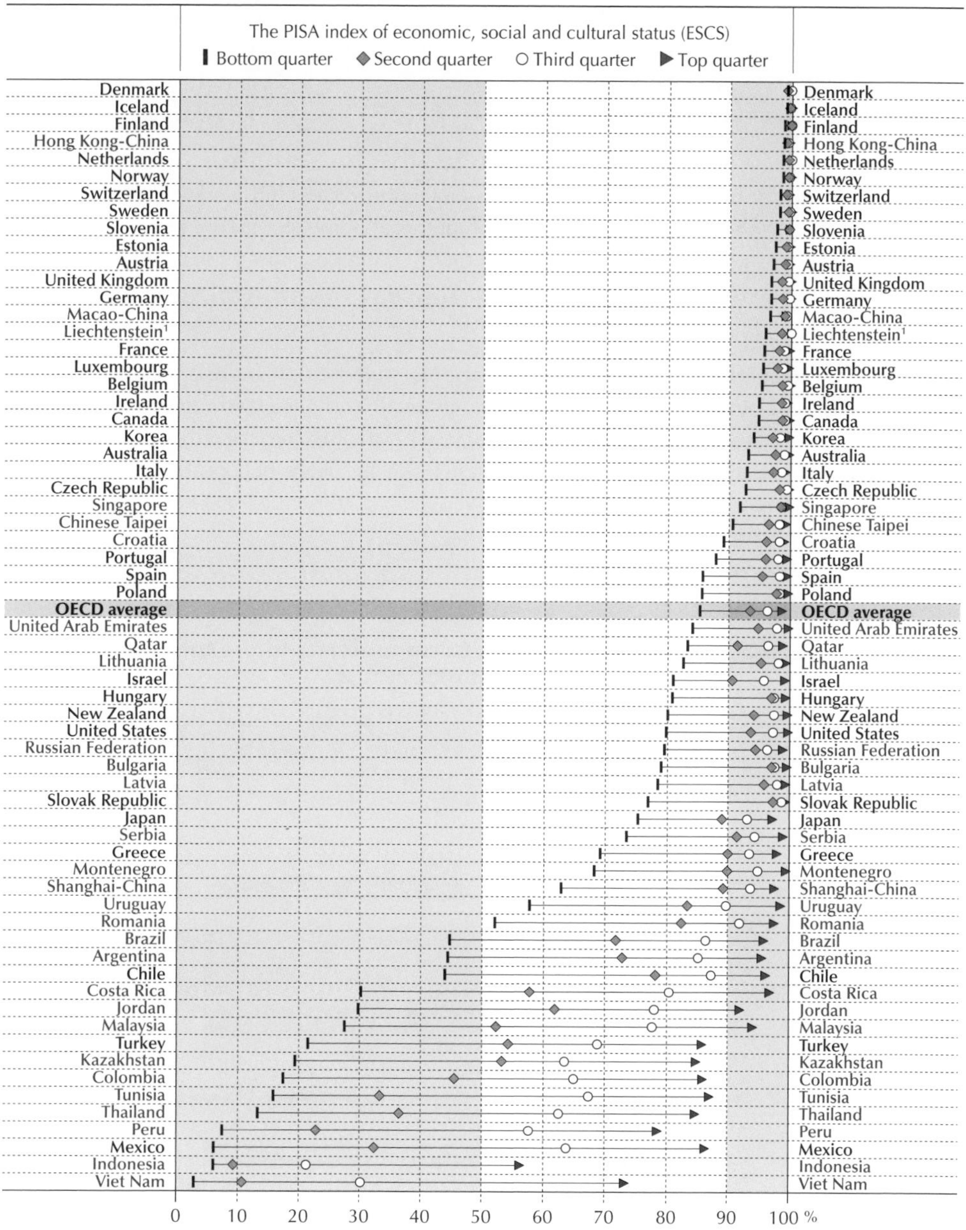
The PISA index of economic, social and cultural status (ESCS)
Bottom quarter
Second quarter
Third quarter
Top quarter
Denmark
Iceland
Finland
Hong Kong-China
Netherlands
Norway
Switzerland
Sweden
Slovenia
Estonia
Austria
United Kingdom
Germany
Macao-China
Liechtenstein[1]
France
Luxembourg
Belgium
Ireland
Canada
Korea
Australia
Italy
Czech Republic
Singapore
Chinese Taipei
Croatia
Portugal
Spain
Poland
OECD average
United Arab Emirates
Qatar
Lithuania
Israel
Hungary
New Zealand
United States
Russian Federation
Bulgaria
Latvia
Slovak Republic
Japan
Serbia
Greece
Montenegro
Shanghai-China
Uruguay
Romania
Brazil
Argentina
Chile
Costa Rica
Jordan
Malaysia
Turkey
Kazakhstan
Colombia
Tunisia
Thailand
Peru
Mexico
Indonesia
Viet Nam
0
10
20
30
40
50
60
70
80
90
100 %

1. The difference between the top and the bottom quarter of ESCS is not statistically significant.

Countries and economies are ranked in descending order of the percentage of students in the bottom quarter of ESCS who have a connection to the Internet at home.

Source: OECD, PISA 2012 Database, Table 5.1a.

StatLink http://dx.doi.org/10.1787/888933253149

In most countries, differences in computer access between advantaged and disadvantaged students shrank between 2009 and 2012 (Figure 5.3 and Table 5.1c); in no country did the gap increase. By 2012, in all countries there were at least as many students in the bottom quarter of socio-economic status as in the top quarter who gained access to computers at home. The narrowing of this core digital divide within most countries means that equity in access to ICT has improved over this three-year period.

Despite the narrowing of this gap, the number of computers available at home differs depending on the household's socio-economic status. In Hungary and Poland, for instance, five out of six advantaged students (84%) have two or more computers at home, compared to only one out of four disadvantaged students. On average across OECD countries, 88% of advantaged students have two or more computers at home, compared to 55% of disadvantaged students (Figure 5.3 and Table 5.1a).

The number of locations where people can go on line, and the possibility of accessing online services "on the go" by using handheld devices, continue to be shaped by socio-economic status. In addition, differences in the quantity of ICT resources available are probably compounded by differences in their quality, which is not measured in PISA. It is likely that households with two or more computers possess at least one newer model, whereas households with a single computer may have an older or less powerful model.

■ Figure 5.3 ■

Change between 2009 and 2012 in access to computers and the Internet at home, by socio-economic status

OECD average

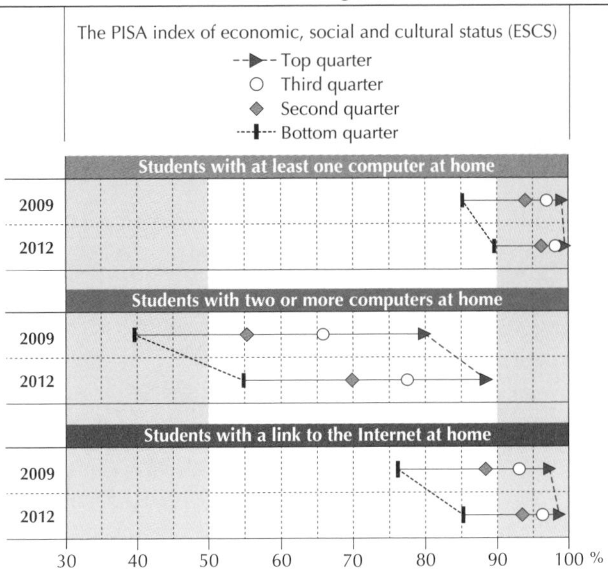
The PISA index of economic, social and cultural status (ESCS)
Top quarter
Third quarter
Second quarter
Bottom quarter
Students with at least one computer at home
Students with two or more computers at home
Students with a link to the Internet at home
2009
2012
30
40
50
60
70
80
90
100 %

Source: OECD, PISA 2012 Database, Tables 5.1a and 5.1b.

StatLink http://dx.doi.org/10.1787/888933253153

That differences in the quantity of computers go hand-in-hand with differences in the ICT services available to students is confirmed by an analysis of unequal access to the Internet. As shown in Figure 5.2, in almost all countries and economies, disadvantaged students reported less Internet access than advantaged students. In countries with relatively little Internet access overall, only the more advantaged students tended to have a connection to the Internet at home. In 40 countries and economies, at least 99% of students in the top quarter of socio-economic status have access to the Internet at home. By contrast, in 15 countries and economies, fewer than one in two students in the bottom quarter of socio-economic status has access to the Internet at home.

Still, on average the gap in Internet access between advantaged and disadvantaged students shrank between 2009 and 2012 (Figure 5.3). It widened only in Indonesia, Kazakhstan, Mexico, Peru and Tunisia, where advantaged students were the main beneficiaries of greater access to the Internet between 2009 and 2012. In all of these countries, fewer than 80% of advantaged students had access to the Internet in 2009 (Tables 5.1a, b and c). These exceptions may thus be the result of different stages in the typical pattern of diffusion of innovation (Rogers, 2010).

Socio-economic and gender differences in early exposure to computers

In 2012, very few students, even among the most disadvantaged, had no experience using computers. But since in many countries/economies the gap in access had closed only recently, disadvantaged students may have less experience using computers than their more advantaged peers do.

On average across OECD countries, only 23% of disadvantaged students had started using computers at the age of 6 or before, as compared to 43% of advantaged students. A similar (and sometimes larger) difference between the two socio-economic groups can be found in all countries that participated in the optional ICT questionnaire. Only in Denmark did more than one in two students from the lowest quarter of socio-economic status start using computers at pre-school age (Figure 5.4).

Similarly, some experience with the Internet is common even among the most disadvantaged students. On average across OECD countries, in 2012 only 1.3% of disadvantaged students had no experience at all using the Internet (Table 5.2).

Nonetheless, some countries have large socio-economic divides in basic use of and experience with computers. In Mexico, the OECD country with the largest inequalities in access to computers, 15% of disadvantaged students had no experience accessing the Internet; of these, a majority (9% of all disadvantaged students) had no experience at all using computers. Only 3% of disadvantaged students in Mexico reported that they first used a computer at age 6 or below (and thus potentially had more than 10 years of experience using computers), compared with 32% of advantaged students (Table 5.2). And socio-economic gaps may be even larger, given that many of the most disadvantaged 15-year-olds in Mexico are not in school anymore.

■ Figure 5.4 ■

Early exposure to computers, by students' socio-economic status

Percentage of students who first used a computer when they were 6 years or younger

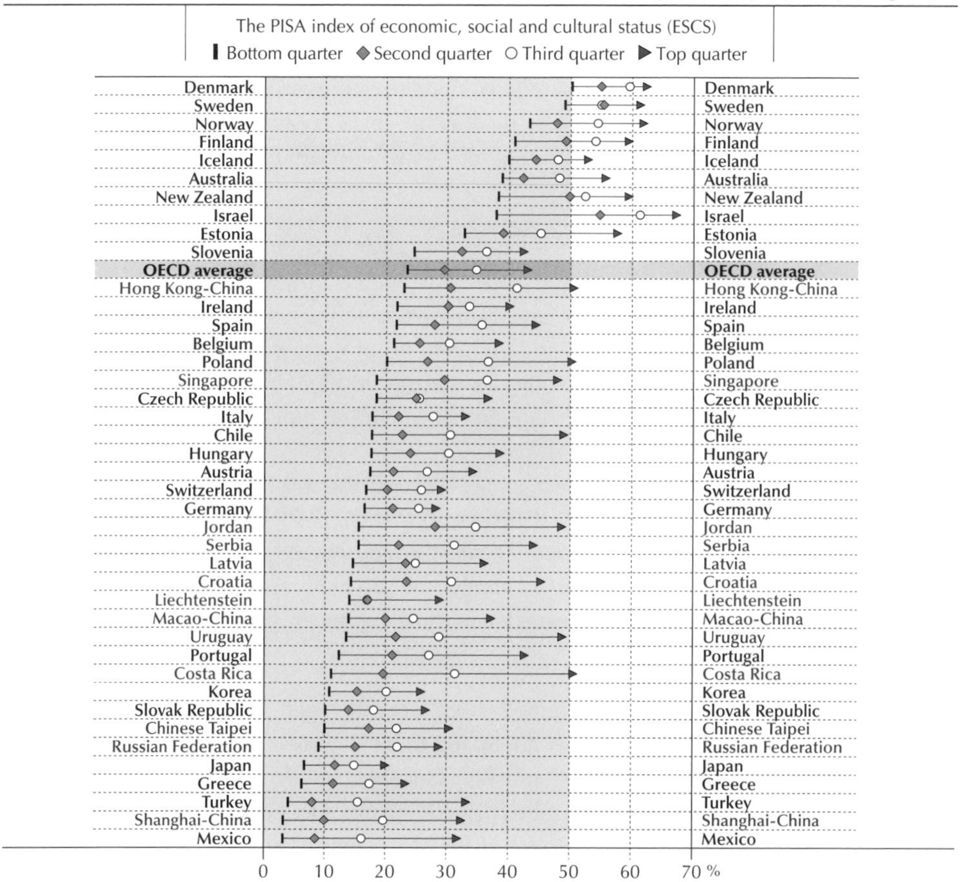
The PISA index of economic, social and cultural status (ESCS)
Bottom quarter
Second quarter
Third quarter
Top quarter
Denmark
Sweden
Norway
Finland
Iceland
Australia
New Zealand
Israel
Estonia
Slovenia
OECD average
Hong Kong-China
Ireland
Spain
Belgium
Poland
Singapore
Czech Republic
Italy
Chile
Hungary
Austria
Switzerland
Germany
Jordan
Serbia
Latvia
Croatia
Liechtenstein
Macao-China
Uruguay
Portugal
Costa Rica
Korea
Slovak Republic
Chinese Taipei
Russian Federation
Japan
Greece
Turkey
Shanghai-China
Mexico
0
10
20
30
40
50
60
70 %

Note: Differences between the top and the bottom quarter of ESCS are statistically significant in all countries and economies.
Countries and economies are ranked in descending order of the percentage of students in the bottom quarter of ESCS who first used a computer when they were 6 years or younger.
Source: OECD, PISA 2012 Database, Table 5.2.
StatLink http://dx.doi.org/10.1787/888933253168

Early exposure to computers and the Internet also differs markedly between boys and girls (Figure 5.5). Boys are significantly more likely than girls to have started using computers early in all but four countries/economies; and in those countries/economies, namely Costa Rica, Hong Kong-China, Japan and New Zealand, the difference is not significant.

The existence of gender gaps in computer experience highlights the importance of non-material barriers in shaping opportunities for digital learning. It is not enough to remove material constraints to ensure that online experiences and skills are equally distributed. Intangible factors, such as cultural norms, count too.

■ Figure 5.5 ■

Early exposure to computers, by gender

Percentage of students who first used a computer when they were 6 years or younger

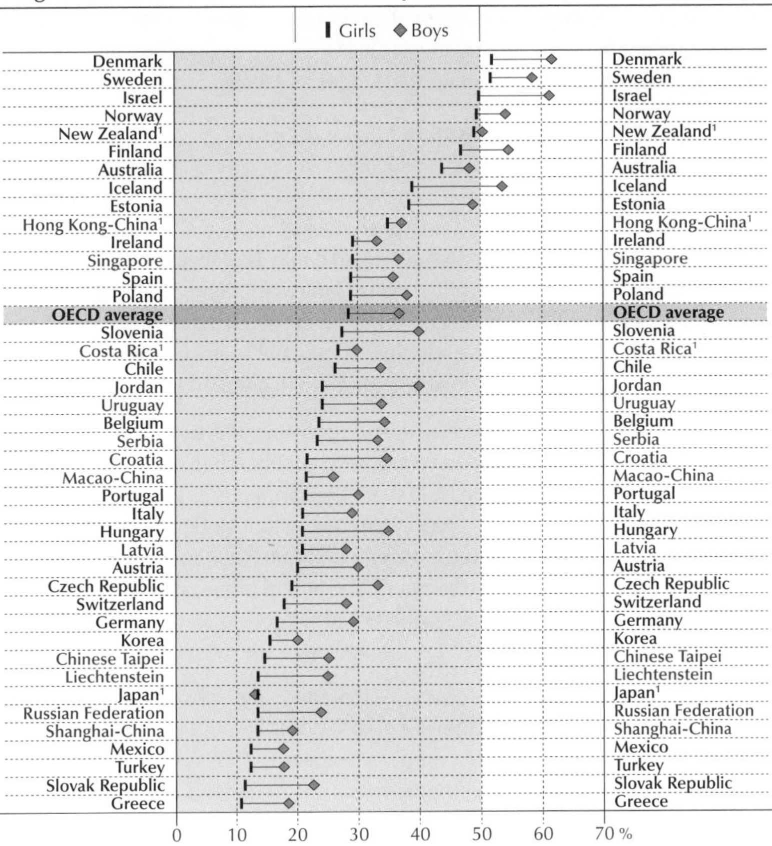

Girls
Boys
Denmark
Sweden
Israel
Norway
New Zealand[1]
Finland
Australia
Iceland
Estonia
Hong Kong-China[1]
Ireland
Singapore
Spain
Poland
OECD average
Slovenia
Costa Rica[1]
Chile
Jordan
Uruguay
Belgium
Serbia
Croatia
Macao-China
Portugal
Italy
Hungary
Latvia
Austria
Czech Republic
Switzerland
Germany
Korea
Chinese Taipei
Liechtenstein
Japan[1]
Russian Federation
Shanghai-China
Mexico
Turkey
Slovak Republic
Greece
0
10
20
30
40
50
60
70 %

1. The difference between boys and girls is not statistically significant.

Countries and economies are ranked in descending order of the percentage of girls who first used a computer when they were 6 years or younger.

Source: OECD, PISA 2012 Database, Table 5.2.

StatLink http://dx.doi.org/10.1787/888933253173

Indeed, given that boys and girls come from all kinds of backgrounds and attend all kinds of schools (at least in countries where participation in schooling at age 15 is universal), differences in their self-reported experience with computers do not reflect material constraints, but rather students' interests and families' and educators' notions about what is suitable for them (see also OECD, 2015). Parents, for instance, may place more restrictions on girls' use of the Internet out of safety concerns.

Gender differences also illustrate the potentially long-lasting consequences of such intangible factors. In restricting girls' access to the Internet more than they do for boys, for instance, parents may undermine girls' feelings of competence. Data from the International Computer and

Information Literacy Study (ICILS) show that in almost all participating countries, girls in the eighth grade feel less confident than boys in their ability to do advanced ICT tasks, such as building a webpage (Fraillon et al., 2014, Table 5.17). Such feelings of incompetence (low self-efficacy) may, in turn, help to explain why, later in life, there are about five times more men than women among those who study computing at the tertiary level (OECD, 2014), or even among those who actively contribute to Wikipedia (Hargittai and Shaw, 2015; Hill and Shaw, 2013).

Rural/urban gaps in Internet access

Because PISA contains information about the location of the school attended by students, rather than the location of the students' home, it can provide only an imprecise picture of rural/urban gaps in access to and use of ICT. Still, PISA data show that in several lower- and middle-income countries, students who attend rural schools have significantly less access to ICT resources at home, particularly when it comes to Internet connections (Tables 5.7a and 5.8). This may be partly the result of poorer fixed and mobile, narrow and broadband infrastructure. The gap in infrastructure is not directly related to students' socio-economic status, but may contribute to socio-economic divides, particularly in countries where poverty is more concentrated in rural, isolated areas.

Data collected from school principals confirm that in several countries, there is a rural/urban divide in connectivity (the possibility of using services offered on line). In Colombia, Indonesia, Mexico and Peru, in particular, rural schools often have as many computers as urban schools, in proportion to the size of their student population. Yet more than one in four students who attend rural schools or schools located in small towns do not have any computer connected to the Internet in their school. By contrast, fewer than one in ten students who attend urban schools do not have access to a computer connected to the Internet at school. In rural schools in these countries, when there are school computers, fewer than half of them are connected to the Internet, on average (Table 5.9a).

A comparison with PISA 2009 identifies countries that made progress in closing rural/urban gaps. In Albania, Indonesia and Uruguay, a large share of schools located in rural areas gained access to an Internet connection for their school computers between 2009 and 2012, possibly as a result of policies to support the economic development of rural areas. As a result, the share of students in rural schools where no computer is connected to the Internet declined rapidly (Table 5.9c).

The role of schools as providers of access to computers and the Internet

In countries where home access to computers and the Internet is strongly related to socio-economic status, schools often play an important role in ensuring that all students have access to ICT resources. In fact, particularly in countries with high levels of income inequality, giving access to ICT resources to all is among the main objectives of ICT policies in education.

In most countries, ICT resources tend to be as good in those schools that serve predominantly disadvantaged students as in more advantaged schools.[1] However, in Costa Rica, Indonesia and Mexico, schools with a disadvantaged student population on average have fewer ICT resources than advantaged schools. A significant share of these disadvantaged schools have no ICT resources at all, higher student/computer ratios, and lower shares of school computers connected to the Internet. In the remaining countries, when there is a difference in the level of ICT resources at school, it is often in favour of disadvantaged schools. In Japan, Korea, Portugal and Tunisia, for instance, there are about half or less than half as many students per computer in disadvantaged schools, compared to advantaged schools (Figure 5.6 and Table 5.5a).

■ Figure 5.6 ■

Student-computer ratio at school, by socio-economic profile of the school

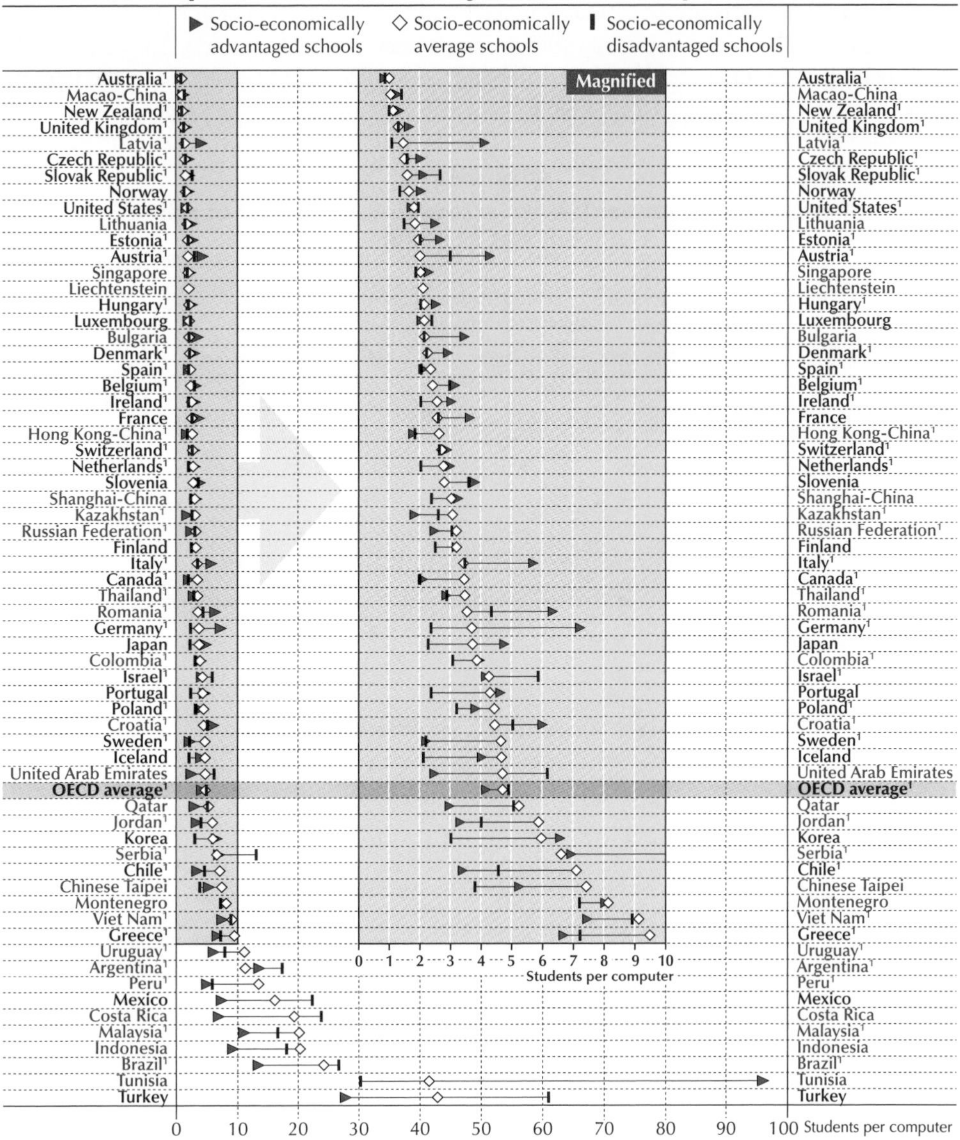
▶ Socio-economically advantaged schools
◇ Socio-economically average schools
❙ Socio-economically disadvantaged schools
Magnified
Australia[1]
Macao-China
New Zealand[1]
United Kingdom[1]
Latvia[1]
Czech Republic[1]
Slovak Republic[1]
Norway
United States[1]
Lithuania
Estonia[1]
Austria[1]
Singapore
Liechtenstein
Hungary[1]
Luxembourg
Bulgaria
Denmark[1]
Spain[1]
Belgium[1]
Ireland[1]
France
Hong Kong-China[1]
Switzerland[1]
Netherlands[1]
Slovenia
Shanghai-China
Kazakhstan[1]
Russian Federation[1]
Finland
Italy[1]
Canada[1]
Thailand[1]
Romania[1]
Germany[1]
Japan
Colombia[1]
Israel[1]
Portugal
Poland[1]
Croatia[1]
Sweden[1]
Iceland
United Arab Emirates
OECD average[1]
Qatar
Jordan[1]
Korea
Serbia[1]
Chile[1]
Chinese Taipei
Montenegro
Viet Nam[1]
Greece[1]
Uruguay[1]
Argentina[1]
Peru[1]
Mexico
Costa Rica
Malaysia[1]
Indonesia
Brazil[1]
Tunisia
Turkey
0 1 2 3 4 5 6 7 8 9 10
Students per computer
0 10 20 30 40 50 60 70 80 90 100 Students per computer

1. The difference between socio-economically advantaged and disadvantaged schools is not statistically significant.

Notes: See Note 1 at the end of this chapter for the definition of socio-economically disadvantaged and advantaged schools. Only schools with at least 10 students in the national modal grade for 15-year-olds are included. The number of students per computer is based on principals' reports about the number of students in the national modal grade for 15-year-olds and on the number of computers available for these students. In schools where no computer is available, the number of students per computer is set at the number of students reported by the principal plus 1.

Countries and economies are ranked in ascending order of the student-computer ratio in schools with an average socio-economic profile.

Source: OECD, PISA 2012 Database, Table 5.5a.

StatLink http://dx.doi.org/10.1787/888933253186

Many disadvantaged students can access computers and the Internet only at school. In Costa Rica, Mexico and Turkey, in particular, more than a third of the most disadvantaged students (those in the bottom quartile of socio-economic status) have access to computers at school, but not at home. Similarly, among the most disadvantaged students, 50% of students in Turkey, 45% in Mexico, 40% in Jordan and 38% in Chile and Costa Rica only have access to the Internet thanks to their school (Figure 5.7 and Table 5.4a).

■ Figure 5.7 ■

Percentage of students with access to the Internet at school, but not at home

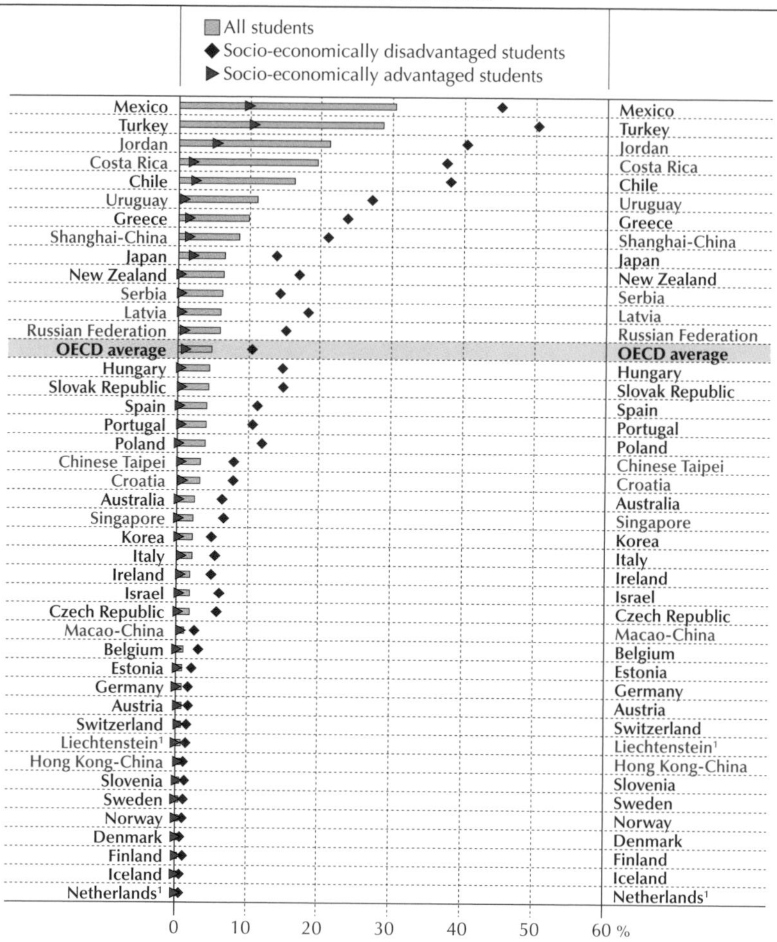
All students
Socio-economically disadvantaged students
Socio-economically advantaged students
Mexico
Turkey
Jordan
Costa Rica
Chile
Uruguay
Greece
Shanghai-China
Japan
New Zealand
Serbia
Latvia
Russian Federation
OECD average
Hungary
Slovak Republic
Spain
Portugal
Poland
Chinese Taipei
Croatia
Australia
Singapore
Korea
Italy
Ireland
Israel
Czech Republic
Macao-China
Belgium
Estonia
Germany
Austria
Switzerland
Liechtenstein¹
Hong Kong-China
Slovenia
Sweden
Norway
Denmark
Finland
Iceland
Netherlands¹
0
10
20
30
40
50
60 %

1. The difference between socio-economically advantaged and disadvantaged students is not statistically significant.
Note: Socio-economically disadvantaged/advantaged students refers to students in the bottom/top quarter of the *PISA index of economic, social and cultural status.*
Countries and economies are ranked in descending order of the percentage of all students who reported having access to an Internet connection at school, but not at home.
Source: OECD, PISA 2012 Database, Table 5.4a.
StatLink http://dx.doi.org/10.1787/888933253199

Still, with the rapid expansion of home ICT resources observed in many countries, the role of schools in creating equitable access is no longer as important as in 2009. In that year, more than half of the most disadvantaged students in Chile, Jordan, the Russian Federation, Turkey and Uruguay had access to the Internet at school, but not at home (Table 5.4b).

DIFFERENCES IN COMPUTER USE RELATED TO SOCIO-ECONOMIC STATUS

This section explores differences in students' use of computers across socio-economic groups. As the divides in access to digital media and resources are closing rapidly – at least in high-income countries – research has started focusing on other aspects of digital inequality (see e.g. Attewell, 2001; Natriello, 2001; Dimaggio et al., 2004; Van Dijk 2005). As Gui (2007) notes, what people do with media is more important than the technologies and connectivity available to them – and also more resistant to change. Indeed, when all barriers that prevent access to new media have been removed, how people use new media still depends on individuals' level of skill, including basic literacy skills, and social support, which vary across socio-economic groups.

Computer use at home

Computer use by students can be first characterised by the amount of time that students spend on line. PISA data show that, on average across OECD countries, the amount of time that students spend on line during weekends does not differ across socio-economic groups. Interestingly, a reverse gap – whereby students from poorer families spend more time on line than students from wealthier families – is observed in 16 out of 29 OECD countries. Disadvantaged students spend at least 15 more minutes per day on line during weekends, compared to advantaged students, in Belgium, Germany, Korea, Shanghai-China, Switzerland and Chinese Taipei (Table 5.12).

Similarly, when the frequency and variety of computer use for leisure, outside of school, are summarised in an index, differences are mostly limited to countries with large gaps in access. In Costa Rica, Jordan and Mexico, the most advantaged students (those from the top quarter of socio-economic status) use computers for leisure more than the OECD average, while students from the bottom quarter are more than one standard deviation below this benchmark. At the same time, in Belgium, Finland, Germany, Sweden, Switzerland and Chinese Taipei, there are no significant differences across socio-economic groups in the average value of the *index of ICT use outside of school for leisure* (Table 5.10).

Yet the specific activities for which students use computers in their free time differ across socio-economic groups. In general, disadvantaged students tend to prefer chat over e-mail, and to play video games rather than read the news or obtain practical information from the Internet (Figure 5.8).

While across OECD countries, a similar proportion of advantaged students (70%) uses e-mail or chats on line at least once a week, on average, the share of disadvantaged students who chat on line (65%) is significantly larger than share of those who use e-mail (56%). And while in most countries/economies there are no differences related to socio-economic status in the use of video games, the influence of socio-economic status is strong when it comes to reading news or obtaining practical information from the Internet (Figure 5.8).

■ Figure 5.8 ■

Common computer leisure activities outside of school, by students' socio-economic status

OECD average values and values for selected countries

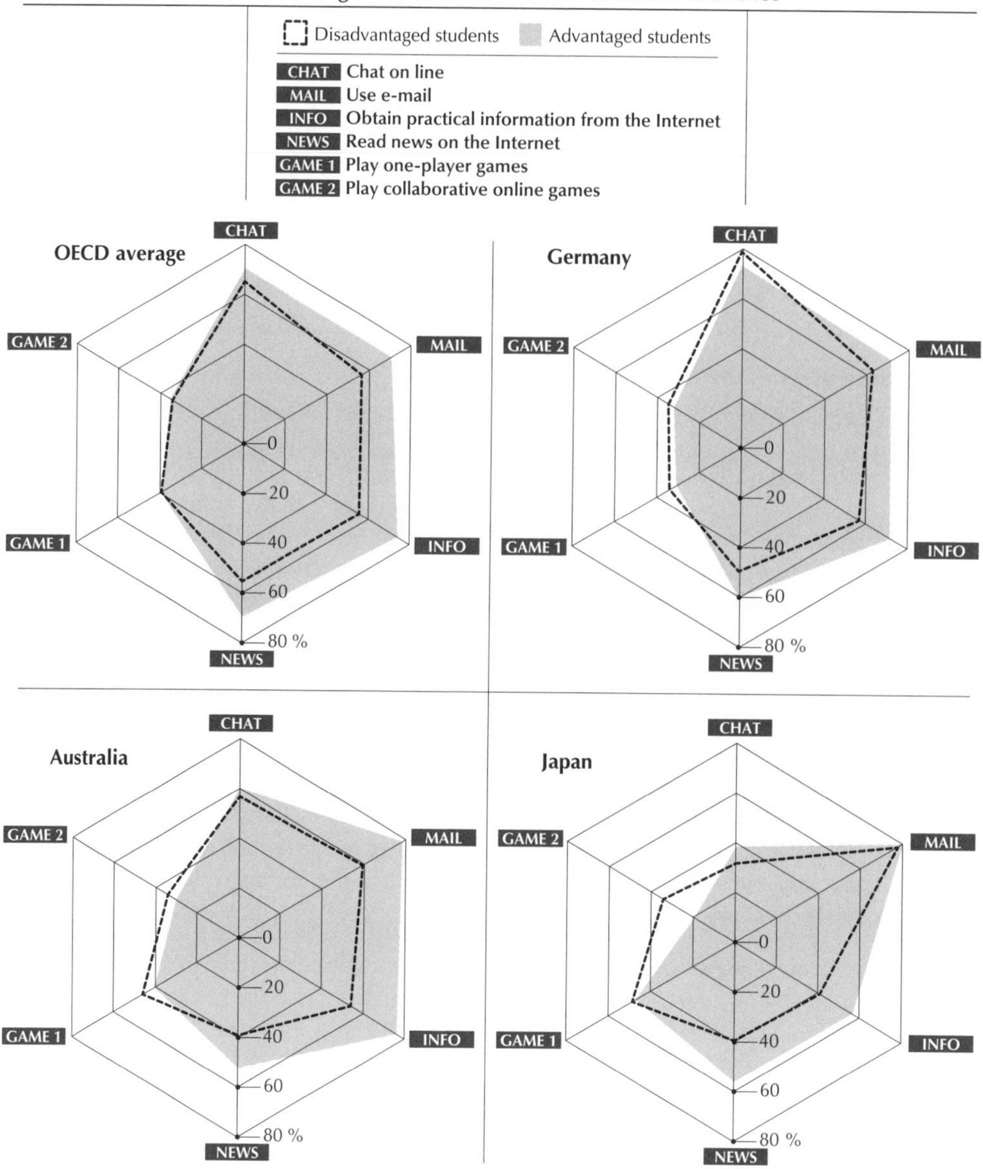
Disadvantaged students
Advantaged students
CHAT Chat on line
MAIL Use e-mail
INFO Obtain practical information from the Internet
NEWS Read news on the Internet
GAME 1 Play one-player games
GAME 2 Play collaborative online games
OECD average
Germany
Australia
Japan
CHAT
MAIL
INFO
NEWS
GAME 1
GAME 2
0
20
40
60
80 %

Notes: The figure shows the percentage of students who engage in each of the selected activities at least once a week. Socio-economically disadvantaged/advantaged students refers to students in the bottom/top quarter of the *PISA index of economic, social and cultural status*.

Source: OECD, PISA 2012 Database, Table 5.11.

StatLink http://dx.doi.org/10.1787/888933253203

Differences in ICT use according to socio-economic groups among 15-year-olds are related to similar differences found in the adult population. An early survey of Swiss adults, for instance, found that more educated people use the Internet more for finding information, whereas less educated adults seem to be particularly interested in the entertainment aspects of the Internet (Bonfadelli, 2002). More recently, a survey in the Netherlands found that low-educated Internet users spent more time on line in their spare time, but those with higher social status used the Internet in more beneficial ways. While more educated people looked for information and personal development opportunities, less educated people spent more time gaming or chatting (Van Deursen and Van Dijk, 2014). The similarity of findings across age groups suggests that socio-economic differences in the use of the Internet and the ability to benefit from its many resources – the so-called second-order digital divide – are closely linked with wider social inequalities.

Computer use at school

When it comes to using ICT at school, differences related to students' socio-economic status are often smaller than those observed when considering ICT use outside of school. In 11 countries and economies, socio-economically disadvantaged students use computers at school more than the most advantaged students. The opposite is true in 10 countries/economies, while in 21 countries and economies, and on average across OECD countries, the difference in computer use between the two groups is not significant (Table 5.10).

During mathematics instruction, disadvantaged students often get more exposure to computers than advantaged students. The use of computers for mathematics teaching and learning (and for other core subjects) may first be introduced in the most challenging classrooms, either because educational disadvantage justifies the extra cost of introducing such tools, or because in these situations teachers and parents are keener to experiment these tools. In five countries and economies, however, advantaged students use ICT in mathematics classes more frequently than disadvantaged students. Denmark and Norway, where the use of computers in mathematics lessons is relatively common, are among these countries (Table 5.10).

HOW PERFORMANCE ON COMPUTER-BASED TESTS IS RELATED TO SOCIO-ECONOMIC STATUS AND FAMILIARITY WITH COMPUTERS

Across all domains assessed in PISA, socio-economic status bears a strong influence on the performance of students; and, as shown above, in some countries disadvantaged students have limited access to ICT devices or less experience in using them. How does the strength of the relationship between the *PISA index of economic, social and cultural status* (ESCS) and performance vary across computer- and paper-based assessments? What does this imply for the relationship between digital skills and familiarity with computers and their uses?

Disparities in performance related to socio-economic status

In the assessment of digital reading and the computer-based assessment of mathematics alike, differences in the *PISA index of economic, social and cultural status* (ESCS) account for 12% of the variation in performance, on average across OECD countries. This is slightly less than in print reading (13%) and significantly less than in mathematics (15%). The impact of socio-economic status on performance is thus weaker in computer-based assessments than in paper-based assessments (Figure 5.9).

■ Figure 5.9 ■

Strength of the relationship between socio-economic status and performance in digital reading and computer-based mathematics

Variation in performance explained by socio-economic status

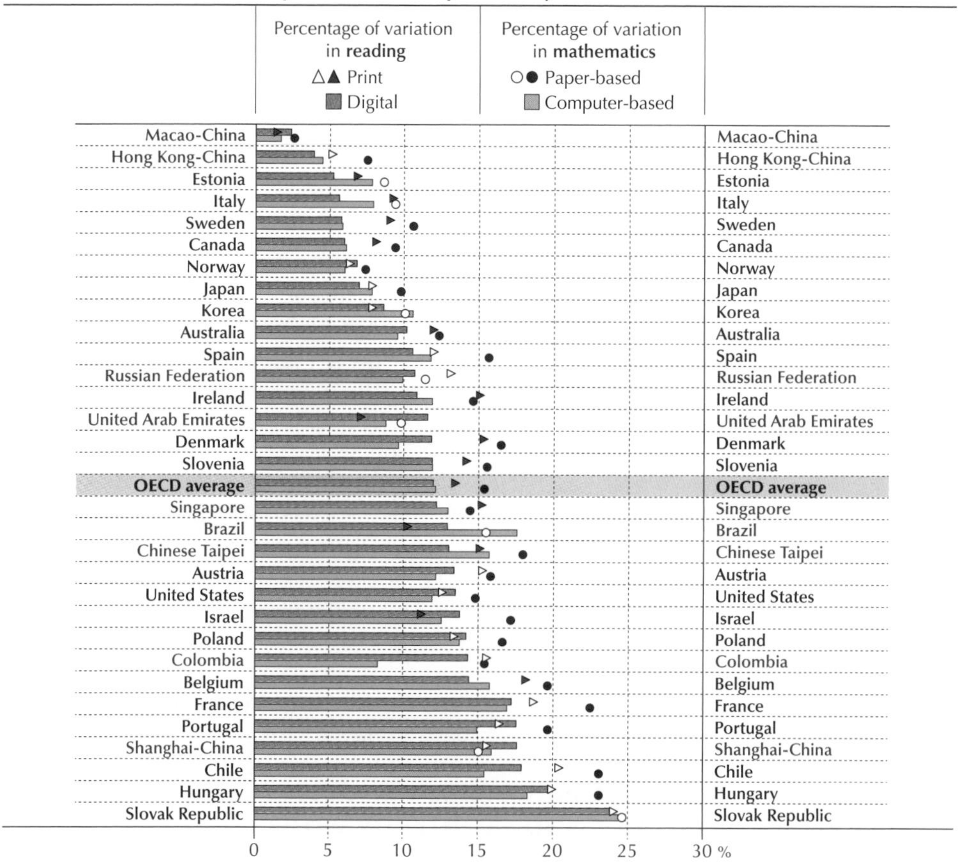
Percentage of variation in reading
Print
Digital
Percentage of variation in mathematics
Paper-based
Computer-based
Macao-China
Hong Kong-China
Estonia
Italy
Sweden
Canada
Norway
Japan
Korea
Australia
Spain
Russian Federation
Ireland
United Arab Emirates
Denmark
Slovenia
OECD average
Singapore
Brazil
Chinese Taipei
Austria
United States
Israel
Poland
Colombia
Belgium
France
Portugal
Shanghai-China
Chile
Hungary
Slovak Republic
0
5
10
15
20
25
30 %

Note: Hollow markers identify countries/economies where the strength of the relationship between the *PISA index of economic, social and cultural status* and performance is not significantly different between computer-based assessments and paper-based assessments of the respective domains.

Countries and economies are ranked in ascending order of the strength of the relationship between performance in digital reading and the PISA index of economic, social and cultural status.

Source: OECD, PISA 2012 Database, Table 5.14.

StatLink http://dx.doi.org/10.1787/888933253212

Furthermore, Figure 5.10 shows that the relationship between socio-economic status and performance on computer-based assessments mostly reflects differences observed in performance on paper-based assessments. On average, students who attain a certain score in PISA mathematics perform equally well in the paper-based and computer-based assessments, regardless of their socio-economic status. In digital reading, small differences in performance remain among students who attain the same score in the paper-based assessment of reading, but come from different socio-economic backgrounds.

In the computer-based assessment of mathematics, in particular, there is little evidence of a specific association between socio-economic status and performance. The observed relationship is accounted for by differences in students' performance in the paper-based mathematics assessment related to socio-economic status. After accounting for such differences, a significant relationship with the *PISA index of economic, social and cultural status* remains in only 4 out of 32 countries/economies (Table 5.15). This implies that differences in performance, related to socio-economic status, in the computer-based assessment of mathematics do not stem from differences in the ability to use computers, but in differences in mathematics proficiency.

By contrast, in digital reading, differences in reading proficiency across socio-economic groups only partially account for differences in performance in digital reading. A small, direct association between socio-economic status and digital reading performance is observed. This direct association most likely stems from differences in navigation and evaluation skills – i.e. those components of reading that are emphasised to a greater extent when reading on line than when reading print. Even in digital reading, however, this direct association accounts for only 0.5% of the variation in performance, while the indirect association (through the effect of socio-economic status on print reading skills) accounts for 11.5% of the variation.

■ Figure 5.10 ■

Relationship among analogue skills, socio-economic status, and performance in computer-based assessments

Variation in performance on computer-based assessments explained by socio-economic status; direct and indirect effects (OECD average)

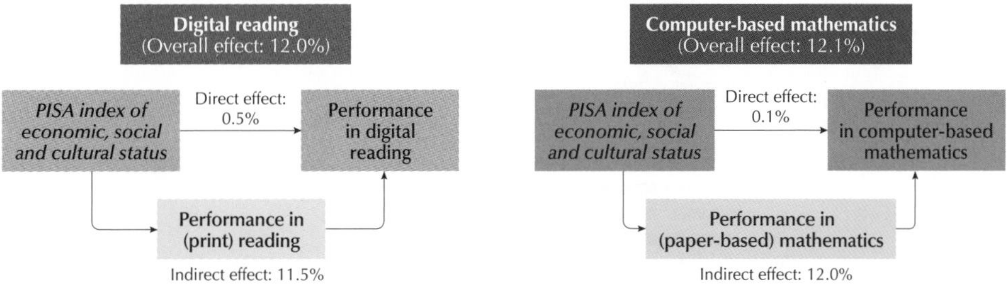
Digital reading
(Overall effect: 12.0%)
PISA index of economic, social and cultural status
Direct effect: 0.5%
Performance in digital reading
Performance in (print) reading
Indirect effect: 11.5%
Computer-based mathematics
(Overall effect: 12.1%)
PISA index of economic, social and cultural status
Direct effect: 0.1%
Performance in computer-based mathematics
Performance in (paper-based) mathematics
Indirect effect: 12.0%

Note: The figure shows that socio-economic status explains 12.0% of the variation in digital reading performance. This is largely the result of the association between socio-economic status and performance in print reading. Only 0.5% of the variation in performance in digital reading is uniquely associated with socio-economic status.
Source: OECD, PISA 2012 Database, Table 5.15.

Previous sections showed that, in their free time, students from the top quarter of socio-economic status read on line and use the Internet to obtain practical information more than disadvantaged students do, even in countries where advantaged and disadvantaged students spend similar amounts of time on line. PISA data cannot show whether reading more on line results in better online reading skills, or the reverse. What they do show, however, is that the differences in use are highly related to differences in students' skills.

Trends in the relationship between digital reading performance and socio-economic status

By analysing how the relationship between digital reading performance and socio-economic status has evolved over time, it is possible to assess whether the bridging of the so-called first digital divide – the fact that access to ICT is now almost universal – also translated into a reduction of the second digital divide – the fact that socio-economic status still has an impact on how well students can use new tools.

Figure 5.11 reports trends in equity for digital reading. In Belgium, Colombia and Poland, where socio-economic status had a strong impact on performance in digital reading in 2009, and in Sweden, the relationship weakened considerably by 2012. In none of these countries was a similar trend observed for print reading (Table 5.16). Meanwhile, in all four countries where equity in digital reading performance improved between 2009 and 2012, equity in access to ICT at home also improved (Figure 5.12).

■ Figure 5.11 ■

Trends in the relationship between digital reading performance and socio-economic status

Variation in digital reading performance explained by socio-economic status (PISA 2009 and PISA 2012)

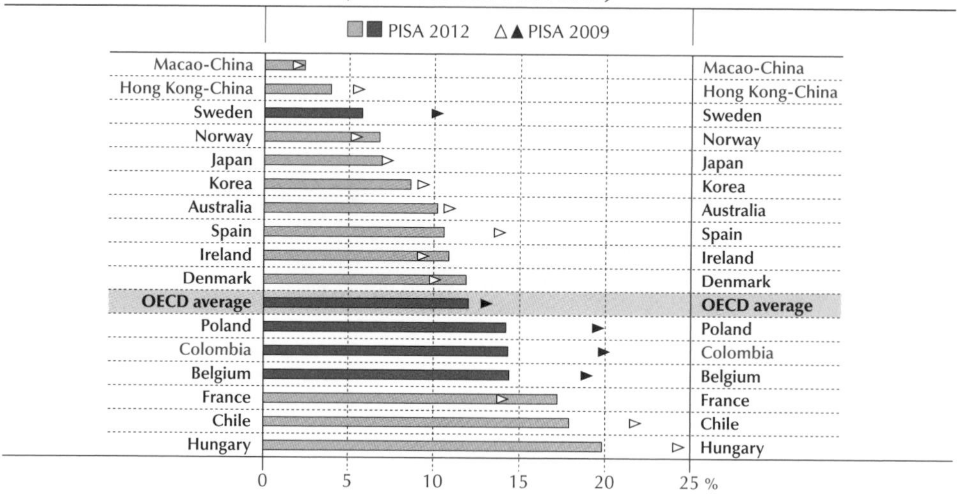
PISA 2012
PISA 2009
Macao-China
Hong Kong-China
Sweden
Norway
Japan
Korea
Australia
Spain
Ireland
Denmark
OECD average
Poland
Colombia
Belgium
France
Chile
Hungary
0
5
10
15
20
25 %

Notes: Countries/economies where the difference between PISA 2009 and PISA 2012 in the percentage of variation in digital reading performance explained by the *PISA index of economic, social and cultural status* is significant is marked in a darker tone. The OECD average refers only to OECD countries represented in this chart.
Countries and economies are ranked in ascending order of the strength of the relationship between performance in digital reading and the PISA index of economic, social and cultural status.
Source: OECD, PISA 2012 Database, Table 5.16.
StatLink http://dx.doi.org/10.1787/888933253226

This suggests that greater equity in digital reading was mostly achieved by reducing the specific impact of socio-economic status on digital skills, rather than the general impact of socio-economic status on reading performance.

■ Figure 5.12 ■

Change between 2009 and 2012 in the "digital access divide" and "digital reading divide"

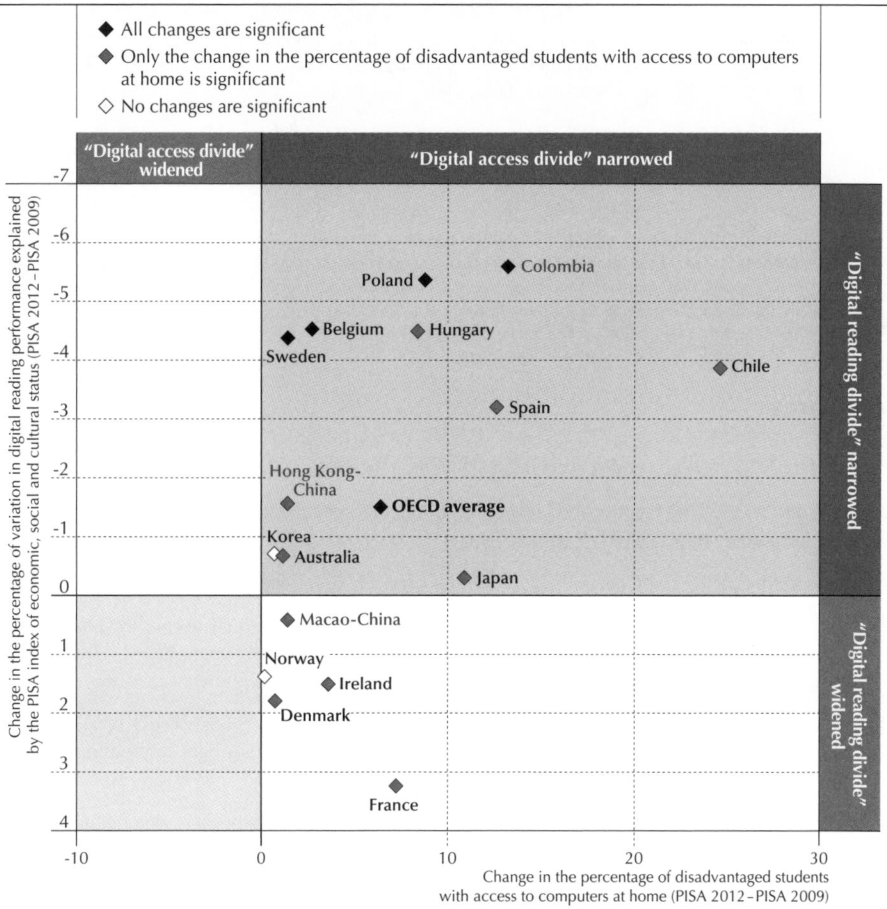
◆ All changes are significant
◆ Only the change in the percentage of disadvantaged students with access to computers at home is significant
◇ No changes are significant
"Digital access divide" widened
"Digital access divide" narrowed
"Digital reading divide" narrowed
"Digital reading divide" widened
Change in the percentage of variation in digital reading performance explained by the PISA index of economic, social and cultural status (PISA 2012 - PISA 2009)
Change in the percentage of disadvantaged students with access to computers at home (PISA 2012 - PISA 2009)
Colombia
Poland
Belgium
Hungary
Sweden
Chile
Spain
Hong Kong-China
OECD average
Korea
Australia
Japan
Macao-China
Norway
Ireland
Denmark
France
-7
-6
-5
-4
-3
-2
-1
0
1
2
3
4
-10
0
10
20
30

Notes: "Disadvantaged students" refers to students in the bottom quarter of the *PISA index of economic, social and cultural status.* The OECD average refers only to OECD countries represented in this chart.
Source: OECD, PISA 2012 Database, Table 5.16.
StatLink http://dx.doi.org/10.1787/888933253235

Note

1. Socio-economically disadvantaged and advantaged schools are identified within individual school systems by comparing the average socio-economic status of the students in the system and the average socio-economic status of the students in each school, using the *PISA index of economic, social and cultural status* (ESCS). Socio-economically disadvantaged schools are those where the school mean ESCS is significantly lower than the country average ESCS (see OECD, 2013, Box IV.3.1).

Chapter 5 tables are available on line at http://dx.doi.org/10.1787/edu-data-en.

Note regarding Israel

The statistical data for Israel are supplied by and under the responsibility of the relevant Israeli authorities. The use of such data by the OECD is without prejudice to the status of the Golan Heights, East Jerusalem and Israeli settlements in the West Bank under the terms of international law.

References

Attewell, P. (2001), "The first and second digital divides", *Sociology of Education*, Vol. 74/3, pp. 252-259.

Bonfadelli, H. (2002), "The Internet and knowledge gaps a theoretical and empirical investigation", *European Journal of Communication,* Vol. 17/1, pp. 65-84.

Compaine, B.M. (2001), *The Digital Divide: Facing a Crisis Or Creating a Myth?*, MIT Press.

Dimaggio, P., E. Hargittai, C. Celeste and **S. Shafer** (2004), "From unequal access to differentiated use: A literature review and agenda for research on digital inequality", in Neckerman, K. (ed.), *Social Inequality*, Russell Sage Foundation, pp. 355-400.

Fraillon, J., J. Ainley, W. Schulz, T. Friedman, and **E. Gebhardt** (2014), "Students' use of and engagement with ICT at home and school", In *Preparing for Life in a Digital Age*, Springer International Publishing, pp. 125-166.

Gui, M. (2007), "Formal and substantial internet information skills: The role of socio-demographic differences on the possession of different components of digital literacy", *First Monday, Vol.* 12/9.

Hargittai, E. and **Y.P. Hsieh** (2013), "Digital inequality", in W.H. Dutton (ed.), *Oxford Handbook of Internet Studies*, Oxford University Press, pp. 129-150.

Hargittai, E. and **A. Shaw** (2015), "Mind the skills gap: The role of internet know-how and gender in differentiated contributions to Wikipedia", *Information, Communication & Society,* Vol. 18/4, pp. 424-442.

Hill, B.M. and **A. Shaw** (2013), "The Wikipedia gender gap revisited: Characterizing survey response bias with propensity score estimation", *PLoS one*, Vol. 8/6.

Natriello, G. (2001), "Bridging the second digital divide: What can sociologists of education contribute?", *Sociology of Education,* Vol. 74/4, pp. 260-265.

OECD (2015), *The ABC of Gender Equality in Education: Aptitude, Behaviour, Confidence*, PISA, OECD Publishing, Paris, http://dx.doi.org/10.1787/9789264229945-en.

OECD (2014), "Indicator C3 How many students are expected to enter tertiary education?", in OECD, *Education at a Glance 2014: OECD Indicators*, OECD Publishing, Paris, http://dx.doi.org/10.1787/eag-2014-24-en.

OECD (2013), *PISA 2012 Results: What Makes Schools Successful (Volume IV): Resources, Policies and Practices*, PISA, OECD Publishing, Paris, http://dx.doi.org/10.1787/9789264201156-en.

OECD (2001), "Understanding the Digital Divide", *OECD Digital Economy Papers*, No. 49, OECD Publishing, Paris, http://dx.doi.org/10.1787/236405667766.

Rogers, E.M. (2010), *Diffusion of Innovations,* 4th edition, Simon ans Schuster, New York.

Stern, M.J., A.E. Adams, and **S. Elsasser** (2009), "Digital inequality and place: The effects of technological diffusion on internet proficiency and usage across rural, suburban, and urban counties", *Sociological Inquiry,* Vol. 79/4, pp. 391-417.

Van Deursen, A.J.A.M. and **J.A.G.M., Van Dijk** (2014), "The digital divide shifts to differences in usage", *New Media & Society*, Vol. 16/3, pp. 507-526.

Van Dijk, J.A.G.M. (2005), *The Deepening Divide: Inequality in the Information Society*, SAGE Publications.

6

How Computers are Related to Students' Performance

Despite considerable investments in computers, Internet connections and software for educational use, there is little solid evidence that greater computer use among students leads to better scores in mathematics and reading. This chapter examines the relationship among computer access in schools, computer use in classrooms, and performance in the PISA assessment.

In the past 15 years, schools and families around the world spent a substantial amount of money on computers, Internet connections, and software for educational use. Yet the benefits of these investments for children's learning are not clear. While relatively abundant research has evaluated the effects of public investments in computers for education on education outcomes, more often than not these evaluations fail to identify any positive association between an increase in computer use and better test scores in mathematics and reading (see Bulman and Fairlie [forthcoming] for a recent review).

A better understanding of how computers affect education outcomes is thus critical for investing in education technology. This chapter explores the relationship among computer access in schools, computer use in classrooms, and performance in PISA assessments.

What the data tell us

- Resources invested in ICT for education are not linked to improved student achievement in reading, mathematics or science.
- In countries where it is less common for students to use the Internet at school for schoolwork, students' performance in reading improved more rapidly than in countries where such use is more common, on average.
- Overall, the relationship between computer use at school and performance is graphically illustrated by a hill shape, which suggests that limited use of computers at school may be better than no use at all, but levels of computer use above the current OECD average are associated with significantly poorer results.

PISA allows for analysing relationships between performance and computer access and use across countries/economies as well as within education systems, across students and schools. The strength of PISA data lies in the wide range of contexts covered. However, in non-experimental, cross-sectional data such as those gathered through PISA, even sophisticated statistical techniques cannot isolate the cause-and-effect relationship among computer access and use of computers, on the one hand, and performance, on the other. With this data, patterns of correlation can be identified, but these must be interpreted carefully, because several alternative explanations could give rise to similar patterns. Box 6.1 discusses in greater detail the problem of identifying causal relationships between computer investments and education outcomes.

This chapter interprets the findings of analyses on PISA data in light of the findings in the wider literature. Experimental findings that can clearly identify causal links in the relationship between computer access and use and academic performance are highlighted in the discussion.

TECHNOLOGY INVESTMENTS AND TRADE-OFFS

When comparing countries/economies whose schools vary in their information and communication technology (ICT) resources, it is important to keep in mind that countries/economies often vary, in related ways, across other dimensions as well. Likewise within countries, differences in the ICT resources of schools may be related to other differences across schools.

Box 6.1. **Interpreting relationships among performance, computer access and use of computers at the system, school and student levels**

Using PISA data, it is possible to relate students' performance to their exposure to computers, as reported by the students themselves or by school principals. It is also possible, at the system level, to relate aggregate indicators of education outcomes to students' average level of exposure to computers within a system – a proxy measure for a country's/economy's effort in integrating information and communication technology (ICT) in education.

There may be several explanations for observing strong relationships between student performance and exposure to computers. These relationships could reflect a cause-and-effect association between computer access/use and performance; but they could also reflect the inverse relationship, whereby (expected) performance drives investment in computers. Countries, schools and families that are less satisfied with their students' performance, for instance, may choose to invest more in new tools or be keener to experiment them in the hope of improving these results. Even in the absence of causal links, these relationships could reflect associations of computer access and use with other variables, such as the resources available, the difficulty of attracting good teachers, etc., which are themselves related to performance.

Within school systems, the main obstacle to interpreting associations as cause-and-effect is the non-random allocation of computers to students, schools, school types and school tracks. Nothing guarantees that students who are more exposed to computers can be compared with students who are less exposed, and that the observed performance differences can be attributed to such differences in exposure. Even when comparing students of similar socio-economic status, those schools and students that have and use computers more differ in several observable and non-observable ways from those that have more limited access to computers, or use them less. For instance, greater availability of computers at school may reflect a principal's capacity to raise funds, the teachers' willingness to lead change, or other principal and teacher characteristics that could not be accounted for in a non-experimental analysis. What students do with computers also depends on what they are able to do, i.e. their level of skill. Non-random selection and reverse causality thus plague within-country analyses, even after accounting for observable differences across students and schools.

The analyses that relate the overall performance of school systems to investments in computers and connectivity, or to levels of computer use at school, run into similar difficulties. A cross-country correlation is a simple measure of the degree to which two variables are associated with each other, but does not prove a causal link between the two, nor the direction of this link. While the correlations are examined after accounting for differences in per capita income, other factors beyond a country's/economy's income level could be related to these variables and explain the association.

In particular, ICT resources are related to the resources available for schools. Countries with low expenditures on education, and low per capita income, tend to have fewer computers per student in their schools than countries with high expenditures on education (Figure 6.1).

■ Figure 6.1 ■

Number of computers available to students and expenditure on education

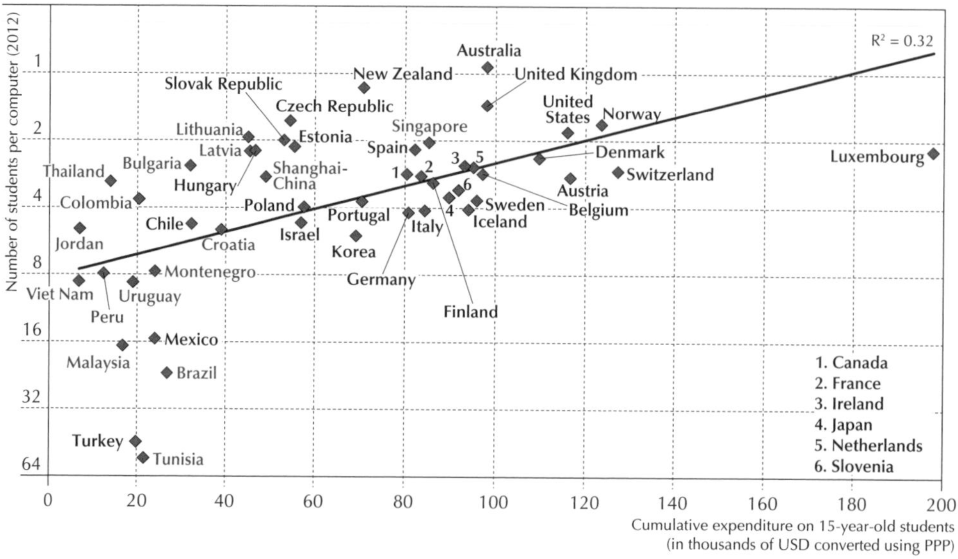
Number of students per computer (2012)
1
2
4
8
16
32
64
$R^2 = 0.32$
Australia
New Zealand
United Kingdom
Slovak Republic
Czech Republic
United States
Norway
Lithuania
Estonia
Singapore
Latvia
Spain
Denmark
Luxembourg
Bulgaria
Shanghai-China
Thailand
Hungary
Switzerland
Austria
Colombia
Poland
Portugal
Sweden
Belgium
Iceland
Chile
Israel
Italy
Jordan
Croatia
Korea
Montenegro
Germany
Viet Nam
Uruguay
Peru
Finland
Mexico
Malaysia
Brazil
Turkey
Tunisia
1. Canada
2. France
3. Ireland
4. Japan
5. Netherlands
6. Slovenia
0
20
40
60
80
100
120
140
160
180
200
Cumulative expenditure on 15-year-old students
(in thousands of USD converted using PPP)

Notes: The horizontal axis reports the cumulative expenditure by educational institutions per student from age 6 to 15, in equivalent USD converted using PPP for GDP. Data for most countries refer to 2010.
Source: OECD, PISA 2012 Database, Table IV.3.1 (OECD, 2013) and Table 2.11.
StatLink http://dx.doi.org/10.1787/888933253247

While investments in computer hardware, software and connectivity appear to increase with the resources spent on education, it is also clear that these investments compete for resources with other priorities. For a given level of resources at the country level, money spent on equipping schools with ICT could have been used for hiring additional teachers, increasing their salaries or investing in their professional development, or spent on other educational resources, such as textbooks. When interpreting the relationship between ICT investments and students' performance in terms of costs and benefits, it is important to include, among the costs, the forgone benefits of alternative uses of money (what economists refer to as the opportunity cost).

Similarly, computer use in classrooms and at home can displace other activities that are conducive to learning, or, instead, increase learning time by reducing recreational time or non-productive uses of classroom time. The net effect of computer use in classrooms and at home is likely to depend on whether computers displace other learning activities or, instead, increase the overall time that is spent learning or the effectiveness of learning processes.

HOW LEARNING OUTCOMES ARE RELATED TO COUNTRIES'/ECONOMIES' INVESTMENTS IN SCHOOL ICT RESOURCES

Figure 6.2 draws a complex picture of the relationship between countries'/economies' performance in PISA and the average level of access to and use of computers at school. While a few of the associations are positive, many correlations are negative, particularly in analyses that account for a country's/economy's income level.

Across countries and economies, the amount of ICT resources available to students is positively related to students' performance. However, much of this association reflects the overall amount of educational resources available to students, as well as school systems' past levels of performance. The strength of the relationship weakens considerably when adjusting the level of ICT resources for the variation in per capita income across countries/economies, and becomes mildly negative when also controlling for the system's average performance in earlier PISA assessments (Figure 6.2).

In fact, PISA data show that for a given level of per capita GDP and after accounting for initial levels of performance, countries that have invested less in introducing computers in school have improved faster, on average, than countries that have invested more. Results are similar across reading, mathematics and science (Figure 6.2).

Figure 6.3, for instance, shows that, between 2003 and 2012, students' performance in mathematics deteriorated in most countries that had reduced their student-computer ratios over the same period (after accounting for differences in per capita GDP).

One possibility is that such school resources were, in fact, not used for learning. But overall, even mesures of ICT use in classrooms and schools show often negative associations with student performance. Average reading proficiency, for instance, is not higher in countries where students more frequently browse the Internet for schoolwork at school. Figure 6.4 shows that in countries where it is more common for students to use the Internet at school for schoolwork, students' performance in reading declined, on average. Similarly, mathematics proficiency tends to be lower in countries/economies where the share of students who use computers in mathematics lessons is larger (Figure 6.2).

An alternative possibility is that resources invested in equipping schools with digital technology may have benefitted other learning outcomes, such as "digital" skills, transitions into the labour market, or other skills different from reading, mathematics and science.

However, the associations with ICT access/use are weak, and sometimes negative, even when results in digital reading or computer-based mathematics are examined, rather than results in paper-based tests (Figure 6.2). In addition, even specific digital reading competencies do not appear to be higher in countries where browsing the Internet for schoolwork is more frequent.

The average quality of students' online navigation, as measured through the *index of task-oriented browsing*, is unrelated to the share of students who frequently use the Internet at school (Figure 6.2). The *index of task-oriented browsing* reflects students' ability to plan and regulate their navigation behaviour on line, and to anticipate, by making an inference based on the available information, whether the target of a link is relevant or not to the task.

■ Figure 6.2 ■

Relationship between students' performance and computer access/use at school

Across all countries and economies

	Mean student performance in PISA 2012				Trends in student performance (annualised change)		Quality of navigation (mean index of task-oriented browsing)
	Mathematics	Reading	Computer-based mathematics	Digital reading	Mathematics	Reading	
A Correlation coefficients[1]							
Average number of computers per student[2]	**0.57**	**0.56**	**0.41**	0.36	-0.15	-0.38	**0.41**
Mean index of ICT use at school	-0.30	-0.30	**-0.47**	**-0.42**	**-0.45**	**-0.51**	-0.20
Mean index of computer use in mathematics lessons	-0.34	-0.38	-0.07	-0.09	-0.02	0.09	-0.05
Share of students browsing the Internet at school for schoolwork at least once a week	-0.23	-0.17	**-0.42**	-0.31	**-0.49**	**-0.55**	-0.06
B Partial correlation coefficients,[3] after accounting for GDP per capita[2]							
Average number of computers per student[2]	0.35	0.32	0.17	0.10	-0.13	-0.29	0.09
Mean index of ICT use at school	**-0.61**	**-0.62**	**-0.67**	**-0.66**	**-0.44**	**-0.50**	**-0.50**
Mean index of computer use in mathematics lessons	-0.26	-0.31	-0.18	-0.23	-0.07	0.05	-0.24
Share of students browsing the Internet at school for schoolwork at least once a week	**-0.55**	**-0.49**	**-0.61**	**-0.54**	**-0.47**	**-0.53**	-0.31
C Partial correlation coefficients,[3] after accounting for GDP per capita[2] and mean performance on the mathematics scale in PISA 2003							
Average number of computers per student[2]	-0.26	-0.23	**-0.40**	**-0.51**	-0.34	-0.29	-0.35
Mean index of ICT use at school	**-0.65**	**-0.50**	**-0.66**	**-0.57**	**-0.47**	**-0.66**	-0.32
Mean index of computer use in mathematics lessons	-0.09	-0.15	-0.01	-0.15	0.08	-0.11	-0.26
Share of students browsing the Internet at school for schoolwork at least once a week	**-0.65**	-0.38	**-0.71**	**-0.43**	**-0.51**	**-0.66**	-0.07

1. The correlation coefficient is a simple measure of association between two variables. It varies between -1 and 1, with 0 indicating no relationship.
2. The average number of computers per student and GDP per capita are measured in logarithms.
3. The partial correlation coefficient is an extension of the correlation coefficient. It corresponds to the correlation between the residuals from the regression of two variables on the confounding variables that need to be accounted for.

Notes: Values above 0.4 indicate strong positive associations and are reported in bold; values below -0.4 indicate strong negative associations and are reported in blue bold.

Each correlation coefficient is based on the highest number of available observations. However, because not all variables are observed across all countries/economies, the sample size varies across cells.

Source: OECD, PISA 2012 Database, Table 6.1.

StatLink http://dx.doi.org/10.1787/888933253256

■ Figure 6.3 ■

Trends in mathematics performance and number of computers in schools

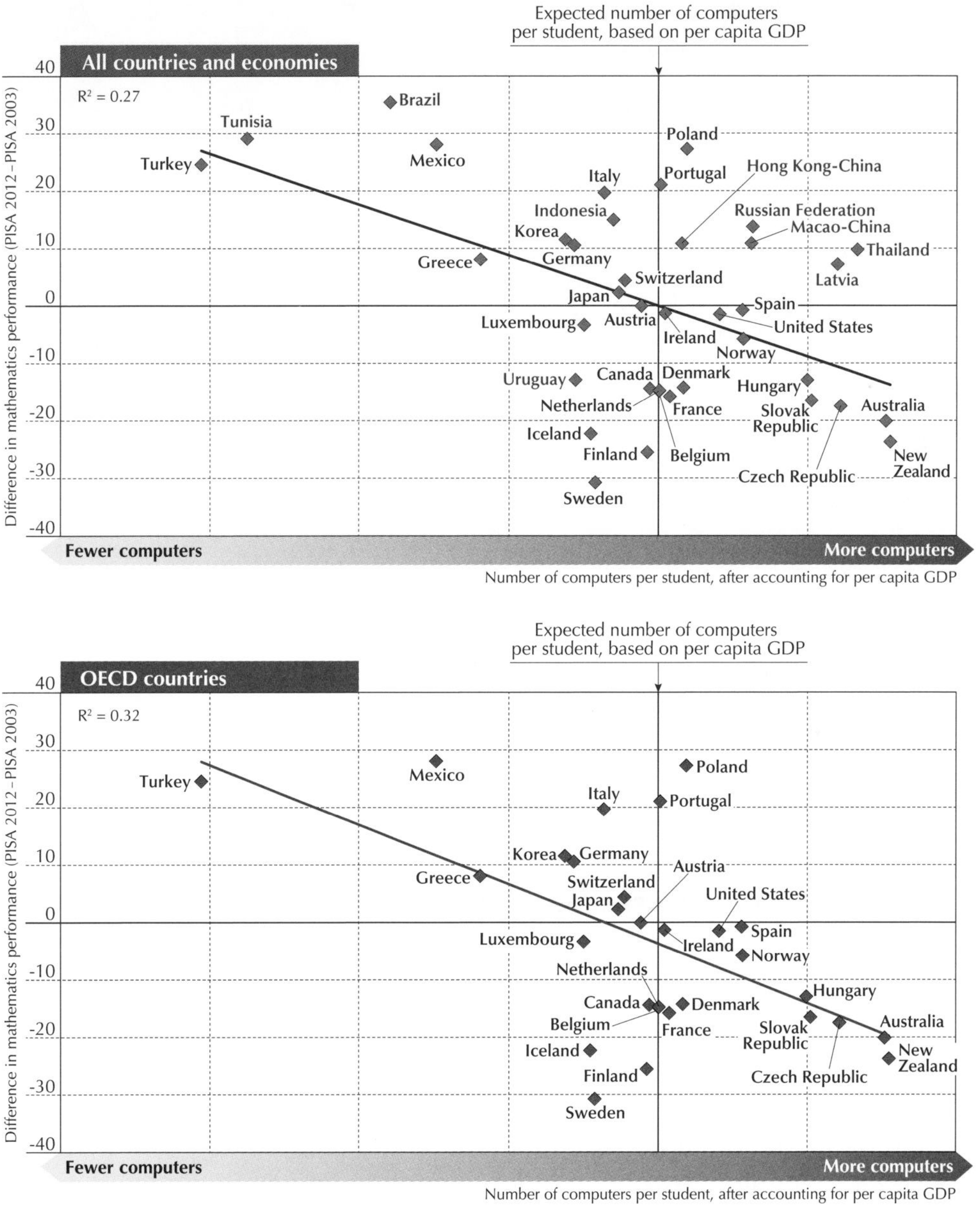
Expected number of computers per student, based on per capita GDP
All countries and economies
R² = 0.27
Difference in mathematics performance (PISA 2012 - PISA 2003)
40
30
20
10
0
-10
-20
-30
-40
Brazil
Tunisia
Turkey
Mexico
Poland
Italy
Portugal
Hong Kong-China
Indonesia
Russian Federation
Macao-China
Korea
Thailand
Greece
Germany
Switzerland
Latvia
Japan
Spain
Luxembourg
Austria
United States
Ireland
Norway
Uruguay
Canada
Denmark
Hungary
Netherlands
France
Slovak Republic
Australia
Iceland
Finland
Belgium
New Zealand
Czech Republic
Sweden
Fewer computers
More computers
Number of computers per student, after accounting for per capita GDP
Expected number of computers per student, based on per capita GDP
OECD countries
R² = 0.32
Difference in mathematics performance (PISA 2012 - PISA 2003)
Turkey
Mexico
Poland
Italy
Portugal
Korea
Germany
Greece
Austria
Switzerland
Japan
United States
Spain
Luxembourg
Ireland
Norway
Netherlands
Hungary
Canada
Denmark
Belgium
France
Slovak Republic
Australia
Iceland
New Zealand
Finland
Czech Republic
Sweden
Fewer computers
More computers
Number of computers per student, after accounting for per capita GDP

Note: The horizontal axis reports residuals from a regression of the student-computer ratio on per capita GDP (both variables are measured in logarithms).

Source: OECD, PISA 2012 Database, Table I.2.3b (OECD, 2014), Table IV.3.2 (OECD, 2013) and Table 2.11.

StatLink http://dx.doi.org/10.1787/888933253262

■ Figure 6.4 ■

Trends in reading performance and proportion of students who frequently browse the Internet for schoolwork at school

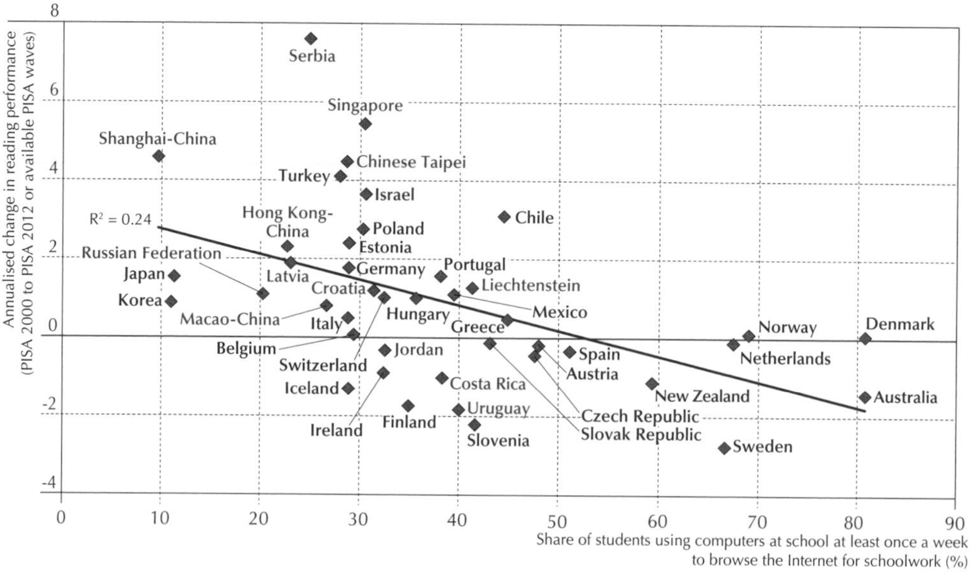
Annualised change in reading performance (PISA 2000 to PISA 2012 or available PISA waves)
8
6
4
2
0
-2
-4
0
10
20
30
40
50
60
70
80
90
Share of students using computers at school at least once a week to browse the Internet for schoolwork (%)
$R^2 = 0.24$
Serbia
Singapore
Shanghai-China
Chinese Taipei
Turkey
Israel
Hong Kong-China
Chile
Poland
Estonia
Russian Federation
Germany
Portugal
Japan
Latvia
Liechtenstein
Croatia
Korea
Hungary
Mexico
Macao-China
Italy
Greece
Norway
Denmark
Belgium
Jordan
Spain
Netherlands
Switzerland
Austria
Iceland
Costa Rica
New Zealand
Australia
Uruguay
Czech Republic
Finland
Ireland
Slovenia
Slovak Republic
Sweden

Notes: The annualised change is the average annual change in PISA score points. It is calculated taking into account all of a country's and economy's participation in PISA.
Source: OECD, PISA 2012 Database, Table I.4.3b (OECD, 2014) and Table 2.1.
StatLink http://dx.doi.org/10.1787/888933253271

In Chapter 4, this index was shown to account for a significant part of the variation in digital reading performance across countries of similar performance in print reading. Among the countries/economies where the quality of students' online navigation is highest, Australia has one of the largest shares of students who frequently browse the Internet at school for schoolwork, Korea one of the smallest, and Singapore an average share (Tables 2.1 and 4.1).

HOW PERFORMANCE IS ASSOCIATED WITH STUDENTS' USE OF ICT FOR SCHOOL

This section compares students within countries/economies, focusing particularly on performance in digital reading and computer-based mathematics, where, in theory, a stronger relationship with exposure to computers can be expected. Do students perform better in digital reading when they read on line more frequently for schoolwork? What is the relationship between students' use of computers during mathematics lessons and their ability to use computers for solving mathematics problems?

When interpreting these relationships, it is important to bear in mind two aspects of the PISA data (see Box 6.1). First, students reported on their use of computers during the current school year, but their performance also depends – and probably to a larger extent – on the learning opportunities and exposure to computers of past school years. In some countries, students who take the PISA test have been in their current school and grade for less than three months. Thus, in PISA data, even frequent use of computers at school might correspond to only short exposures.

Second, both the current level of performance and the current level of computer use might be the consequence of past performance levels. In most systems, 15-year-old students are either no longer in comprehensive schools or are streamed or grouped by ability in mathematics lessons. Variations in the use of computers might relate to the track or ability group of students. In other words, users and non-users might be very different from each other to start with, in terms of their aptitude, behaviour and disposition towards learning and school.

Analyses discussed in this section account for differences in socio-economic status across students and schools, but cannot account for past performance levels and for several other important determinants of students' exposure to computers at school.

Use of computers at school

The *index of ICT use at school* measures how frequently students engage in a variety of activities, such as browsing the Internet at school, using e-mail at school, chatting on line at school, and using computers for practice and drilling in foreign-language classes. Higher values of this index correspond to more frequent and more varied uses.

Figure 6.5 (left panel) shows that students who make slightly below-average use of computers at school have the highest performance in digital reading. Overall, the relationship is graphically illustrated by a hill shape, which suggests that limited use of computers at school may be better than no use at all, but levels of computer use above the current OECD average are associated with significantly poorer results.

■ Figure 6.5 ■

Students' skills in reading, by index of ICT use at school

OECD average relationship, after accounting for the socio-economic status of students and schools

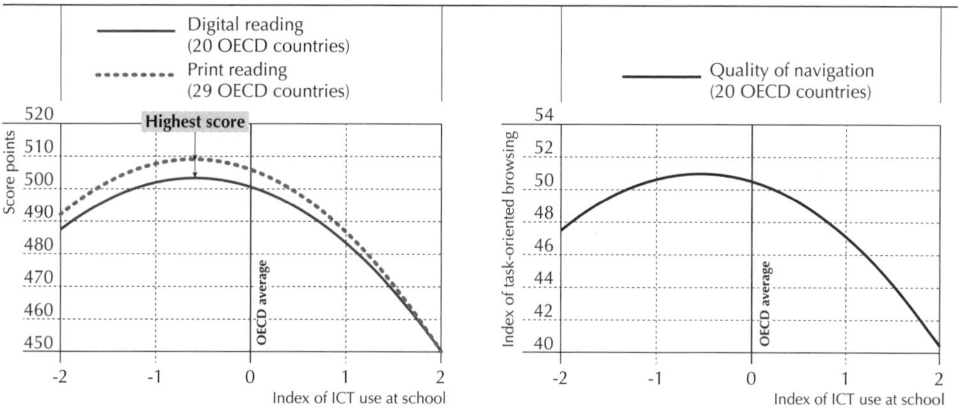
Digital reading
(20 OECD countries)
Print reading
(29 OECD countries)
Highest score
Score points
520
510
500
490
480
470
460
450
OECD average
-2
-1
0
1
2
Index of ICT use at school
Quality of navigation
(20 OECD countries)
Index of task-oriented browsing
54
52
50
48
46
44
42
40
OECD average
-2
-1
0
1
2
Index of ICT use at school

Notes: The lines represent the predicted values of the respective outcome variable, at varying levels of the *index of ICT use at school*, for students with a value of zero on the *PISA index of economic, social and cultural status* (ESCS), in schools where the average value of ESCS is zero.
Quality of navigation refers to students' ability to plan and regulate their navigation behaviour on line; this is measured by the *index of task-oriented browsing* (see Chapter 4).
Source: OECD, PISA 2012 Database, Table 6.2.
StatLink http://dx.doi.org/10.1787/888933253280

Figure 6.5 also shows that the relationship between computer use and performance is similar across digital and print reading; this suggests that even specific online reading skills do not benefit from high levels of computer use at school. This is confirmed by the right-hand panel, which relates the *index of task-oriented browsing* – an indicator of students' navigation and evaluation skills in online texts – to the *index of ICT use at school*. Even such specific online reading skills do not appear to benefit from more intensive use of computers at school.

Overall, using computers at school does not seem to confer a specific advantage in online reading. In detail, however, the relationship between performance and the frequency of use varies across activities.

The decline in performance associated with greater frequency of certain activities, such as chatting on line at school and practicing and drilling, is particularly large (Figure 6.6). Students who frequently engage in these activities may be missing out on other more effective learning activities. Students who never or only very rarely engage in these activities have the highest performance.

In contrast, for browsing the Internet or using e-mail, the relationship with reading skills becomes negative only when the frequency increases beyond "once or twice a week" (Figure 6.6). Thus, encouraging students to read on line, in moderation, may have positive effects on reading more generally. Teachers who offer a diverse range of materials to read can promote engagement with reading, particularly among boys (OECD, 2015). In 16 out of 25 countries/economies with available data, students who browse the Internet at school once or twice a month score above students who never do so on the PISA digital reading scale. In addition, the highest quality of navigation is attained by students who reported browsing the Internet at school "once or twice a week", suggesting that practice with online navigation in a school setting can be particularly important for specific skills related to online reading (Table 6.3c).

There are also significant differences across countries (Table 6.2, and Tables 6.3a through 6.3i). In Australia, in particular, more frequent browsing of the Internet at school – even the most frequent browsing – is associated with gains in digital reading skills. Australia is among the countries where students use computers at school the most.

Use of computers in mathematics lessons

The *index of computer use in mathematics lessons* measures whether teachers or students use computers during mathematics lessons, and for which tasks. Higher values on this index correspond to more mathematics tasks being performed with computers, particularly by students.

Across OECD countries, students who do not use computers in mathematics lessons tend to perform better in the paper-based and the computer-based assessment of mathematics (Figures 6.7 and 6.8). This may reflect, to a large extent, the fact that advanced mathematics classes rely less on computers than more applied mathematics classes. However, even the ability to use computers as a mathematical tool – a skill that is only assessed in the computer-based assessment of mathematics – appears to benefit little from greater use of computers in mathematics classes, as shown in the right panel of Figure 6.7.

■ Figure 6.6 ■

Frequency of computer use at school and digital reading skills

OECD average relationship, after accounting for the socio-economic status of students and schools

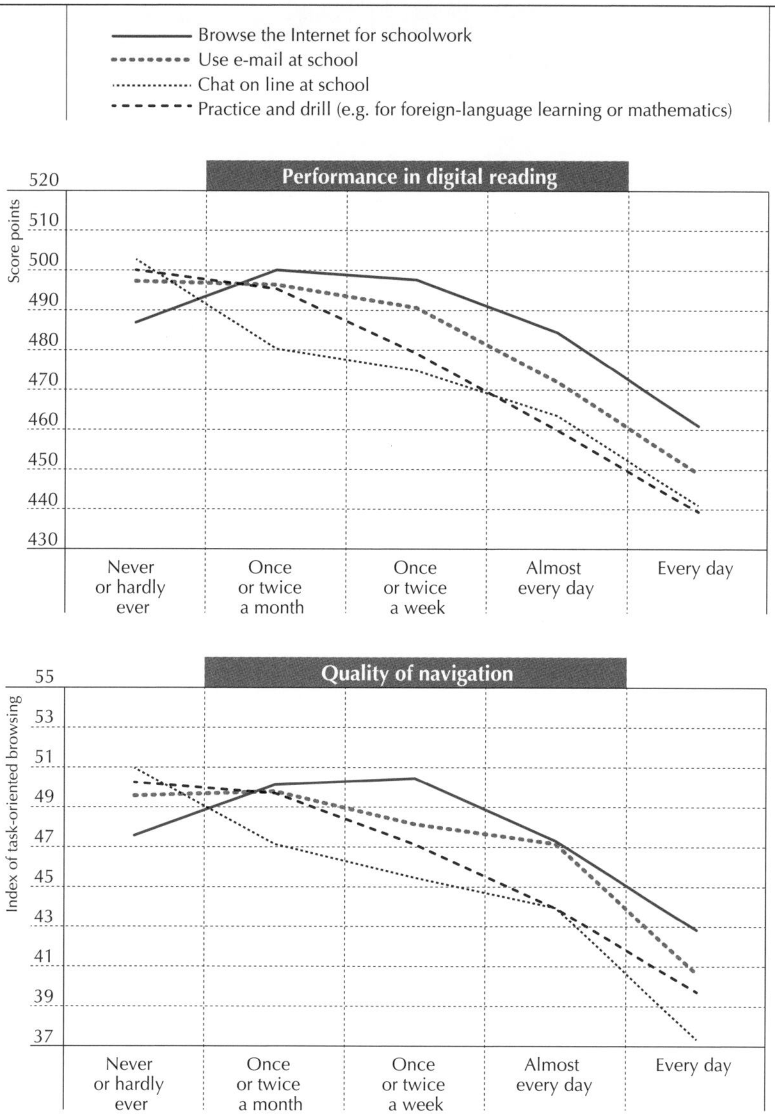
Browse the Internet for schoolwork
Use e-mail at school
Chat on line at school
Practice and drill (e.g. for foreign-language learning or mathematics)
Performance in digital reading
Score points
520
510
500
490
480
470
460
450
440
430
Never or hardly ever
Once or twice a month
Once or twice a week
Almost every day
Every day
Quality of navigation
Index of task-oriented browsing
55
53
51
49
47
45
43
41
39
37
Never or hardly ever
Once or twice a month
Once or twice a week
Almost every day
Every day

Notes: The charts plot the predicted values of the respective outcome variables for students with a value of zero on the *PISA index of economic, social and cultural status* (ESCS), in schools where the average value of ESCS is zero.

Quality of navigation refers to students' ability to plan and regulate their navigation behaviour on line; this is measured by the *index of task-oriented browsing* (see Chapter 4).

Source: OECD, PISA 2012 Database, Tables 6.3a, b, c and g.

StatLink http://dx.doi.org/10.1787/888933253296

■ Figure 6.7 ■

Performance in computer-based and paper-based mathematics, by index of computer use in mathematics lessons

OECD average relationship, after accounting for the socio-economic status of students and schools

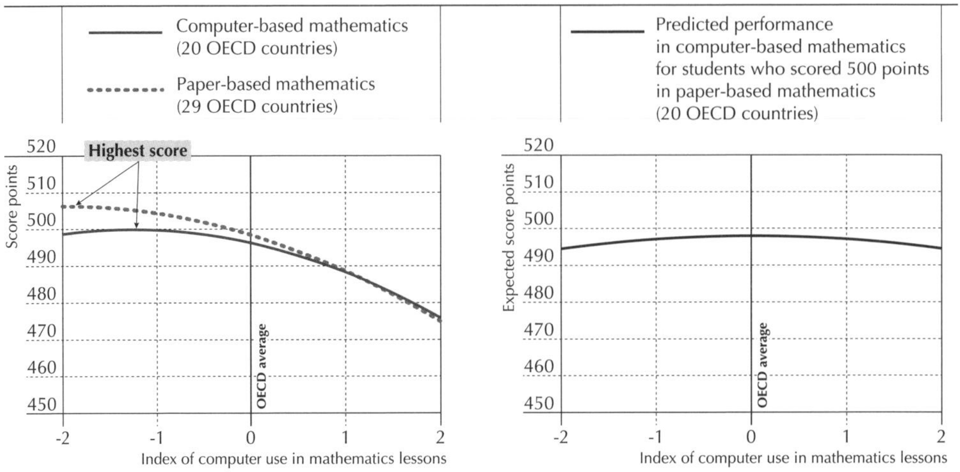
Computer-based mathematics (20 OECD countries)
Paper-based mathematics (29 OECD countries)
Predicted performance in computer-based mathematics for students who scored 500 points in paper-based mathematics (20 OECD countries)
Highest score
Score points
Expected score points
520
510
500
490
480
470
460
450
OECD average
-2
-1
0
1
2
Index of computer use in mathematics lessons

Notes: The lines represent the predicted values of the respective outcome variable, at varying levels of the *index of computer use in mathematics lessons,* for students with a value of zero on the *PISA index of economic, social and cultural status* (ESCS), in schools where the average value of ESCS is zero.
Source: OECD, PISA 2012 Database, Table 6.4.
StatLink http://dx.doi.org/10.1787/888933253302

Irrespective of the specific tasks involved, students who do not use computers in mathematics lessons perform better in mathematics assessments than students who do use computers in their mathematics lesson, after accounting for differences in socio-economic status (Figure 6.8).

There are, however, exceptions to this negative relationship. In Belgium, Denmark and Norway, there is a positive association between computer use in mathematics lessons and performance in the computer-based assessment of mathematics, particularly when the comparison accounts for differences in students' socio-economic status and in schools' socio-economic profile. Students who use computers during mathematics lessons tend to score higher than students who do not (Table 6.4, and Tables 6.5a through 6.5g). Denmark and Norway, too, are among the countries where students use computers at school the most.

Use of computers outside of school for schoolwork

The relationship between reading skills and using computers for schoolwork outside of school is, at first glance, similar to the relationship between reading skills and using computers for schoolwork at school. The *index of ICT use outside of school for schoolwork* measures how frequently students do homework on computers, browse the Internet for schoolwork, use e-mail for communications related to school, visit the school website, and/or upload or download materials on it. Higher values of this index correspond to more frequent and more varied uses.

■ Figure 6.8 ■

Computer use in mathematics lessons and performance in computer-based mathematics

OECD average relationship, after accounting for the socio-economic status of students and schools

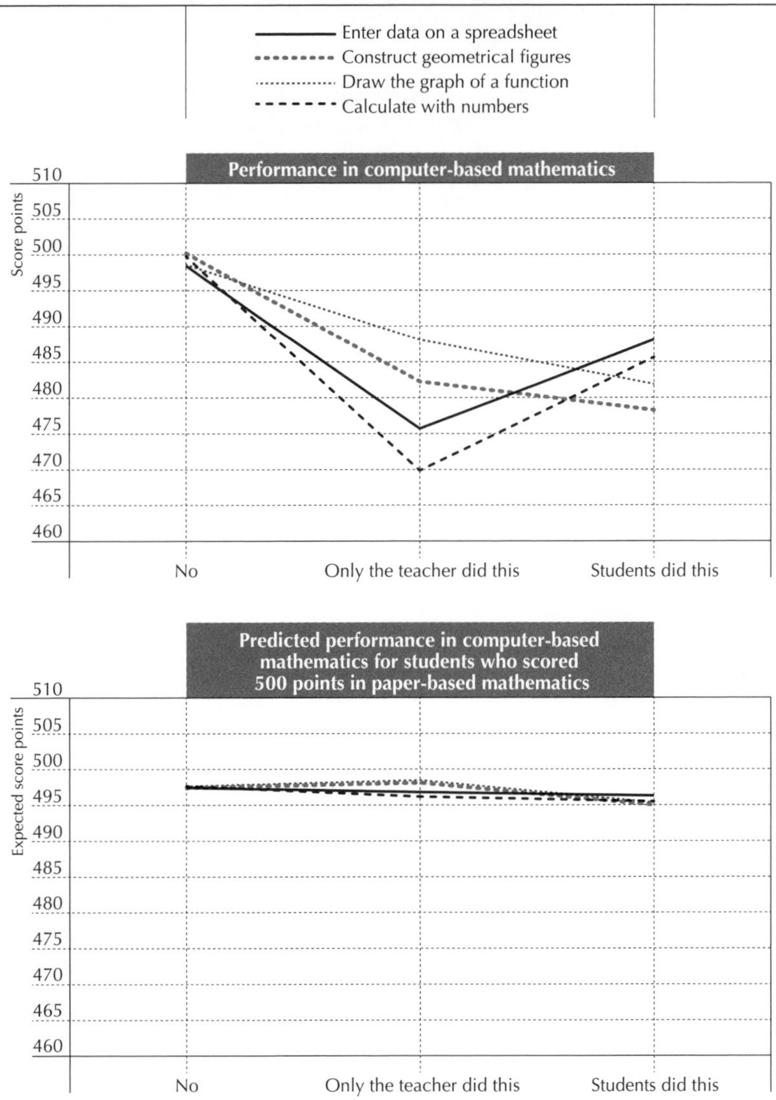
Enter data on a spreadsheet
Construct geometrical figures
Draw the graph of a function
Calculate with numbers
Performance in computer-based mathematics
Score points
510
505
500
495
490
485
480
475
470
465
460
No
Only the teacher did this
Students did this
Predicted performance in computer-based mathematics for students who scored 500 points in paper-based mathematics
Expected score points
510
505
500
495
490
485
480
475
470
465
460
No
Only the teacher did this
Students did this

Notes: The top chart plots the predicted values of performance in computer-based mathematics for students with a value of zero on the *PISA index of economic, social and cultural status* (ESCS), in schools where the average value of ESCS is zero. The bottom chart plots the predicted values of performance in computer-based mathematics for students who scored 500 points in paper-based mathematics, have a value of zero on the index, and are in schools where the average value of ESCS is zero.

Source: OECD, PISA 2012 Database, Tables 6.5a, b, c and d.

StatLink http://dx.doi.org/10.1787/888933253318

Students who use computers for schoolwork outside of school to a moderate degree perform best in both digital and print reading – higher than students who never use computers at all. When computer use increases beyond the OECD average, however, the relationship turns negative. This hill-shaped relationship is also observed when considering the quality of students' navigation (*index of task-oriented browsing*) (Figure 6.9).

■ Figure 6.9 ■

Students' skills in reading, by index of ICT use outside of school for schoolwork

OECD average relationship, after accounting for the socio-economic status of students and schools

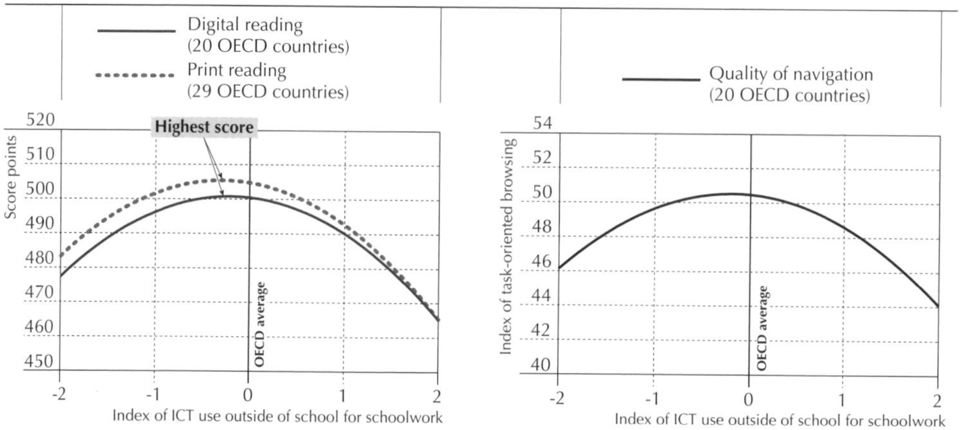
Digital reading
(20 OECD countries)
Print reading
(29 OECD countries)
Highest score
Score points
520
510
500
490
480
470
460
450
OECD average
-2
-1
0
1
2
Index of ICT use outside of school for schoolwork
Quality of navigation
(20 OECD countries)
Index of task-oriented browsing
54
52
50
48
46
44
42
40
OECD average
-2
-1
0
1
2
Index of ICT use outside of school for schoolwork

Notes: The lines represent the predicted values of the respective outcome variable, at varying levels of the *index of ICT use outside of school for schoolwork,* for students with a value of zero on the *PISA index of economic, social and cultural status* (ESCS), in schools where the average value of ESCS is zero.
Quality of navigation refers to students' ability to plan and regulate their navigation behaviour on line; this is measured by the *index of task-oriented browsing* (see Chapter 4).
Source: OECD, PISA 2012 Database, Table 6.6.
StatLink http://dx.doi.org/10.1787/888933253329

The two homework activities listed in the ICT familiarity questionnaire (doing homework on computers, and browsing the Internet for schoolwork) show a similar hill-shaped relationship with performance. Students who never do these activities on computers, and students who do them every day, are the two groups with the lowest performance in the assessment of digital reading. When considering communication activities among students and with teachers, such as using e-mail to communicate with other students, there is no difference in average performance between students who never use a computer for these activities, and students who do so up to once or twice a week (Figure 6.10).

When interpreting these results, it is important to bear in mind that what students do when they are free to choose how to spend their time depends on their skills (what they are able to do) and their dispositions towards learning more generally. For example, the group of students who rarely use computers for doing homework outside of school includes those students who rarely do any homework outside of school, irrespective of whether they do so with computers or not.

■ Figure 6.10 ■

Frequency of computer use outside of school for schoolwork and digital reading skills

OECD average relationship, after accounting for the socio-economic status of students and schools

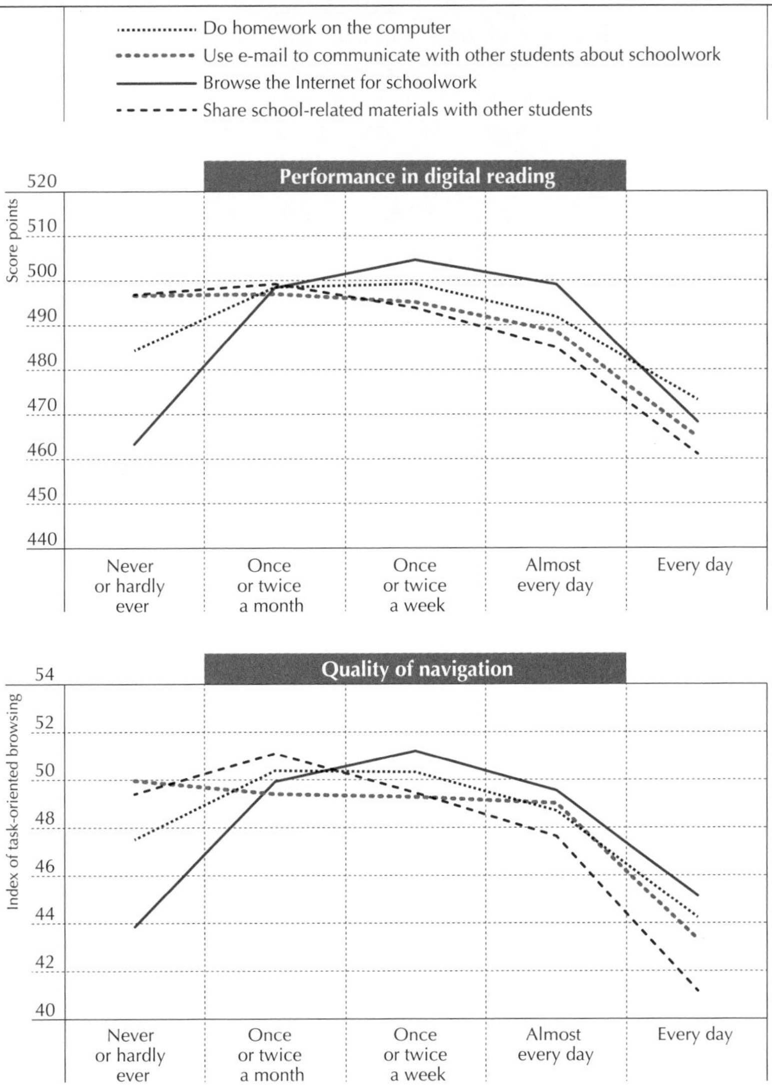
Do homework on the computer
Use e-mail to communicate with other students about schoolwork
Browse the Internet for schoolwork
Share school-related materials with other students
Performance in digital reading
Score points
520
510
500
490
480
470
460
450
440
Never or hardly ever
Once or twice a month
Once or twice a week
Almost every day
Every day
Quality of navigation
Index of task-oriented browsing
54
52
50
48
46
44
42
40
Never or hardly ever
Once or twice a month
Once or twice a week
Almost every day
Every day

Notes: The charts plot the predicted values of the respective outcome variables for students with a value of zero on the *PISA index of economic, social and cultural status* (ESCS), in schools where the average value of ESCS is zero.
Quality of navigation refers to students' ability to plan and regulate their navigation behaviour on line; this is measured by the *index of task-oriented browsing* (see Chapter 4).
Source: OECD, PISA 2012 Database, Tables 6.7a, b, f and g.
StatLink http://dx.doi.org/10.1787/888933253338

The relationship between doing homework on computers and performance might reflect students' engagement with school, in general, rather than their use of computers for school, in particular.

USE OF COMPUTERS AT HOME FOR LEISURE AND DIGITAL READING PERFORMANCE

Students use computers at home for playing games, to remain in contact with friends, and for all sorts of leisure activities, such as downloading music, reading news, or simply browsing the Internet for fun. The frequency and variety of leisure activities in which students engage when using computers at home is summarised in an *index of ICT use outside of school for leisure*.

Figure 6.11 shows the hill-shaped relationship between the uses of computers at home for leisure and digital reading performance. Moderate users tend to perform better than both intensive users and rare users. The figure also shows a similar, hill-shaped relationship with print reading. In this latter case, however, rare users perform better than intensive users (those with the highest values on this index).

■ Figure 6.11 ■

Students' skills in reading, by index of ICT use outside of school for leisure

OECD average, after accounting for the socio-economic status of students and schools

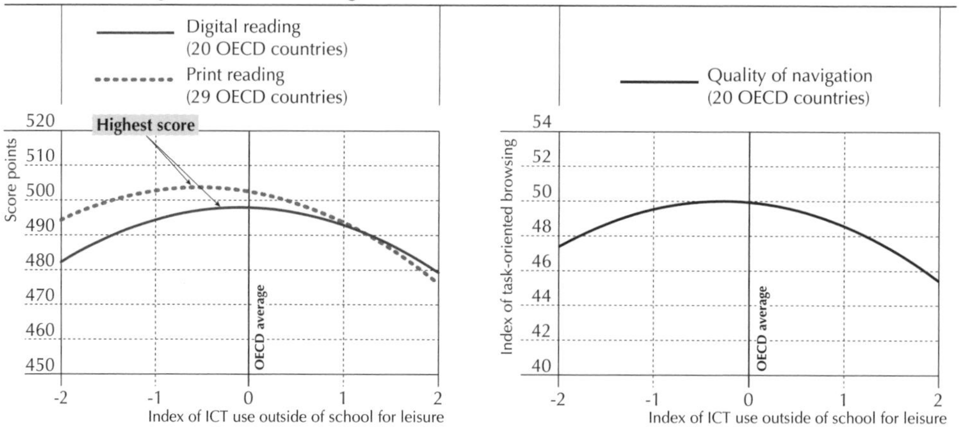
Digital reading (20 OECD countries)
Print reading (29 OECD countries)
Highest score
Score points
520
510
500
490
480
470
460
450
OECD average
-2
-1
0
1
2
Index of ICT use outside of school for leisure
Quality of navigation (20 OECD countries)
Index of task-oriented browsing
54
52
50
48
46
44
42
40
OECD average
-2
-1
0
1
2
Index of ICT use outside of school for leisure

Notes: The lines represent the predicted values of the respective outcome variable, at varying levels of the *index of ICT use outside of school for leisure,* for students with a value of zero on the *PISA index of economic, social and cultural status* (ESCS), in schools where the average value of ESCS is zero.
Quality of navigation refers to students' ability to plan and regulate their navigation behaviour on line; this is measured by the *index of task-oriented browsing* (see Chapter 4).
Source: OECD, PISA 2012 Database, Table 6.8.
StatLink http://dx.doi.org/10.1787/888933253343

Students who use computers most intensely differ in many ways from students who use computers rarely, if at all. Computer use, itself, may be the result, rather than the cause, of different levels of digital skills. For these reasons, it is not possible to interpret these associations as simple cause-effect relationships. Nevertheless, these patterns indicate that it is not necessary to use computers frequently to perform well in digital reading.

■ Figure 6.12 ■

Frequency of ICT use outside of school for leisure and digital reading skills

OECD average relationship, after accounting for the socio-economic status of students and schools

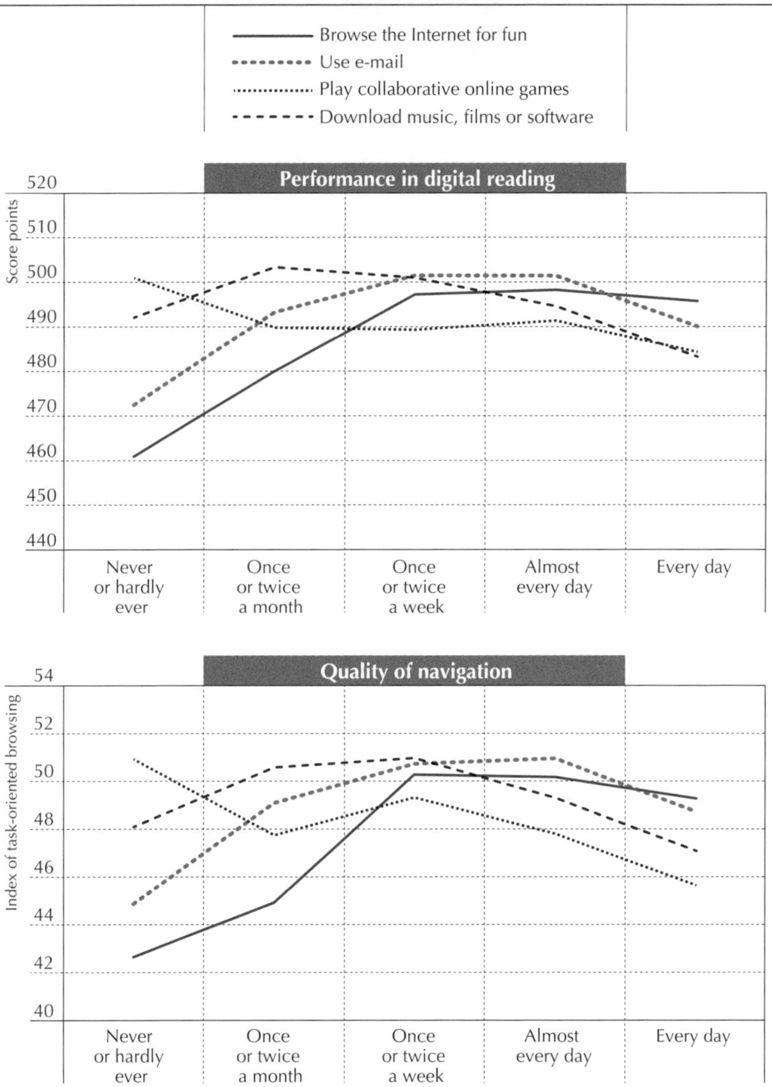
Browse the Internet for fun
Use e-mail
Play collaborative online games
Download music, films or software
Performance in digital reading
Score points
520
510
500
490
480
470
460
450
440
Never or hardly ever
Once or twice a month
Once or twice a week
Almost every day
Every day
Quality of navigation
Index of task-oriented browsing
54
52
50
48
46
44
42
40
Never or hardly ever
Once or twice a month
Once or twice a week
Almost every day
Every day

Notes: The charts plot the predicted values of the respective outcome variables for students with a value of zero on the *PISA index of economic, social and cultural status* (ESCS), in schools where the average value of ESCS is zero.

Quality of navigation refers to students' ability to plan and regulate their navigation behaviour on line; this is measured by the *index of task-oriented browsing* (see Chapter 4).

Source: OECD, PISA 2012 Database, Tables 6.9b, c, f and i.

StatLink http://dx.doi.org/10.1787/888933253359

In fact, Figure 6.12 shows that the relationship between leisure activities on computers and performance in digital reading varies depending on the specific activity. Some activities, such as browsing the Internet for fun or using e-mail, are more positively related to proficiency in online reading than others, such as playing collaborative games on line or downloading music or films from the Internet. Better online readers do more of the former, and less of the latter.

These differences across different activities must be interpreted in light of the fact that students select their leisure activities, in part, based on what they enjoy most; and this, in turn, depends on how well they are able to handle the task. Students who read more tend to be better readers; in turn, better readers are likely to feel rewarded by reading more. Reading engagement and reading proficiency sustain each other in a reciprocal relationship.

RESEARCH EVIDENCE ON THE IMPACT OF COMPUTER USE ON STUDENT PERFORMANCE

Overall, the most frequent pattern that emerges in PISA data when computer use is related to students' skills is a weak or sometimes negative association between investment in ICT use and performance. While the correlational nature of this finding makes it difficult to draw guidance for policy from it, the finding is remarkably similar to the emerging consensus in the research literature, based on studies that use more rigorously designed evaluations.

Several studies have assessed the impact on education outcomes of allocating more resources for ICT in schools. Most recent research in this field has been conducted using "natural experiments", whereby the given reality of the situation creates a control group that can be compared to the "treated" group, which in this case represents the schools that receive the additional resources. The majority of these studies finds that such policies result in greater computer use in "treated" schools, but only few studies find positive effects on education outcomes, even when the new resources did not displace other investments (Bulman and Fairlie, forthcoming). Evidence resulting from such "natural experiments" in Israel (Angrist and Lavy, 2002), the Netherlands (Leuven et al., 2007), California (Goolsbee and Guryan, 2006) and Peru (Cristia, Czerwonko and Garofalo, 2014) agrees with the finding of limited, and sometimes negative, effects on traditional performance indicators, such as test scores, grades in national examinations, and incidence of dropout.

Few studies are based on controlled experiments, whereby treatment and control groups are created by a random draw. A randomised evaluation of the "Computers for Education" programme in Colombia (Barrera-Osorio and Linden, 2009) finds limited effects on learning, but also finds that additional computers did not translate into increased use of computers for instruction.

As an exception to these findings, Machin, McNally and Silva (2007) report performance gains from increased funding for ICT equipment among primary schools in England. These authors use a change in the rules governing the allocation of funds across local education authorities, around the year 2000, to compare schools (or rather, local education authorities) that gained additional funds under the new rules to those whose resources decreased or remained constant.

Other studies have assessed the impact of specific uses of ICT on education outcomes. Experimental evaluations of specific uses of computers for instructional purposes – such as educational software – tend to report positive results more often (Bulman and Fairlie, forthcoming). However, to interpret these findings it is crucial to determine whether the introduction of computer-assisted instruction increases learning time overall or displaces other learning activities.

In his review of the effectiveness of computer-assisted instruction, based on 81 meta-analyses of research published over the past 30 years, Hattie (2013) finds that the effect on learning is neither larger nor smaller than the typical effect found from other well-intentioned teaching interventions, on average. As a result, if computer use replaces similarly effective teaching activities, the net effect may be zero.

Furthermore, the specific uses promoted in the context of experimental evaluation studies may be better than the average uses that "normal" teachers promote in their classrooms. In their analysis of TIMSS data, which links, for the same student, differences in computer use across subjects (mathematics and science) to differences in performance, Falck, Mang and Woessmann (2015) find that mathematics results are unrelated to computer use, while science results are positively related to certain uses ("looking up ideas and information") and negatively related to others ("practicing skills and procedures").

Effects, indeed, are likely to vary depending on the context and the specific uses. In their assessment of the literature on computer-assisted instruction, Hattie and Yates (2013) report stronger effects when computers were supplementing traditional teaching, rather than seen as its alternative. According to these authors, positive effects were achieved in interventions that followed the same principles of learning that apply for traditional teaching as well: computers were particularly effective when used to extend study time and practice, when used to allow students to assume control over the learning situation (e.g. by individualising the pace with which new material is introduced), and when used to support collaborative learning.

Rigorous experimental evidence on the effect of home computer use on students' performance in school is more limited. Three recently published experiments report mixed evidence. Exploiting a sharp discontinuity in eligibility rules for a computer-vouchers programme for families with school-aged children in Romania, Malamud and Pop-Eleches (2011) find mixed evidence on impacts, with some outcomes, such as school grades, deteriorating for the eligible students, and other outcomes, such as computer skills and cognitive skills measured with Raven's progressive matrices, improving. In a randomised trial in California, where free computers where given to students in grades 6-10 who previously had none, no effects were found on grades, test scores, credits earned, or engagement with school (Fairlie and Robinson, 2013). Finally, in a randomised trial in Peru, about 1 000 primary school children selected by a lottery received a free laptop computer for home use. Five months after receiving the computer, these children reported greater use of computers overall and were more proficient in using them than non-recipients. No effects were found however on reading and mathematics scores, on cognitive skills, and on more general ICT proficiency; while teachers reported that recipients of free computers exerted less effort at school compared to non-recipients (Beuermann et al., 2015).

Overall, the evidence from PISA, as well as from more rigorously designed evaluations, suggests that solely increasing access to computers for students, at home or at school, is unlikely to result in significant improvements in education outcomes. Furthermore, both PISA data and the research evidence concur on the finding that the positive effects of computer use are specific – limited to certain outcomes, and to certain uses of computers.

Chapter 6 tables are available on line at http://dx.doi.org/10.1787/edu-data-en.

Note regarding Israel

The statistical data for Israel are supplied by and under the responsibility of the relevant Israeli authorities. The use of such data by the OECD is without prejudice to the status of the Golan Heights, East Jerusalem and Israeli settlements in the West Bank under the terms of international law.

References

Angrist, J. and **V. Lavy** (2002), "New evidence on classroom computers and pupil learning", *Economic Journal,* Vol. 112/482, pp. 735-765.

Barrera-Osorio, F. and **L.L. Linden** (2009), "The use and misuse of computers in education : Evidence from a randomized experiment in Colombia", *World Bank Policy Research Working Paper Series*, No. 4836.

Beuermann, D.W., J. Cristia, S. Cueto, O. Malamud and **Y. Cruz-Aguayo** (2015), "One laptop per child at home: Short-term impacts from a randomized experiment in Peru", *American Economic Journal: Applied Economics,* Vol. 7/2, pp. 53-80.

Bulman, G. and **R.W. Fairlie** (forthcoming), "Technology and education: Computers, software, and the Internet", in Hanushek, R., S. Machin and L. Woessmann (eds.), *Handbook of the Economics of Education*, Vol. 5, North Holland, Amsterdam.

Cristia, J., A. Czerwonko and **P. Garofalo** (2014), "Does technology in schools affect repetition, dropout and enrollment? Evidence from Peru", *IDB Working Paper Series*, No. IDB-WP-477, Inter-American Development Bank, Research Department.

Fairlie, R.W. and **J. Robinson** (2013), "Experimental evidence on the effects of home computers on academic achievement among schoolchildren", *American Economic Journal: Applied Economics,* Vol. 5/3, pp. 211-240.

Falck, O., C. Mang and **L. Woessmann** (2015), "Virtually no effect? Different uses of classroom computers and their effect on student achievement", *IZA Discussion Paper*, No. 8939.

Goolsbee, A. and **J. Guryan** (2006), "The impact of internet subsidies in public schools", *The Review of Economics and Statistics*, Vol. 88/2, pp. 336-347.

Hattie, J. (2013), *Visible Learning: A Synthesis of Over 800 Meta-Analyses Relating to Achievement*, Routledge, United Kingdom.

Hattie, J. and **G.C.R. Yates** (2013), *Visible Learning and the Science of How We Learn*. Routledge, United Kingdom.

Leuven, E., M. Lindahl, H. Oosterbeek and **D. Webbink** (2007), "The effect of extra funding for disadvantaged pupils on achievement", *The Review of Economics and Statistics,* Vol. 89/4, pp. 721-736.

Machin, S., S. McNally and **O. Silva** (2007), "New technology in schools: Is there a payoff?", *Economic Journal,* Vol. 117/522, pp. 1145-1167.

Malamud, O. and **C. Pop-Eleches** (2011), "Home computer use and the development of human capital", *The Quarterly Journal of Economics*, Vol. 126/2, pp. 987-1027.

OECD (2015), *The ABC of Gender Equality in Education: Aptitude, Behaviour, Confidence*, PISA, OECD Publishing, Paris, http://dx.doi.org/10.1787/9789264229945-en.

OECD (2013), *PISA 2012 Results: What Makes Schools Successful (Volume IV): Resources, Policies and Practices*, PISA, OECD Publishing, Paris, http://dx.doi.org/10.1787/9789264201156-en.

7

Using Log-File Data to Understand What Drives Performance in PISA (Case Study)

In computer-based tests, machines keep track (in log files) of – and, if so instructed, could analyse – all the steps and actions students take in finding a solution to a given problem. This chapter uses three tasks from the PISA 2012 computer-based reading assessment to illustrate how process data recorded by the assessment can enhance educators' ability to monitor students' test-taking behaviour and measure their skills.

Information and communication technology (ICT) tools have the potential to improve education and teaching in several ways. In the domain of assessment, digital tools can improve precision and efficiency of measurements, and expand the kinds of knowledge and skills that can be assessed (e.g. problem solving [OECD, 2014]). Perhaps more important, ICT tools make it easier for students to identify their learning needs as they participate in the assessment. Indeed, computers' interactive nature, rapid feedback loops and powerful analytical possibilities can be harnessed in the interest of universal learning principles. When digital tools support students' engagement with challenging material, thus extending learning time and practice, or help students to assume control over the learning situation, by individualising the pace with which new material is introduced or by providing immediate feedback, students probably learn more.

Bunderson, Inouye and Olsen (1988) were among the first to describe the potential of "intelligent measurement". In their vision, computers could provide the kind of advice that, in the past, only experts could give to learners, and only if they closely monitored learners' progress (an extremely time-consuming activity). In computer-administered tasks, machines keep track of all the steps and actions taken towards a solution (in log files). If correctly instructed, computers could also analyse those actions along with students' performance on the tasks. Thus, computers could eventually produce not only static test scores, but also an interpretation of scores (a profile) and personalised feedback for learners and their instructors.

Yet more than 25 years later, this vision of intelligent measurement is still far from being implemented on a large scale. One reason for the slow progress is the scarcity of studies investigating the use of process data (log-file data) for analysing students' learning. As Csapó et al. (2012) note, it is very difficult to "make sense of the hundreds of pieces of information students may produce when engaging in a complex assessment" (p. 216).

What the data tell us

- In computer-based tests, log files record information about the timing and type of actions students perform while trying to solve tasks. Analyses of log files allow for investigating how fluently students read, how persistent they are in trying to solve challenging problems and, more generally, analysing differences in how students handle tasks.
- Students who need a long time to read and understand a simple test question are likely to lack fluency in reading, as well as other basic reading skills. Data culled from one task in the digital reading assessment show that students in Brazil, Chile, Colombia, Hungary and the United Arab Emirates are significantly more likely to read slowly than students in other countries. In contrast, in Japan, Korea, and other countries with small shares of low performers in reading, few students read slowly.
- The largest proportions of students who could solve a complex digital reading task in less than the seven minutes usually required to succeed were observed in Australia, Canada, France and the United States. But when also considering students who persisted beyond seven minutes to solve the problem correctly, other countries and economies – notably Hong Kong-China, Ireland, Japan, Macao-China, Shanghai-China and Singapore – performed on par with or sometimes better than the former group of countries.

This chapter uses three assessment items, or tasks, to illustrate how process data recorded by computer-based assessments enhance the ability to measure students' behaviour and skills. All three items analysed here belong to a same test unit (*SERAING*), which means that they share a common text as stimulus material.

The case study is organised as follows. First, the general features of the unit *SERAING* are introduced. In addition to providing the context for the later analyses, this unit illustrates how students' skills in digital reading were assessed in PISA 2012. Next, students' reading fluency, their persistence, and their navigation behaviour are analysed, drawing on comparisons of students across countries and across performance levels.

All findings in this section are based on a limited number of tasks, sometimes on a single task. For this reason, they should be interpreted with caution. Further research is necessary to generalise and corroborate results.

DESCRIPTION OF THE UNIT *SERAING*

The three items analysed in greater detail here were chosen to illustrate the range of navigation demands in the PISA assessment. Figure 7.1 shows that the tasks in the unit *SERAING* span the full range of navigation difficulties.

■ Figure 7.1 ■

How text processing and navigation demands vary across tasks in the unit *SERAING*

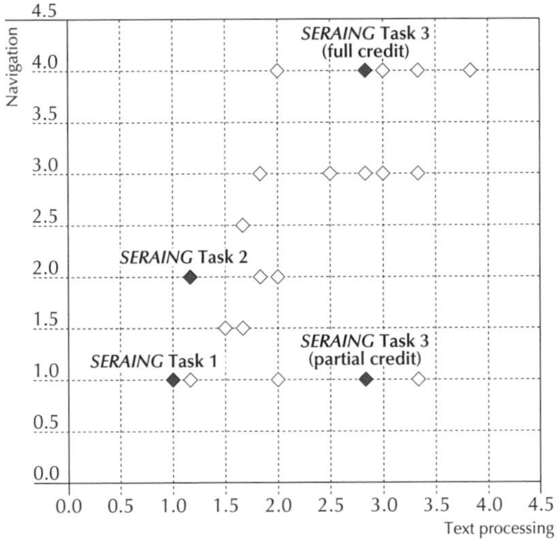
Navigation
4.5
4.0
3.5
3.0
2.5
2.0
1.5
1.0
0.5
0.0
SERAING Task 3
(full credit)
SERAING Task 2
SERAING Task 3
(partial credit)
SERAING Task 1
0.0
0.5
1.0
1.5
2.0
2.5
3.0
3.5
4.0
4.5
Text processing

Notes: The horizontal axis shows experts' ratings of text-processing demands; the vertical axis shows experts' ratings of navigation demands (both ratings are expressed on a 1-4 scale, with 4 corresponding to the most difficult).
Each diamond represents one or more tasks in the PISA 2012 assessment of digital reading.
Source: OECD (2011), *PISA 2009 Results: Students on Line: Digital Technologies and Performance (Volume VI)*, p. 43, http://dx.doi.org/10.1787/9789264112995-en.
StatLink http://dx.doi.org/10.1787/888933253361

■ Figure 7.2 ■

Screenshots of webpages used in the unit *SERAING*

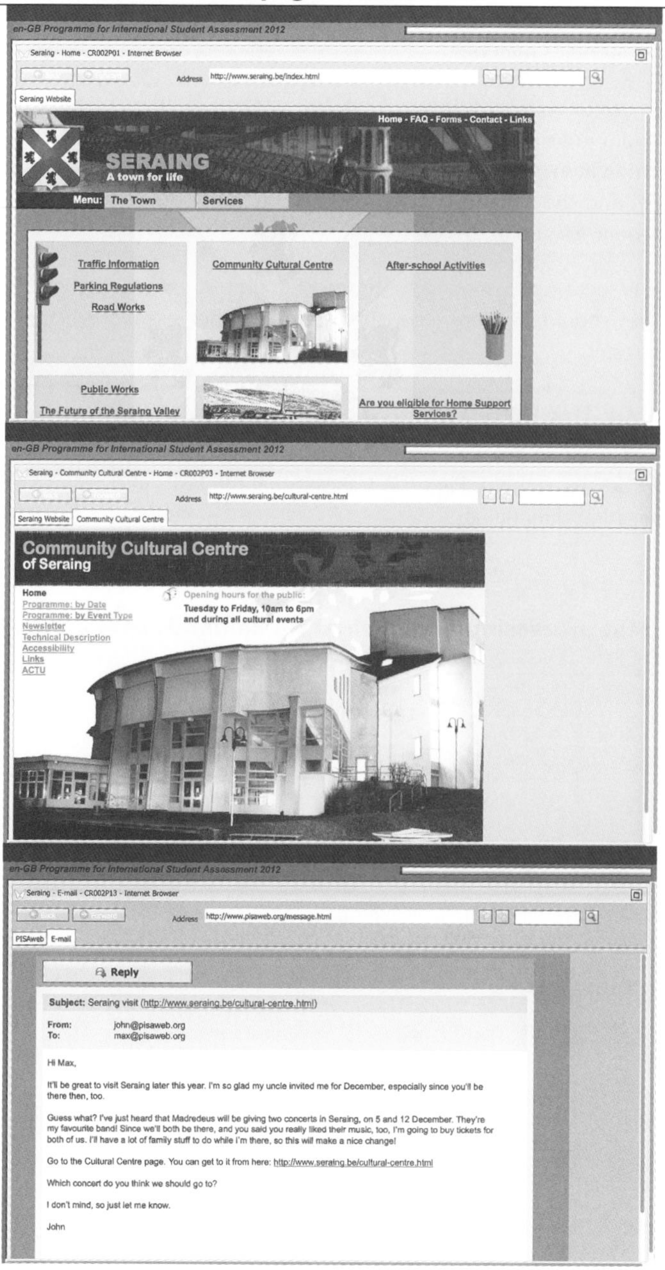
en-GB Programme for International Student Assessment 2012
Seraing - Home - CR002P01 - Internet Browser
Address http://www.seraing.be/index.html
Seraing Website
Home - FAQ - Forms - Contact - Links
SERAING
A town for life
Menu: The Town Services
Traffic Information
Parking Regulations
Road Works
Community Cultural Centre
After-school Activities
Public Works
The Future of the Seraing Valley
Are you eligible for Home Support Services?
en-GB Programme for International Student Assessment 2012
Seraing - Community Cultural Centre - Home - CR002P03 - Internet Browser
Address http://www.seraing.be/cultural-centre.html
Seraing Website Community Cultural Centre
Community Cultural Centre of Seraing
Home
Programme: by Date
Programme: by Event Type
Newsletter
Technical Description
Accessibility
Links
ACTU
Opening hours for the public:
Tuesday to Friday, 10am to 6pm and during all cultural events
en-GB Programme for International Student Assessment 2012
Seraing - E-mail - CR002P13 - Internet Browser
Address http://www.pisaweb.org/message.html
PISAweb E-mail
Reply
Subject: Seraing visit (http://www.seraing.be/cultural-centre.html)
From: john@pisaweb.org
To: max@pisaweb.org
Hi Max,
It'll be great to visit Seraing later this year. I'm so glad my uncle invited me for December, especially since you'll be there then, too.
Guess what? I've just heard that Madredeus will be giving two concerts in Seraing, on 5 and 12 December. They're my favourite band! Since we'll both be there, and you said you really liked their music, too, I'm going to buy tickets for both of us. I'll have a lot of family stuff to do while I'm there, so this will make a nice change!
Go to the Cultural Centre page. You can get to it from here: http://www.seraing.be/cultural-centre.html
Which concert do you think we should go to?
I don't mind, so just let me know.
John

Source: Australian Consortium for Educational Research (2015), "PISA examples of computer-based items: Digital Reading 2012: *SERAING*", http://cbasq.acer.edu.au/index.php?cmd=toEra2012 (accessed 30 April 2015).

The items are briefly described below and are available for viewing on the website of the Australian Consortium for Educational Research (http://cbasq.acer.edu.au/index.php?cmd=toEra2012 [accessed 30 April 2015]). The extent and nature of text-processing skills and navigation required in each of the tasks can be best appreciated by trying to solve the items.

The unit *SERAING* is built around the fictional website of the Belgian city of Seraing (Figure 7.2). The unit comprises three tasks. Box 7.1 summarises the main characteristics of each task. The first two tasks measure students' proficiency in "accessing and retrieving" information. In an online environment, this involves searching for information by interacting with the available navigation tools, using knowledge of the typical structures encountered on line and feedback received along the way as a guide. To limit the search difficulty, both tasks provide directions to guide and orient students ("Look at the Seraing home page", "Find the page for…"). The third task is classified as "complex" because several cognitive processes are involved at the same time to solve this task. As in previous tasks, students need to search and locate information, and are provided with explicit directions to assist them. They also need to "integrate and interpret" the information found, contrasting two concert descriptions, and to reflect on these descriptions in light of their personal preferences, in order to justify a choice of one concert over the other. All aspects of the reading framework ("access and retrieve", "integrate and interpret", "reflect and evaluate": see OECD, 2013a) are important, making this a "complex" item. Answers given to this last item were scored by trained coders.

Box 7.1. **General description of tasks in the unit *SERAING***

TASK 1

Question stem: Look at the Seraing home page. What are the dates of the Heritage Days?

Answer format: Simple multiple choice (4 options)

Framework aspect: Access and retrieve

Difficulty on the digital reading scale: 248 points (below Level 1b)

Number of pages available for navigation: 21

Minimum number of navigation steps required for locating the necessary information: 0 (but scrolling is required)

TASK 2

Question stem: Find the page for the Seraing Community Cultural Centre. Which film will be shown in the first week of November?

Answer format: Simple multiple choice (4 options)

Framework aspect: Access and retrieve

Difficulty on the digital reading scale: 382 points (Level 1a)

Number of pages available for navigation: 21

Minimum number of navigation steps required for locating the necessary information: 3

...

TASK 3

Question stem: Open the e-mail inbox and read John's e-mail message to Max. Click on "Reply" and write a reply to John from Max. In the reply, recommend which concert to buy tickets for (5 December or 12 December). Explain why this concert would be more enjoyable, referring to the concert descriptions.

Click on "Send your message" to send the reply.

Answer format: Constructed response, expert coded

Framework aspect: Complex

Difficulty on the digital reading scale: 570 points (Level 4) for full credit, 547 points (Level 3) for partial credit. Partial credit is given to students who could indicate their preference and give an explanation, but their explanation is not related to concert descriptions. No credit is given to students who could indicate the preference, but did not give any explanation.

Number of pages available for navigation: 25

Minimum number of navigation steps required for locating the necessary information: 11

Over 38 000 students from 32 countries participating in the assessment of digital reading were given these tasks. Process data are available for 38 506 students for the first task, 38 370 for the second, and 37 474 for the third task. The unit appeared at the end of one of the two test clusters, which means that half of the students were administered this unit before reaching the middle of the 40-minute test session, and half of the students at the very end.

On average across OECD countries, 38% of students received full credit for all three tasks in this unit, 43% solved two out of three tasks correctly, 16% solved only one task correctly, and 4% of students did not solve any task correctly, among students with available process data and excluding students who did not reach this unit in the test (Table 7.6). In general, the proportion of correct answers across countries/economies is in line with the ranking of countries and economies by their mean performance on the digital reading scale.[1]

Throughout the case study, the behaviour of strong and weak students will be contrasted by comparing students who received full credit for all three tasks and students who solved at most one of the three tasks correctly. As defined here, the groups of strong and weak students account for 38% and 20% of the student population, respectively.

HOW FLUENTLY CAN STUDENTS READ?

Good readers are able to process the words and sentences they read fast and accurately (Catts et al., 2002), as if they were listening to a natural voice rather than reading a text. In simple tasks where the stimulus material contains a short explicit direction, *initial reaction time* can be used to measure reading fluency. Initial reaction time refers to the amount of time, measured in seconds, from the moment the student sees the item to the first action a student takes.[2] This measure can be extracted from process data recorded automatically by the test-administration platform.

Although it was not designed for this purpose, Task 2 in the unit *SERAING* offers a good setting to measure and compare reading fluency across students. When students reach Task 2 in the unit, they have already had the opportunity to familiarise themselves with the homepage of Seraing – the stimulus material – in Task 1. The only material that is new to them is the question in the bottom part of the screen, which states: "Find the page for the Seraing Community Cultural Centre. Which film will be shown in the first week of November?" The phrase "Community Cultural Centre" prominently appears at the centre of the homepage. Initial reaction time on this task typically corresponds to the time it takes students to click on this link; it is therefore most likely related to the time it takes to read and understand the question, and only to a limited extent to other processes (such as locating the information, developing a plan, etc.).

Figure 7.3 shows how the initial reaction time varies across students of different proficiency in (digital) reading. The weakest students – those who are able to solve at most one of the three *SERAING* tasks correctly – have the longest reaction times, on average, indicating that many of these students may lack fluency in decoding words and sentences.

■ Figure 7.3 ■

Initial reaction time on Task 2 in the unit *SERAING*, by performance categories

Median time between the start of the task and the first mouse click, in seconds (OECD average)

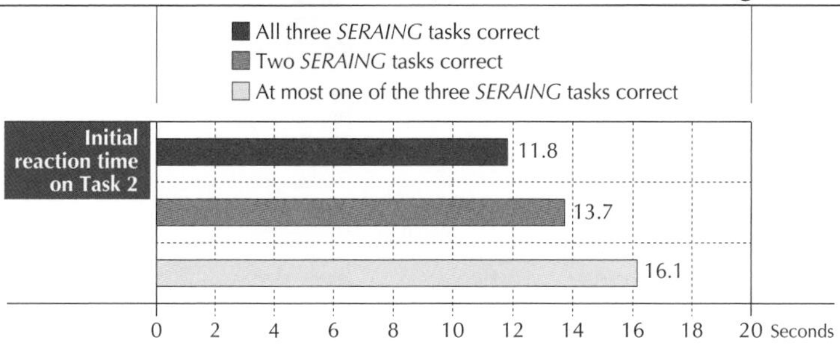
All three SERAING tasks correct
Two SERAING tasks correct
At most one of the three SERAING tasks correct
Initial reaction time on Task 2
11.8
13.7
16.1
0
2
4
6
8
10
12
14
16
18
20
Seconds

Note: Because time indicators typically have a skewed distribution and some very large outliers, the median time (50th percentile) is shown in this figure.

Source: OECD, PISA 2012 Database, Table 7.1.

StatLink http://dx.doi.org/10.1787/888933253377

On average across OECD countries, 10% of students have reaction times shorter than 6 seconds, while another 10% of students take 28 seconds or more to react (Table 7.1). Further analyses show that reaction time is negatively related to success in this simple task. Some 83% of the fastest students (those who reacted in under 6 seconds) went on to answer the question correctly, while only 46% of the slowest students (those who reacted in over 28 seconds) answered the question correctly.[3] The latter group is thus likely to have poor fluency in reading and difficulties related to basic reading skills. But how are these students distributed across countries?

In some countries, such as Brazil, Chile, Colombia, Hungary and the United Arab Emirates, students are significantly more likely to read slowly than in Japan, Korea, and other East Asian countries and economies. The fact that this variation across countries is strongly related to the variation in the proportion of low performers in (print) reading may indicate that one reason behind students' difficulties in reading is insufficient basic skills, such as the automatic decoding of words (Figure 7.4).

■ Figure 7.4 ■

Relationship between long reaction time on Task 2 in the unit *SERAING* and low performance in reading

Across countries and economies

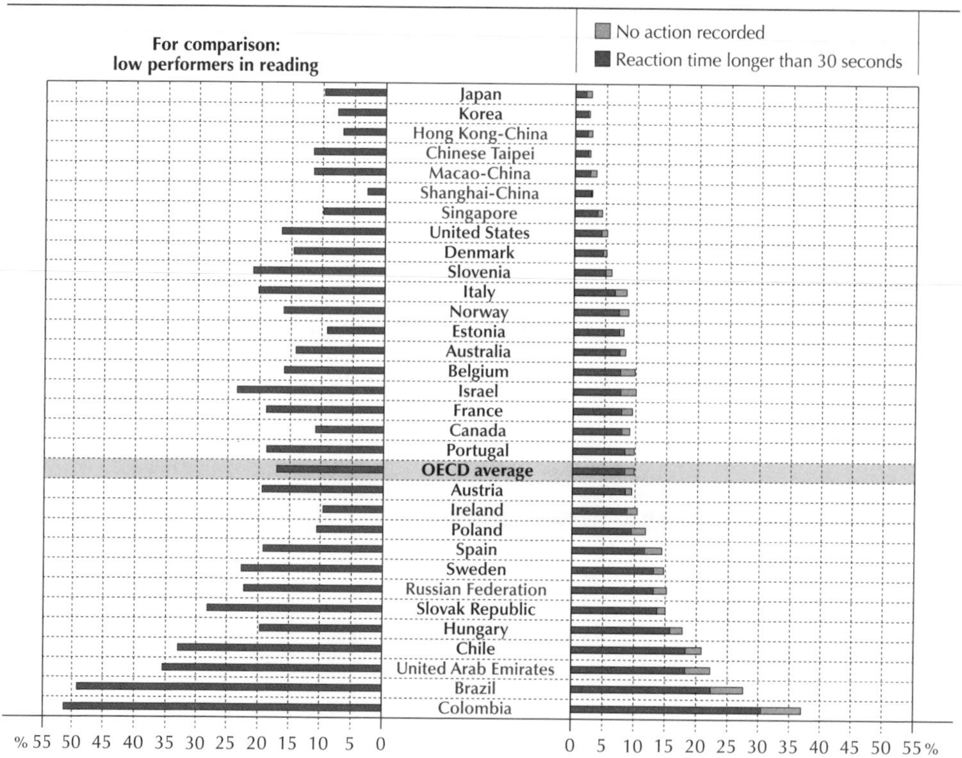
For comparison: low performers in reading
No action recorded
Reaction time longer than 30 seconds
Japan
Korea
Hong Kong-China
Chinese Taipei
Macao-China
Shanghai-China
Singapore
United States
Denmark
Slovenia
Italy
Norway
Estonia
Australia
Belgium
Israel
France
Canada
Portugal
OECD average
Austria
Ireland
Poland
Spain
Sweden
Russian Federation
Slovak Republic
Hungary
Chile
United Arab Emirates
Brazil
Colombia
% 55 50 45 40 35 30 25 20 15 10 5 0
0 5 10 15 20 25 30 35 40 45 50 55 %

Countries and economies are ranked in ascending order of the percentage of students whose reaction time is longer than 30 seconds.

Source: OECD, PISA 2012 Database, Table 7.1.

StatLink http://dx.doi.org/10.1787/888933253389

By identifying a lack of reading fluency as a possible reason behind the large proportion of low-performing students, the analysis of log files in digital reading can also indicate possible ways to improve the reading skills of low performers and adjust instruction to better serve their needs. The high correlation (0.90), across countries and economies, between the percentage of students performing below Level 2 in print reading, and the percentage of students whose initial reaction time exceeds 30 seconds shows that reaction time is a good predictor of mastery of basic reading skills (Table 7.1). Further research would be needed, however, to ensure that measures of reading fluency based on reaction time are comparable across languages.[4]

HOW DO STUDENTS ALLOCATE EFFORT AND TIME TO TASKS?

Timing measures may not only function as indicators of how fluently students process certain cognitive tasks; they may also indicate the degree of effort and motivation. For this reason, they are often difficult to interpret.

Time on task is calculated as the total time spent on a task from start to finish. How is time on task related to performance? If longer times indicate greater care in completing the task, then better-performing students may spend more time on a task. At the same time, more proficient students work more fluently and thus faster on tasks, and this could explain a negative association between success and time on task (Goldhammer et al., 2014).

Which effect dominates – greater care or greater fluency – is a matter of empirical investigation, and may vary depending on task demands, as well as on external time pressures.[5] Tasks that lend themselves to automatic processing will give rise to a negative association between time on task and performance. Tasks that instead require students to regulate their cognitive processing more, and that cannot be solved without the active engagement of students, will give rise to positive associations.

■ Figure 7.5 ■

Time on tasks in the unit *SERAING*, by performance categories

Median time spent on each task, in seconds (OECD average)

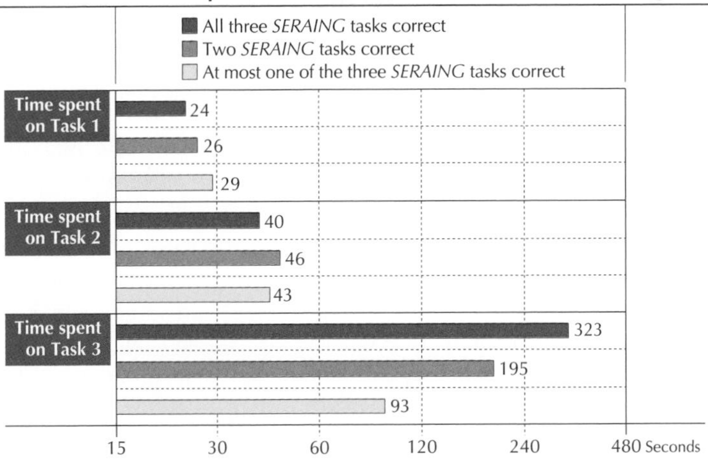
All three SERAING tasks correct
Two SERAING tasks correct
At most one of the three SERAING tasks correct
Time spent on Task 1
24
26
29
Time spent on Task 2
40
46
43
Time spent on Task 3
323
195
93
15
30
60
120
240
480 Seconds

Note: The horizontal axis is in logarithmic scale: each tick corresponds to a doubling in the value.
Source: OECD, PISA 2012 Database, Table 7.2.
StatLink http://dx.doi.org/10.1787/888933253392

The third and most difficult task in the unit *SERAING* illustrates the complex relationship between time on task and performance (Figure 7.5). In Tasks 1 and 2 of this unit, the strongest students, i.e. those who are able to solve all three *SERAING* tasks correctly, work faster than weaker students, on average. This is consistent with the observation that these tasks are relatively straightforward. Even Task 2 lends itself to automatic processing. Although it requires several steps to find the solution, students who follow the expected path do not run into unexpected

impasses, and the type of navigation they are asked to perform – narrowing down the search while moving towards a solution – is relatively linear, and corresponds to a familiar structure that is often encountered on line.

In contrast, several features make Task 3 more demanding. To start, students need to work on two websites at the same time (a webmail site and the Seraing website). They must use several navigation tools (tabs and links), and need to navigate back and forth across pages. In addition, students need to use their short-term memory to contrast two descriptions and then encapsulate one of the differences found in these descriptions in an argument stating their preference. Not surprisingly, the strongest students are those who take the longest time to reach a solution. Indeed, this task requires high levels of metacognitive regulation in order to select a strategy, apply adequate cognitive processes at each step, and sustain effort throughout the task.

Success rates on Task 3 vary significantly across countries. For the most part, these differences are in line with overall performance differences across countries/economies. The main exception is Korea, where fewer students solved the task correctly than across OECD countries, on average (Tables 3.1 and 7.3).

Analyses of time spent on this task reveal that students' willingness and ability to sustain and regulate effort in demanding tasks may play a major role in between-country differences in performance. On average across OECD countries, 41% of students received full credit for Task 3; 32% of students were able to solve the task correctly in less than seven minutes; and a further 9% took seven minutes or longer to solve this task correctly (Table 7.3). The latter group of students shows remarkable persistence in a task that may be at the upper limit of their ability.[6]

Figure 7.6 shows that in Australia, Canada, France and the United States, more than four in ten students were able to solve Task 3 correctly in less than seven minutes, a higher proportion than on average across OECD countries. However, after including slower but persistent students who were able to solve Task 3 accurately, but needed more than seven minutes to do so, other countries performed on par with or sometimes better than this group of countries. In Singapore, 38% of students succeeded on this task after spending more than seven minutes working on it – making it the most successful country in completing this task. In Hong Kong-China, Ireland, Japan, Macao-China and Shanghai-China, more than one in six students belong to this group of relatively slow, but highly persistent students.[7]

These first results based on log files show how measures of students' use of time during the PISA test can be related to cognitive and non-cognitive aspects of students' performance at both ends of the performance distribution. The findings relate the variation in students' reaction time and time on task to their ease with and motivation to complete different tasks. Further work is required to investigate the robustness of findings based on case studies. Such work may also extend the analyses of timing data recorded in log files to other aspects, such as task dependencies and order effects. Does the time required to solve the previous task influence students' willingness and ability to solve the next task? Do students allocate time and effort differently at the beginning and end of the test? Do students strategically allocate time to tasks, skipping questions when they recognise them as "too hard to crack"?

■ Figure 7.6 ■

Students' perseverance and success

Percentage of students who succeed on Task 3 in the unit SERAING, *by time spent on the task*

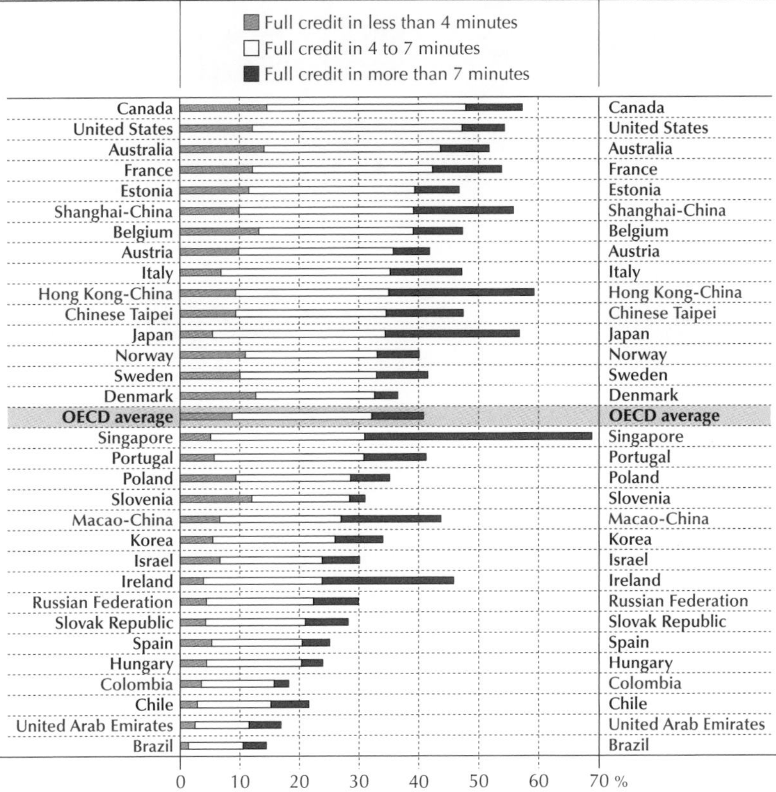
Full credit in less than 4 minutes
Full credit in 4 to 7 minutes
Full credit in more than 7 minutes
Canada
United States
Australia
France
Estonia
Shanghai-China
Belgium
Austria
Italy
Hong Kong-China
Chinese Taipei
Japan
Norway
Sweden
Denmark
OECD average
Singapore
Portugal
Poland
Slovenia
Macao-China
Korea
Israel
Ireland
Russian Federation
Slovak Republic
Spain
Hungary
Colombia
Chile
United Arab Emirates
Brazil
0
10
20
30
40
50
60
70 %

Countries and economies are ranked in descending order of the percentage of students who solved Task 3 in less than seven minutes and obtained full credit for their solution.
Source: OECD, PISA 2012 Database, Table 7.3.
StatLink http://dx.doi.org/10.1787/888933253404

HOW DO STUDENTS NAVIGATE A SIMPLE WEBSITE?

The unit *SERAING* is built around the fictional website of a city (Seraing). The structure of Seraing's website corresponds to a hierarchical hypertext, a relatively common structure encountered on line (Figure 7.7). Hierarchical hypertexts have a branching structure that resembles a tree and have been found to facilitate information retrieval, compared to linear or networked structures (Mohageg, 1992). The typical navigation sequences on these websites have one beginning (the "home page") but many possible endings, depending on decisions made by the reader. Readers who search for information in hierarchical sites typically move to the next level at each step, thus narrowing down their search. In addition to movements across levels along "branches", in Seraing's website students could also move across pages belonging to the same hierarchical level by means of a navigation menu, a feature that is often present in real websites as well.

■ Figure 7.7 ■

Hierarchical structure of Seraing's fictitious website

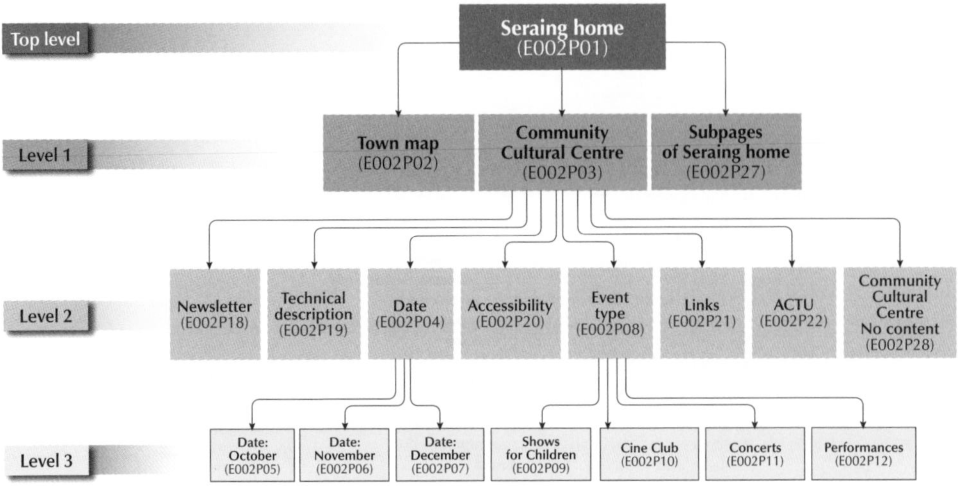
Top level
Seraing home (E002P01)
Level 1
Town map (E002P02)
Community Cultural Centre (E002P03)
Subpages of Seraing home (E002P27)
Level 2
Newsletter (E002P18)
Technical description (E002P19)
Date (E002P04)
Accessibility (E002P20)
Event type (E002P08)
Links (E002P21)
ACTU (E002P22)
Community Cultural Centre No content (E002P28)
Level 3
Date: October (E002P05)
Date: November (E002P06)
Date: December (E002P07)
Shows for Children (E002P09)
Cine Club (E002P10)
Concerts (E002P11)
Performances (E002P12)

Note: "Top Level", "Level 1", "Level 2" and "Level 3" indicate hierarchical levels: Level 3 pages can only be accessed from the Top Level by going through a Level 1 and a Level 2 page first.

Source: Australian Consortium for Educational Research (2015), "PISA examples of computer-based items: Digital Reading 2012: *SERAING*", http://cbasq.acer.edu.au/index.php?cmd=toEra2012 (accessed 30 April 2015).

Figure 7.8 shows which pages are available for navigation and were coded as relevant in each task. Pages are identified by a title that describes the content, and by a unique code (not visible to the student) used for the purpose of analysis. The first and second tasks in the unit *SERAING* start on the home page, which is the website's top-level page. Several thematic portals can be found at the first level, and detailed information is provided at the second and third levels. The third task starts on a mailing website; students can reach Seraing's website by clicking on a link embedded in an e-mail. As shown in the figure, there is only one relevant page in Task 1; there are six relevant pages in Task 2, which form two efficient navigation paths; and there are 12 task-relevant pages in Task 3, seven of which appear on Seraing's website, and five appear on the mailing website.

Several links on the website were intentionally "broken", and students who clicked on them landed on pages with "no content available", and received immediate feedback inviting them to go back to the previous page. There are two such pages, one at Level 1 of the hierarchy, one at Level 2. These pages may not be perceived as the same page by students but are counted as such throughout this report.

Successful and unsuccessful navigation in Task 2 in the unit *SERAING*

Task 2 in the unit *SERAING* corresponds to a relatively common, if simple, online search task. The task requires students to identify the movie to be shown in the Community Cultural Centre during the first week of November, information they can find on the third level of the hierarchy.

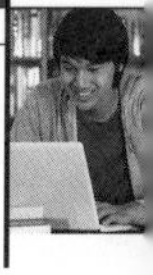

■ Figure 7.8 ■

List of page codes and relevant pages in the unit *SERAING*

PAGE TYPE
- S Starting page
- R Relevant page
- N Non-relevant page
- (blank) Not available for this task

PAGE CODE	PAGE NAME	Task 1 (CR002Q01)	Task 2 (CR002Q03)	Task 3 (CR002Q05)
E002P01	Seraing: home	S	S	N
E002P02	Town map	N	N	N
E002P03	Community Cultural Centre	N	R	R
E002P04	Community Cultural Centre: Date	N	R	R
E002P05	Community Cultural Centre: Date – October	N	N	N
E002P06	Community Cultural Centre: Date – November	N	R	N
E002P07	Community Cultural Centre: Date – December	N	N	R
E002P08	Community Cultural Centre: Event type	N	R	R
E002P09	Community Cultural Centre: Event type – Shows for children	N	N	N
E002P10	Community Cultural Centre: Event type – Cine club	N	R	
E002P11	Community Cultural Centre: Event type – Concerts	N	N	R
E002P12	Community Cultural Centre: Event type – Performances	N	N	N
E002P13	Email reading			R
E002P14	Community Cultural Centre: Event type – Madredeus 1	N	N	R
E002P15	Community Cultural Centre: Concerts – Madredeus 2	N	N	R
E002P16	Send email			R
E002P17	Email frame			R
E002P18	Community Cultural Centre: Newsletter	N	N	N
E002P19	Community Cultural Centre: Technical description	N	N	N
E002P20	Community Cultural Centre: Accessibility	N	N	N
E002P21	Community Cultural Centre: Links	N	N	N
E002P22	Community Cultural Centre: ACTU	N	N	N
E002P27	Subpages of Seraing home page without content	N	N	N
E002P28	Subpages of Community Cultural Centre without content	N	N	N
E002P29	Confirmation for sending the reply email			R
E002P30	Email home			S
	Number of relevant pages in each task	**1**	**6**	**12**

Note: The PISA digital reading unit *SERAING* can be seen at the website http://cbasq.acer.edu.au/index.php?cmd=toEra2012 (accessed 30 April 2015).

On average, four out of five of students across OECD countries solved this task correctly (Table 7.5). The most efficient navigation sequence involves visiting three pages beyond the starting page (three steps) (Figure 7.9). Students may fail this unit either because they make wrong decisions at one or more points in their navigation, or because they fail to continue navigating for as long as required.

Figure 7.9 contrasts the behaviour of successful and unsuccessful students. The figure shows the main navigation paths in this task (not all paths are shown). Arrows indicate possible steps along these paths: blue arrows indicate task-relevant steps (from relevant to relevant pages), whereas black dotted arrows indicate other kinds of steps (missteps, corrections, and task-irrelevant steps). For each step shown in these figures, a number counts the frequency with which it is recorded in students' log files. Students could exit the navigation to give an answer or move to the next task at any point; such decisions are shown by grey arrows.

■ Figure 7.9 ■

Navigation behaviour in Task 2 in the unit *SERAING*

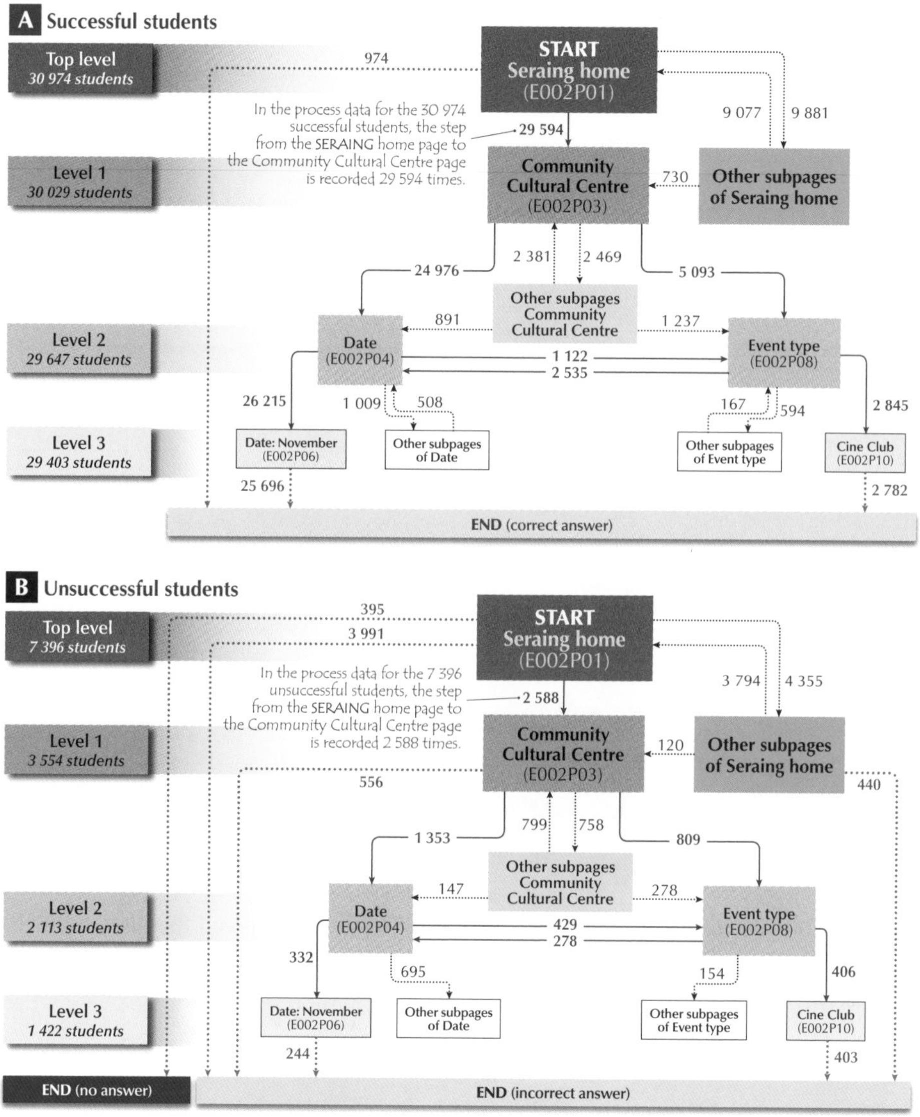
A Successful students
Top level
30 974 students
Level 1
30 029 students
Level 2
29 647 students
Level 3
29 403 students
START
Seraing home
(E002P01)
974
In the process data for the 30 974 successful students, the step from the SERAING home page to the Community Cultural Centre page is recorded 29 594 times.
29 594
9 077
9 881
Community Cultural Centre
(E002P03)
730
Other subpages of Seraing home
2 381
2 469
24 976
5 093
Other subpages Community Cultural Centre
891
1 237
Date
(E002P04)
Event type
(E002P08)
1 122
2 535
26 215
1 009
508
167
594
2 845
Date: November
(E002P06)
Other subpages of Date
Other subpages of Event type
Cine Club
(E002P10)
25 696
2 782
END (correct answer)
B Unsuccessful students
Top level
7 396 students
Level 1
3 554 students
Level 2
2 113 students
Level 3
1 422 students
395
3 991
START
Seraing home
(E002P01)
In the process data for the 7 396 unsuccessful students, the step from the SERAING home page to the Community Cultural Centre page is recorded 2 588 times.
2 588
3 794
4 355
Community Cultural Centre
(E002P03)
120
Other subpages of Seraing home
556
440
799
758
1 353
809
Other subpages Community Cultural Centre
147
278
Date
(E002P04)
Event type
(E002P08)
429
278
332
695
154
406
Date: November
(E002P06)
Other subpages of Date
Other subpages of Event type
Cine Club
(E002P10)
244
403
END (no answer)
END (incorrect answer)

Notes: The figure shows the main pages available for viewing and the main navigation paths in this task (not all paths are shown). Blue and black dotted arrows indicate possible steps between pages: blue arrows indicate task-relevant steps (from relevant to relevant pages), whereas black dotted arrows indicate other kinds of steps (missteps, corrections, and task-irrelevant steps). Grey dotted arrows indicate the last page visited before ending navigation. For each step shown in these figures, the number of cases recorded in log files is indicated next to the arrows (numbers are unweighted).
Pages are placed based on their position at different levels in the hierarchical hypertext. Relevant pages are highlighted in blue. Non-relevant pages having the same position in the hierarchy were grouped to simplify exposition.
Source: OECD, PISA 2012 Database, Table 7.4.

Figure 7.9 clearly shows the two efficient navigation sequences. The first goes through the "Date" page, the second through the "Event type" page. Panel A in this figure shows that successful students were more likely to visit the "Date" page than the "Event type" page, after reaching the portal of the Community Cultural Centre. This may be related to the fact that the former link appears above the latter in the navigation menu, and is therefore more prominent. It is also likely that students who solved this task perceived a closer match between the question and the stimulus text for the former link ("November" – "Date") than for the latter ("film" – "Event type"). Indeed, some students who initially followed the "Event type" path reverted to the "Date" path in their next step, when continuing on the "Event type" branch would have required them to match the question stem ("film") with "Cine-club" among a list of 12 possibilities (including some potentially overlapping categories, such as "Various" or "Shows for children").

The top-left part of Figure 7.9 also shows that some 1 571 students (30 974 minus 29 403), representing 5% of all students who solved this item correctly, did not, in fact, reach the third level of Seraing's website during their navigation, but nevertheless gave the correct answer. Of the 30 974 students who gave the correct answer, only 29 403 reached Level 3. If their log files are complete, this means that they gave a guess answer. Given that this is a multiple-choice item where students had to select among four options, it can be estimated that for each correct guess, there should be about three times as many incorrect guesses. Indeed, further analyses show that 5 251 students, representing 71% of the unsuccessful students, similarly tried to give an answer, despite the fact that they had not reached the third level of Seraing's website.

Why did students fail to answer this question correctly? Panel B in Figure 7.9 shows that a majority of the unsuccessful students (3 991 students) did not perform any action other than attempt a guess answer. It also shows that, among the remaining students, those who did navigate the website had relatively unfocused browsing behaviour, on average. Visits to non-relevant pages are much more likely to be observed among students who failed the task.

Differences between successful and unsuccessful students in the quantity and quality of navigation are confirmed by the indicators of navigation used in Chapter 4. Figure 7.10 shows that successful students had longer navigation sequences (four navigation steps) than unsuccessful students (three navigation steps), on average. It also shows that unsuccessful students had a larger number of non-task-relevant steps (missteps, corrections, task-irrelevant steps) than successful students, whose typical navigation sequence included the three required task-relevant steps. In short, the navigation of successful students is characterised by longer sequences and a more careful selection of pages to visit.

Overall, it is possible to distinguish four reasons for failing to solve this task, three of which are related to navigation. First, students may not have navigated the website and simply remained on the Seraing home page. Second, students may have ended their navigation at some point along the task-relevant path before reaching the page containing the crucial information to solve the task. Third, students may have deviated from the task-relevant navigation path, ending their navigation on a non-relevant page – perhaps they were lost after a misstep. Finally, some students may have completed their navigation as expected, by visiting either the "November" or the "Cine-club" page, but nevertheless failed to give the correct answer.

■ Figure 7.10 ■

Quality and quantity of navigation steps in Task 2 in the unit *SERAING*, by performance on the task

OECD average values

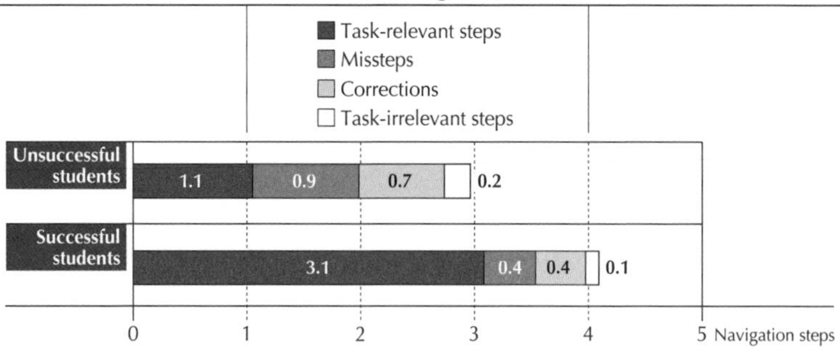
Task-relevant steps
Missteps
Corrections
Task-irrelevant steps
Unsuccessful students
1.1
0.9
0.7
0.2
Successful students
3.1
0.4
0.4
0.1
0
1
2
3
4
5 Navigation steps

Source: OECD, PISA 2012 Database, Table 7.5.

StatLink http://dx.doi.org/10.1787/888933253410

■ Figure 7.11 ■

Navigation behaviour of students unsuccessful on Task 2 in the unit *SERAING*

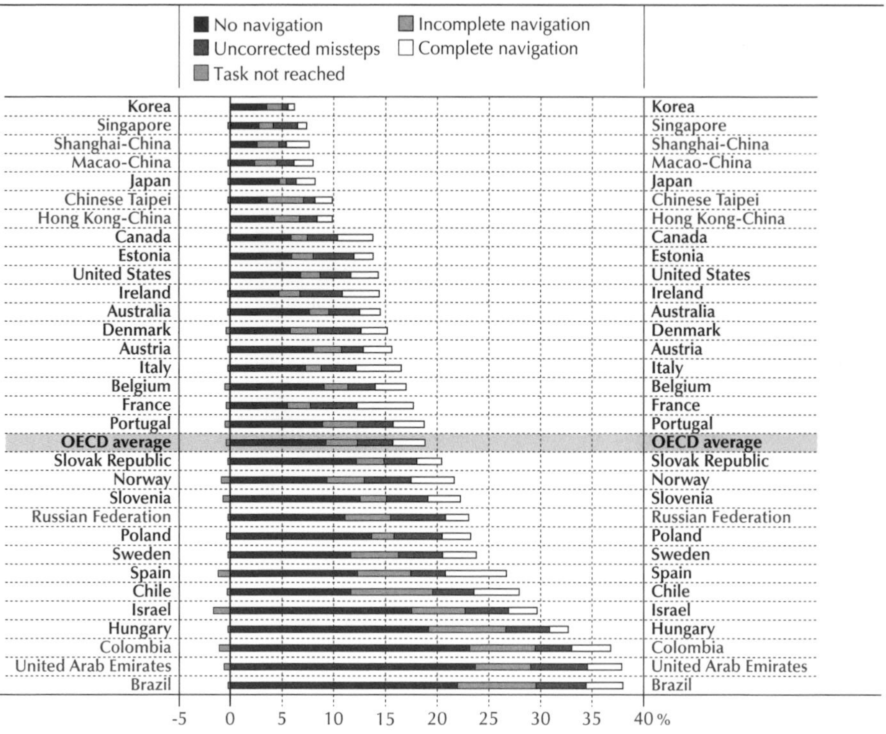
No navigation
Uncorrected missteps
Task not reached
Incomplete navigation
Complete navigation
Korea
Singapore
Shanghai-China
Macao-China
Japan
Chinese Taipei
Hong Kong-China
Canada
Estonia
United States
Ireland
Australia
Denmark
Austria
Italy
Belgium
France
Portugal
OECD average
Slovak Republic
Norway
Slovenia
Russian Federation
Poland
Sweden
Spain
Chile
Israel
Hungary
Colombia
United Arab Emirates
Brazil
-5
0
5
10
15
20
25
30
35
40 %

Countries and economies are ranked in ascending order of the share of students with no credit for Task 2 in the unit SERAING.

Source: OECD, PISA 2012 Database, Table 7.5.

StatLink http://dx.doi.org/10.1787/888933253420

Across all countries/economies, most students who were unsuccessful in this item have navigation-related mistakes recorded in their log files. In detail, on average across OECD countries, 9% of students did not attempt any navigation step in this item. However, in Korea, Macao-China, Shanghai-China, Singapore and Chinese Taipei, less than 4% of students did not try to navigate in this item. By contrast, an average of 3% of students completed the navigation but still failed to select the correct answer; in Spain and France, this was the case for more than 5% of students (Figure 7.11).

IMPLICATIONS OF THE CASE STUDY FOR COMPUTER-BASED ASSESSMENTS

The analyses of reaction time and of time on task, as well as the detailed description of students' navigation behaviour, based on data recorded in log files for a single unit in digital reading, illustrate three advantages of computer-based assessments.

First, the detailed information on the interactions of unsuccessful students with assessment tasks may be used to improve the ability to measure proficiency at lower ends of the performance distribution. In particular, the scoring rubrics could be expanded to give partial credit for certain elementary processes observed in isolation, in addition to giving credit for the joint product of these processes (task success). For example, partial credit could be awarded to students who understand the simple instruction "Find the page for the Community Cultural Centre" and click on the corresponding link.

Second, log files often reveal to a greater extent than students' answers alone what the most frequent mistakes are, and allow for investigating the reasons behind them. This information, in turn, can be used to identify learners' profiles and improve teaching practices. In mathematics, there is a long tradition of identifying common mistakes on assessment tasks in order to diagnose misconceptions and weaknesses among students. Teachers use this to inform instruction and design learning experiences (OECD, 2005; Wiliam, 2010). Furthermore, existing studies at the national level have similarly analysed the traces left by students on PISA paper booklets (OECD, 2013b; DEPP, 2007). However, such analyses have been limited by the fact that few students (about 10% in the case of France) actually leave traces of their reasoning on paper booklets. The data captured by a computer system can expand the possibilities for such analyses – at lower cost.

In addition, the above analysis shows that several invalid test-taking behaviours, such as guessing, can be detected in on-screen tests. This, in turn, may lead to significant gains in the precision of performance measures derived from test answers. In the PISA computer-based assessment of problem solving, for instance, several multiple-choice items were designed to require certain interactions to arrive at the correct solution and were scored as correct only if these interactions had been recorded in log files (OECD, 2014).

Notes

1. The correlation of the sum of scores on *SERAING* tasks with the latent performance measure (PV1CREA) is 0.68.

2. "Action" refers here to mouse clicks only (on a link, a tab, on an answer option, or elsewhere on the page). Mouse scrolls or keyboard strokes are not recorded in the data used for this analysis.

3. Percentages refer to the pooled sample with students from all countries and economies.

4. There are only few studies in which comparable, timed fluency tasks were administered across languages and orthographies. Most of these are not based on representative samples, focus on younger students, and are confined to European languages (e.g. Frith, Wimmer and Landerl, 1998; Mann and Wimmer, 2002; Seymour et al., 2003). It is not clear how well their results can be generalised to the population level and to later stages in the development of reading proficiency, and how other languages would compare (also see Abadzi, 2011).

5. The PISA computer-based test in 2012 was a timed test: students had 40 minutes to complete all questions in their forms. Questions had been used in a Field Trial, and the length of test forms was determined, after the Field Trial, to ensure that approximately 80% of all students (across countries) would complete the test without running into the time limit.

6. Only full-credit answers are considered here, for two reasons. First, there were few students who received partial credit. Second, students could have received partial credit without navigating the Seraing website at all, at least in theory. Only students receiving full credit demonstrate the kind of skills that justify the classification of this item as "complex" within the reading framework.

7. Between-country differences do not change much by whether students see this task towards the middle of the test, or at the end of it. See Table 7.3 for full results.

Chapter 7 tables are available on line at http://dx.doi.org/10.1787/edu-data-en.

Note regarding Israel

The statistical data for Israel are supplied by and under the responsibility of the relevant Israeli authorities. The use of such data by the OECD is without prejudice to the status of the Golan Heights, East Jerusalem and Israeli settlements in the West Bank under the terms of international law.

References

Abadzi, H. (2011), Reading fluency measurements in EFA FTI partner countries: Outcomes and improvement prospects, *Partnership for Education (GPE) Working Paper Series on Learning,* No. 1, World Bank, http://documents.worldbank.org/curated/en/2011/09/18042914/reading-fluency-measurements-efa-fti-partner-countries-outcomes-improvement-prospects.

Australian Consortium for Educational Research (2015), "PISA examples of computer-based items: Digital Reading 2012: *SERAING*", http://cbasq.acer.edu.au/index.php?cmd=toEra2012 (accessed 30 April 2015).

Bunderson, C.V., D.K. Inouye and **J.B. Olsen** (1988), "The four generations of computerized educational measurement", *ETS Research Report Series,* Vol. 1988/1, pp. i-148.

Catts, H.W., M. Gillispie, L.B. Leonard, R.V. Kail and **C.A. Miller** (2002), "The role of speed of processing, rapid naming, and phonological awareness in reading achievement", *Journal of Learning Disabilities,* Vol. 35/6, pp. 510-525.

Csapó, B., J. Ainley, R.E. Bennett, T. Latour and **N. Law** (2012), "Technological issues for computer-based assessment", in P. Griffin, B. McGaw and E. Care (eds.), *Assessment and Teaching of 21st Century Skills*, Springer Netherlands, pp. 143-230.

DEPP (2007), "Résultats des français par champs mathématiques (Chapter 5)", in *L'évaluation internationale PISA 2003 : Compétences des élèves français en mathématiques, compréhension de l'écrit et sciences*, Les Dossiers, No. 180, Direction de l'évaluation, de la prospective et de la performance (DEPP), Ministère de l'éducation nationale, de l'enseignement supérieur et de la recherche, http://media.education.gouv.fr/file/83/1/4831.pdf.

Frith, U., H. Wimmer and **K. Landerl** (1998), "Differences in phonological recoding in German- and English-speaking children", *Scientific Studies of Reading,* Vol. 2/1, pp. 31-54.

Goldhammer, F., J. Naumann, A. Stelter, K. Tóth, H. Rölke and **E. Klieme** (2014), "The time on task effect in reading and problem solving is moderated by task difficulty and skill: Insights from a computer-based large-scale assessment", *Journal of Educational Psychology,* Vol. 106/3, pp. 608-626.

Mann, V. and **H. Wimmer** (2002), "Phoneme awareness and pathways into literacy: A comparison of German and American children", *Reading and Writing,* Vol. 15/7-8, pp. 653-682.

Mohageg, M.F. (1992), "The influence of hypertext linking structures on the efficiency of information retrieval", *Human Factors,* Vol. 34/3, pp. 351-367.

OECD (2014), *PISA 2012 Results: Creative Problem Solving (Volume V): Students' Skills in Tackling Real-Life Problems*, PISA, OECD Publishing, Paris, http://dx.doi.org/10.1787/9789264208070-en.

OECD (2013a), *PISA 2012 Assessment and Analytical Framework: Mathematics, Reading, Science, Problem Solving and Financial Literacy*, PISA, OECD Publishing, Paris, http://dx.doi.org/10.1787/9789264190511-en.

OECD (2013b), "Strengths and Weaknesses of American Students in Mathematics", in OECD, *Lessons from PISA 2012 for the United States*, OECD Publishing, Paris, http://dx.doi.org/10.1787/9789264207585-5-en.

OECD (2011), *PISA 2009 Results: Students On Line: Digital Technologies and Performance (Volume VI)*, PISA, OECD Publishing, Paris, http://dx.doi.org/10.1787/9789264112995-en.

OECD (2005), *Formative Assessment: Improving Learning in Secondary Classrooms*, OECD Publishing, Paris, http://dx.doi.org/10.1787/9789264007413-en.

Seymour, P.H.K., M. Aro and **J. Erskine** and collaboration with **COST Action A8 network** (2003), "Foundation literacy acquisition in European orthographies", *British Journal of Psychology*, Vol. 94, pp. 143-174.

Wiliam, D. (2010), "The role of formative assessment in effective learning environments", in *The Nature of Learning: Using Research to Inspire Practice*, OECD Publishing, Paris, http://dx.doi.org/10.1787/ 9789264086487-8-en.

8

Implications of Digital Technology for Education Policy and Practice

For the first time, today's parents and teachers have little, if any, experience with the tools that children are going to use every day in their adult lives. This chapter discusses the implications for education policy of the need to equip students with the fundamental skills required to participate fully in hyper-connected, digitised societies.

Using complex tools to solve everyday problems is a defining attribute of our species. Generation after generation, parents raised their children to use the tools with which they were familiar. Later on, some of the more ingenious children tweaked their ancestors' tools and invented new ones. But never before the advent of electronic computers and, more recently, of Internet-based services, did such a large fraction of humanity change their everyday habits and tools in such a short time. Within a couple of decades, the tools used in most trades and for such basic acts as communicating, gathering information, keeping records of the past or drawing plans about the future were replaced by digital ones. For the first time, today's parents and teachers have little, if any, experience with the tools that children are going to use every day in their adult lives.

It is easy to feel overwhelmed by the changes that occurred over the past few generations. Surely such a deep and rapid evolution, affecting our daily lives, must have consequences on the processes and content of education as well; the abundance of irrational fears or enthusiasms about the impacts of technology on our lives would have anyone believe so. But is there evidence to confirm it? This report aims to document the changes that occurred – and did not occur – in the education and lives of young people following the rise of digital technology using data from the OECD Programme for International Student Assessment (PISA).

In the past 25 years, schools and families around the world spent a substantial amount of money on computers, Internet connections, and software for educational use (Chapters 1 and 2). By 2012, in most OECD countries less than 2% of 15-year-old students lived in households without computers (Figure 1.1). And in half of the 34 OECD countries, 15-year-old students went to schools that had at least one computer connected to the Internet available for every three students. In Australia, an early leader in investments in educational technology (OECD, 1999), there was one such computer for every student (Table 2.11).

Empowering young people to become full participants in today's digital public space, equipping them with the codes and tools of their technology-rich world, and encouraging them to use online learning resources – all while exploring the use of digital technologies to enhance existing education processes, such as student assessment (Chapter 7) or school administration – are goals that justify the introduction of computer technology into classrooms.

DIGITAL TOOLS ARE OFTEN COMPLEMENTARY TO SKILLS, BOTH BASIC AND ADVANCED

Technological changes in society raise fundamental questions about the role of education and schools. What should students know and be able to do? What is the value of knowledge that has been traditionally acquired in school, when so much information is available on line?

Most schools and teachers did not directly influence the pace at which computers were introduced into workplaces; nor did they decide that personal communications should happen over the Internet, rather than in face-to-face meetings or using the telephone. Yet the skills that are typically learned at school play a crucial role in determining whether a student adopts digital technology and can benefit from it.

Today, even simple interactions and transactions often require writing and reading, rather than speaking and listening – e.g. asking information from a help-desk, making a professional appointment, sharing information with team members, etc. As a consequence, students who leave school without sufficient reading and writing skills may be even less able to participate fully in economic, social and civic life than they were in the past.

The increasing importance of reading and writing in daily life is one of the reasons why the benefits of digital technologies are unevenly shared across high-skilled and low-skilled individuals. In addition, the fact that computers and digitally enhanced machines, or robots, can perform many tasks at a lower cost than human workers means that the skills that complement new technologies are in increasing demand. The greatest benefits accrue to those who have the ability to design digital solutions, adapting or creating machine algorithms to fit one's needs. These capacities build on advanced reasoning and problem-solving skills and require good mastery of symbolic and formal language. They often build on related skills acquired in mathematics courses.

TEACH THE FOUNDATION SKILLS THAT ARE NEEDED IN A DIGITAL ENVIRONMENT

In a world that is rapidly embracing digital technology as the main medium of communication, students need to be able to gather and use online information (Chapter 3). They must be familiar with the text formats encountered on line in order to learn to navigate through the web critically and successfully. As a matter of fact, the typical texts encountered on line require certain reading processes, such as evaluating the trustworthiness of sources, drawing inferences from multiple texts, and navigating within and across pages, more than do traditional printed texts. All of these processes can be learned and practiced in school settings (Chapter 4).

Reading in the digital medium builds on reading skills acquired in a non-digital environment, but also relies on good navigation skills. Navigation, in turn, requires metacognitive regulation, the ability to organise complex hypertext structures into a coherent mental map, experience in evaluating the relevance of pages, and a repertoire of effective strategies for reading on line. Without these, students find themselves digitally adrift.

The most successful countries and economies in the PISA digital reading assessment have similar visions of the importance of digital skills for today's students. But they differ in the level of use of information and communication technologies (ICT) in schools.

Singapore and Korea, the two highest-performing countries in digital reading (Chapter 3) and among those countries where the quality of students' web-navigation behaviour is highest (Chapter 4), have excellent broadband infrastructure (ITU, 2014) and high levels of familiarity with computers among 15-year-olds students (Chapter 1). Yet students are not more exposed to the Internet in school than are students on average across OECD countries. Despite this, most students have a good mastery of the strategies that assist them in online navigation – in addition to performing strongly in all domains assessed in PISA. This suggests that many evaluation and navigation skills may be acquired more easily if students are already proficient in higher-order thinking and reasoning processes in other domains.

In Australia, another high-performing country where students demonstrate strong ability in browsing the web, the Internet is used during school hours to a greater extent than in any other country that participated in the optional ICT familiarity questionnaire in PISA 2012 (Chapter 2). ICT is represented in two ways in the Australian Curriculum – within the "Technologies learning area curriculum"; and through the "ICT general capability", which is embedded across all learning areas of the curriculum. The learning continuum for the ICT general capability describes the knowledge, skills, behaviours and dispositions that students can reasonably be expected to develop at particular stages of schooling.[1] This framework guides teachers and industry in creating the educational resources that promote proficiency in the use of electronic sources of information, and helps to ensure that students develop useful skills in their time on line, such as planning a search, locating information on a website, evaluating the usefulness of information, and assessing the credibility of sources.

Studying online resources at school can not only help to develop digital reading skills, but also expand the diversity of topics, genres, and sources that are used in class. Greater diversity of reading materials, in turn, can lead to greater enjoyment of reading. PISA data collected in 2009 show that the share of students who do not read anything for enjoyment increased since 2000 (OECD, 2010a). Yet there's no question that reading anything for enjoyment is better for student performance than reading nothing. By including, among learning resources, those reading materials that are favourites among the students who read for enjoyment, teachers can promote the habit of reading to the largest number of students (OECD, 2015a).

INVEST IN SKILLS TO PROMOTE EQUAL OPPORTUNITIES IN A DIGITAL WORLD

Differences in access to digital resources across students of different socio-economic status have narrowed considerably over recent years, to the point where, in all but five OECD countries with available data, disadvantaged students spend at least as much time on line as advantaged students do (Table 5.12).[2] Yet, even with equal access, not all students have the knowledge and skills to be able to benefit from the resources that are available to them.

In the past, the convergence of goods and services, including those related to education, onto online platforms was sometimes described as a great opportunity to bridge existing inequalities in access to offline equivalents (think of online encyclopaedias and massive open online courses). And indeed, affordable and widespread ICT devices, particularly mobile phones, have created many opportunities to bring education, health and financial services to poor or marginalised populations (OECD, 2015b). But the ability to benefit from new technologies seems to increase with individuals' and societies' skill levels. Therefore, the move to online services may mitigate purely economic disadvantage, but amplify the disadvantage that stems from a lack of access to a quality education in the early and primary school years.

The results presented in Chapter 5 imply that in developed countries, differences in the uptake and use of Internet resources are related to the unequal distribution of skills, more than to unequal access to such resources. In our increasingly digital world, deep and pre-existing social and cultural divides also cut into civic engagement in online fora, participation in online learning, and the ability to search on line for a better job (e.g. Van Deursen and Van Dijk, 2014).

What can schools do to help all students make the most of their access to digital tools? Results show that if current gaps in reading, writing and mathematics skills are not narrowed, inequalities in digital skills will persist, even if all Internet services were available free of charge. The cost of Internet services is often only of secondary importance when it comes to participating in status-enhancing activities.

This means that to reduce inequalities in the ability to benefit from digital tools, countries need to improve equity in education first. Ensuring that every child reaches a baseline level of proficiency in reading and mathematics will do more to create equal opportunities in a digital world than can be achieved by expanding or subsidising access to high-tech devices and services.

RAISE AWARENESS OF THE POSSIBLE HARMFUL ASPECTS OF INTERNET USE

When every child has access to the Internet, parents and teachers can use the educational resources that are available on line to foster children's learning. Yet unlimited access to the Internet can also have negative consequences for children's development. Those in charge of educating today's "connected" learners are confronted with a number of new (or newly relevant) issues, from "information overload" to plagiarism, from protecting children from online risks (fraud, violations of privacy, online bullying) to setting an adequate and appropriate media diet (OECD, 2012a; OECD, 2014).

Previous studies had found negative impacts of extended screen time on adolescents' sleep (Cain and Gradisar, 2010; Hysing et al., 2015), physical activity (Melkevik et al., 2010) and social well-being (Richards et al., 2010). Based on the available research evidence, several national public health authorities have warned about the possible negative consequences of increased screen time (e.g. House of Commons Health Committee, 2014, p. 85) and issued guidelines that recommend limiting children's recreational screen time, typically to less than two hours per day (e.g. Council on Communications and Media, 2013; Population Health Division, 2015).

PISA data confirm and extend these findings (Chapter 1). They show that 15-year-olds who spend more than six hours on line every day are particularly at risk of suffering from lower emotional well-being and of behaving in problematic ways at school, such as arriving late for class or skipping days of school. While these findings cannot demonstrate the direction of causality, they suggest that well-being at school is strongly related to the electronic media diet outside of school. Parents, schools and health professionals can work together to monitor and plan children's use of new media.

Schools should educate students as critical consumers of Internet services and electronic media, helping them to make informed choices and avoid harmful behaviours. They can also raise awareness in families about the risks that children face on line and how to avoid them (OECD, 2012b). In addition to protecting children from online threats, parents must help children to balance leisure uses of ICT with time for other recreational activities that do not involve screens, such as sports and, equally important, sleep.

DEVELOP COHERENT PLANS, INCLUDING TEACHER TRAINING, FOR USING ICT IN THE CLASSROOM

Plans for technology in education sometimes promised to improve the efficiency of education processes, delivering better results at lower cost (OECD, 1999; OECD, 2010b). Yet the link from

more technology to better results is far from direct, with many actors involved in making the required changes happen. And the costs are not limited to devices that need to be bought; they include teachers to train, resources to develop and buildings to adapt, as well as the foregone benefits of alternative uses of that money (opportunity costs).

Evidence from PISA shows only a weak or sometimes negative association between the use of ICT in education and performance in mathematics and reading, even after accounting for differences in national income and in the socio-economic status of students and schools (Chapter 6). In most countries, students who make some use of the Internet at school, for instance, tend to be better at reading, particularly when it comes to understanding and navigating online texts, than students who never browse the Internet for schoolwork at school. But other activities, such as using drilling and practice software for mathematics or languages, show a clear negative relationship with performance. And more frequent, daily browsing of the Internet at school is also generally associated with lower performance (Australia is a rare exception to this pattern).

The most rigorous impact studies also show no effects of investments in computers on students' non-digital performance. While there is too little credible evidence on this issue, positive findings are limited to certain contexts and certain uses of ICT. These include when computer software and Internet connections help to increase study time and practice, or allow teachers to provide optimal learning opportunities to students, in which students assume control over their own learning and/or learn collaboratively (see Chapter 6 for a full discussion and references).

The conclusion that emerges is that schools and education systems are, on average, not ready to leverage the potential of technology. Gaps in the digital skills of both teachers and students, difficulties in locating high-quality digital learning resources from among a plethora of poor-quality ones, a lack of clarity on the learning goals, and insufficient pedagogical preparation for blending technology meaningfully into lessons and curricula, create a wedge between expectations and reality. If these challenges are not addressed as part of the technology plans of schools and education ministries, technology may do more harm than good to the teacher-student interactions that underpin deep conceptual understanding and higher-order thinking.

LEARN FROM PAST EXPERIENCE TO IMPROVE THE EFFECTIVENESS OF FUTURE INVESTMENTS IN TECHNOLOGY

When it comes to decisions about investments in technology, it is easy to discard evidence from past experience by pointing at the many differences between "there and then", and "here and now". The devices themselves are likely to differ, if not in shape (laptops rather than desktops; tablets rather than interactive whiteboards) at least in their capabilities. Yet unless past disappointment with technology in education can convincingly be attributed to the limitations of hardware (and it rarely can), changing the device will not help to avoid the pitfalls encountered in previous large-scale education technology plans. Technology can amplify great teaching, but great technology cannot replace poor teaching. In schools as well as in other organisations, technology often increases the efficiency of already-efficient processes, but it may also make inefficient processes even more so.[3]

Certainly, some of the intended goals of current and past ICT initiatives are difficult to measure. For instance, it is sometimes argued that digital technologies should be seen as a support for "a more flexible, learner-centred notion of education" that helps to develop curiosity, creativity, collaboration and other "soft skills" vital to 21st-century societies (Livingstone, 2011).

Many other potential benefits fall outside of what PISA can measure through the performance of 15-year-old students. The fact that this report does not document them does not imply that they do not exist. For example, technology provides great platforms for collaboration among teachers and for their participation in continuous professional development, thus empowering them as knowledge professionals and change leaders.

Still, countries and education systems can do more to improve the effectiveness of their investments in ICT by being both gradually accepting and sceptical. They can more clearly identify the goals they want to achieve by introducing technology in education, and strive to measure progress towards these goals, experimenting with alternative options too. This kind of clarity in planning would enable them, and other countries and systems, to learn from past experience, gradually improving on previous iterations and creating the conditions that support the most effective uses of ICT in schools.

Despite the many challenges involved in integrating technology into teaching and learning, digital tools offer a great opportunity for education. Indeed, in many classrooms around the world, technology is used to support quality teaching and student engagement, through collaborative workspaces, remote and virtual labs, or through the many ICT tools that help connect learning to authentic, real-life challenges. Teachers who use inquiry-based, project-based, problem-based or co-operative pedagogies often find a valuable partner in new technologies; and industry is developing several technologies (learning analytics and serious games, for example) that promise to exploit the rapid feedback loops afforded by computers to support real-time, formative assessments, thus contributing to more personalised learning (Johnson et al., 2014).

What this shows is that the successful integration of technology in education is not so much a matter of choosing the right device, the right amount of time to spend with it, the best software or the right digital textbook. The key elements for success are the teachers, school leaders and other decision makers who have the vision, and the ability, to make the connection between students, computers and learning.

Notes

1. The ICT general capability is one of the seven "general capabilities" that inform teaching and learning across all school subjects in Australia. The learning continuum for ICT general capability comprises five dimensions: "Applying social and ethical protocols and practices when using ICT", "Investigating with ICT", "Creating with ICT", "Communicating with ICT", and "Managing and operating ICT". In the ICT general capability curriculum documents, learning goals are further articulated across the year levels from Foundation to Year 10, with examples related to subject areas. This recognises that students develop their ICT capability around its use as well as their ability to transfer and apply it in other settings. Furthermore, the Australian National Assessment Program (NAP) includes a triennial sample population assessment to monitor students' ICT literacy at the system and national level (Australian Curriculum, Assessment and Reporting Authority, 2015; Santiago et al., 2011).

2. Among OECD countries, the exceptions are: Chile, Mexico, Poland, Portugal, the Slovak Republic and Slovenia. Data are not available for Canada, France, Luxembourg, the United Kingdom and the United States.

3. Microsoft founder Bill Gates expressed this in the following way: "The first rule of any technology used in a business is that automation applied to an efficient operation will magnify the efficiency. The second is that automation applied to an inefficient operation will magnify the inefficiency" (Gates, Myhrvold, and Rinearson, 1995, p.136).

References

Australian Curriculum, Assessment and Reporting Authority (2015), "F-10 Curriculum: General Capabilities: Information and Communication Technology (ICT) Capability", *Australian Curriculum Website* www.australiancurriculum.edu.au (accessed 1 June 2015).

Cain, N. and **M. Gradisar** (2010), "Electronic media use and sleep in school-aged children and adolescents: A review", *Sleep Medicine*, Vol. 11/8, 735-742.

Council on Communications and Media (2013), "Children, adolescents, and the media", *Pediatrics*, Vol. 132, pp. 958-961.

Gates, B., N. Myhrvold and **P. Rinearson** (1995), *The Road Ahead*, Viking, New York.

House of Commons Health Committee (2014), *HC 342 - Children's And Adolescents' Mental Health and CAMHS*, The Stationery Office.

Hysing, M., S. Pallesen, K.M. Stormark, R. Jakobsen, A.J. Lundervold and **B. Sivertsen** (2015), "Sleep and use of electronic devices in adolescence: results from a large population-based study", *BMJ Open*, Vol. 5/1.

Johnson, L., S. Adams Becker, V. Estrada and **A. Freeman** (2014), *NMC Horizon Report: 2014 K-12 Edition*, The New Media Consortium, Austin Texas.

ITU (2014), *Measuring the Information Society Report*, International Telecommunication Union, Geneva.

Livingstone, S. (2011), "Critical reflections on the benefits of ICT in education", *Oxford Review of Education*, Vol. 38/1, pp. 9-24.

Melkevik, O., T. Torsheim, R.J. Iannotti and **B. Wold** (2010), "Is spending time in screen-based sedentary behaviors associated with less physical activity: A cross national investigation", *International Journal of Behavioral Nutrition and Physical Activity*, Vol. 7/46.

OECD (2015a), *The ABC of Gender Equality in Education: Aptitude, Behaviour, Confidence*, PISA, OECD Publishing, Paris, http://dx.doi.org/10.1787/9789264229945-en.

OECD (2015b), *Innovation Policies for Inclusive Development*, OECD Publishing, Paris, http://dx.doi.org/10.1787/9789264229488-en.

OECD (2014), "Trends Shaping Education 2014 Spotlight 5: Infinite Connections", www.oecd.org/edu/ceri/Spotlight%205-%20Infinite%20Connections.pdf.

OECD (2012a), "Emerging issues for education", in OECD, *Connected Minds: Technology and Today's Learners*, OECD Publishing, Paris, http://dx.doi.org/10.1787/9789264111011-9-en.

OECD (2012b), *The Protection of Children Online, Recommendation of the OECD Council*, OECD Publishing, Paris, www.oecd.org/sti/ieconomy/childrenonline_with_cover.pdf.

OECD (2010a), "Trends in attitudes and student-school relations", in OECD, *PISA 2009 Results: Learning Trends: Changes in Student Performance Since 2000 (Volume V)*, OECD Publishing, Paris, http://dx.doi.org/10.1787/9789264091580-9-en.

OECD (2010b), "The policy debate about technology in education", in OECD, *Are the New Millennium Learners Making the Grade?: Technology Use and Educational Performance in PISA 2006*, OECD Publishing, Paris, http://dx.doi.org/10.1787/9789264076044-4-en.

OECD (1999), "Indicator E6: Computers in schools and their use", in *Education at a Glance 1998: OECD Indicators*, OECD Publishing, Paris, http://dx.doi.org/10.1787/eag-1998-en.

Population Health Division (2015), "Australia's Physical Activity and Sedentary Behaviour Guidelines", *Australian Government Department of Health*, www.health.gov.au/internet/main/publishing.nsf/content/health-pubhlth-strateg-phys-act-guidelines#apa1317 (accessed 31 March 2015).

Richards, R., R. McGee, S.M. Williams, D. Welch and **R.J. Hancox** (2010), "Adolescent screen time and attachment to parents and peers", *Archives of Pediatrics & Adolescent Medicine, Vol.* 164/3, 258-262.

Santiago, P., G. Donaldson, J. Herman and **C. Shewbridge** (2011), *OECD Reviews of Evaluation and Assessment in Education: Australia 2011*, OECD Reviews of Evaluation and Assessment in Education, OECD Publishing, Paris, http://dx.doi.org/10.1787/9789264116672-en.

Van Deursen, A.J.A.M. and **J.A.G.M. Van Dijk** (2014), "The digital divide shifts to differences in usage", *New Media & Society*, Vol. 16/3, pp. 507-526.

Annex A

TECHNICAL NOTES ON ANALYSES IN THIS VOLUME

The following annexes are available in electronic form only at www.oecd.org/pisa:

Annex A.1: Classification of computer-based mathematics tasks, by whether they require the use of computers to solve problems

Annex A.2: PISA 2012 computer-based assessment log files

Annex A.3: Technical notes on analyses in Chapter 4

Annex B

LIST OF TABLES AVAILABLE ON LINE

ANNEX B

LIST OF TABLES AVAILABLE ON LINE

The following tables are available in electronic form only at http://dx.doi.org/10.1787/edu-data-en.

...

Chapter 7 How computers are related to students' performance

ORGANISATION FOR ECONOMIC CO-OPERATION AND DEVELOPMENT

The OECD is a unique forum where governments work together to address the economic, social and environmental challenges of globalisation. The OECD is also at the forefront of efforts to understand and to help governments respond to new developments and concerns, such as corporate governance, the information economy and the challenges of an ageing population. The Organisation provides a setting where governments can compare policy experiences, seek answers to common problems, identify good practice and work to co-ordinate domestic and international policies.

The OECD member countries are: Australia, Austria, Belgium, Canada, Chile, the Czech Republic, Denmark, Estonia, Finland, France, Germany, Greece, Hungary, Iceland, Ireland, Israel, Italy, Japan, Korea, Luxembourg, Mexico, the Netherlands, New Zealand, Norway, Poland, Portugal, the Slovak Republic, Slovenia, Spain, Sweden, Switzerland, Turkey, the United Kingdom and the United States. The European Union takes part in the work of the OECD.

OECD Publishing disseminates widely the results of the Organisation's statistics gathering and research on economic, social and environmental issues, as well as the conventions, guidelines and standards agreed by its members.

OECD PUBLISHING, 2, rue André-Pascal, 75775 PARIS CEDEX 16
(98 2015 02 1P) ISBN 978-92-64-23954-8 – 2015-05